*Contentious Spirits*

ASIAN AMERICA
*A series edited by Gordon H. Chang*

The increasing size and diversity of the Asian American population, its growing significance in American society and culture, and the expanded appreciation, both popular and scholarly, of the importance of Asian Americans in the country's present and past—all these developments have converged to stimulate wide interest in scholarly work on topics related to the Asian American experience. The general recognition of the pivotal role that race and ethnicity have played in American life, and in relations between the United States and other countries, has also fostered this heightened attention.

Although Asian Americans were a subject of serious inquiry in the late nineteenth and early twentieth centuries, they were subsequently ignored by the mainstream scholarly community for several decades. In recent years, however, this neglect has ended, with an increasing number of writers examining a good many aspects of Asian American life and culture. Moreover, many students of American society are recognizing that the study of issues related to Asian America speaks to, and may be essential for, many current discussions on the part of the informed public and various scholarly communities.

The Stanford series on Asian America seeks to address these interests. The series will include works from the humanities and social sciences, including history, anthropology, political science, American studies, law, literary criticism, sociology, and interdisciplinary and policy studies.

*A full list of titles in the Asian America series can be found online at www.sup.org/asianamerica*

# Contentious Spirits

RELIGION IN KOREAN AMERICAN

HISTORY, 1903–1945

*David K. Yoo*

STANFORD UNIVERSITY PRESS

STANFORD, CALIFORNIA

2010

Stanford University Press
Stanford, California
© 2010 by the Board of Trustees of the
Leland Stanford Junior University

Library of Congress Cataloging-in-Publication Data

Yoo, David.
   Contentious spirits : religion in Korean American history,
1903–1945 / David K. Yoo.
      p.  cm. — (Asian America)
   Includes bibliographical references and index.
   ISBN 0-8047-6928-0 (cloth : alk. paper) —
   ISBN 0-8047-6929-7 (pbk. : alk. paper)
   1. Korean Americans—Religion.  2. Korean Americans—
Hawaii—History—20th century.  3. Korean Americans—
California—History—20th century.  4. United States—
Emigration and immigration—Religious aspects—Christianity.
5. United States—Emigration and immigration—Social aspects.
I. Title.  II. Series: Asian America.

BR563.K67Y66  2010
277.3'082089957—dc22

                             2009029256

Printed in the United States of America on acid-free,
archival-quality paper

Typeset at Stanford University Press in 11/14 Garamond

*For Ruth and our boys*

# Contents

# Acknowledgments

If writing a book can be compared to running a marathon, then the acknowledgments represent a welcome opportunity to thank the many people who made it possible to cross the finish line. My gratitude goes first to the remarkable people and institutions represented in these pages. The richness and diversity of their stories deserve to be documented and told, and it is a privilege to have contributed to that storytelling. Many people have served as guides along the way, and the Reverend Steven Jhu, Michael Kim, the Reverend Kwang-Jin Kim, Elder Stuart Ahn, the Reverend Woong-min Kim, and Donna Lee introduced me to key individuals and provided access to important documents and records. Sustained conversations with the Reverend T. Samuel Lee and the Reverend Tom Choi gave me valuable perspectives on the role of religion in Korean American history in Hawai'i and on the mainland.

Every historian owes much to librarians and archivists, and I thank James Cartwright and Sherman Seki of the University of Hawai'i at Manoa for their assistance. Ken Klein, Sun-Yoon Lee, and Joy Kim of the USC East Asian Library offered generous support in accessing their collections. Thanks to the staffs of the libraries of the Claremont Colleges, the Claremont School of Theology, Drew University, and Fuller Seminary. In particular, the Inter-Library Loan Department at the Claremont Colleges ably processed my many requests. For research assistance in Claremont, I acknowledge the good work of Amber Ariate and Herb Ruffin. Hyung-ju Ahn's guidance regarding the newspaper, the *Shinhan Minbo* (New Korea), helped with the material on California, as did Yeo-Jin Rho's translation assistance with Korean-language materials.

A number of institutions provided support that contributed to the research and writing of this project. An Institute of American Cultures Postdoctoral Fellowship from UCLA provided a wonderful year at the Asian American Studies Center. Similarly, the Los Angeles–based research benefited from a faculty fellowship from the John Randolph Haynes and Dora Haynes Foundation. For the chance to share work in progress, I thank colleagues and staff members at the Academy of Korean Studies in South Korea; the Asian American Program at Princeton Seminary; the Center for Korean Studies at UCLA; the Center for Korean Studies at the University of Hawai'i at Manoa; the Department of Asian American Studies at the University of California, Irvine; and the Korean Society for American History, Seoul, Korea.

Conversations with colleagues over the years have sustained the lengthy process of writing this book, and I am grateful for people who have listened, suggested, commented, challenged, and encouraged: Emily Anderson, Eiichiro Azuma, Rudy Busto, Joan Bryant, Peter Cha, Laura Mariko Cheifetz, Jane Iwamura, Russell Jeung, David Kyuman Kim, Jung Ha Kim, Lili Kim, Richard Kim, Stacy Kitahata, Kenneth Lee, Sang Hyun Lee, Pyong Gap Min, Rodger Nishioka, Mary Paik, Su Pak, Wayne Patterson, Christen Sasaki, Tim Tseng, Duncan Williams, and Karen Yonemoto. Two individuals, the late Yuji Ichioka and the late Steffi San Buenaventura, will not get to read the finished product, but they both contributed much to what appears here. In addition, APARRI (the Asian Pacific American Religions Research Initiative) has been a great source of community. Kudos are due to Fumitaka Matsuoka and Chris Chua for their caretaking of the organization and to my fellow managing board members.

I have been fortunate over the years to teach and work at the Claremont Colleges, and I thank all of my colleagues in the Department of History at Claremont McKenna College, especially Diana Selig and Albert Park, who read parts of the manuscript, and Diana Selig and Arthur Rosenbaum, with whom I have talked about this project on and off for quite some time. The staff members of the Faculty Support Center have provided much appreciated assistance. The Intercollegiate Department of Asian American Studies has been a great support, and I thank Linus Yamane and Kathy Yep for the various times I shared some about what was happening with the project. Special thanks to Madeline Gosiaco for helping me with the production and technical aspects of the book. I have also had the opportunity to talk other colleagues in Claremont about this project, including Dean Adachi, Hal Barron, Stephen Davis, Gaston Espinosa, Mark and Jeney Hearn, Minju Kim, and Rita Roberts.

A long time ago, I spoke with Gordon Chang about this project, and I am very glad to be joining the series on Asian America published by Stanford University Press. Both he and editor Stacy Wagner have guided the process with wisdom and care. Many thanks to press staff Jessica Walsh, John Feneron, and Ariane De Pree-Kajfez and to copyeditor Mary Ray Worley. In addition, the two outside readers for the press provided helpful comments and questions.

Friends and family have been such a source of support, fun, hospitality, and much more. In Hawai'i, Brian Niiya and Karen Umemoto let me stay at their place and provided some great home-cooked meals. I first met Gary Pak through his novels and short stories, and I am thankful for the friendship that has developed over plate lunches, and talk story. It is an honor to have Gary's artwork grace the cover of the book. In southern California, so many friends have made the lives of my family far richer, and though I cannot name everyone, a special shout-out to the Chaks, Soon and Esther Chung, the Hoang-Rappaports, Jae and Kristi Lee, Judy Lee, the Ums, the Yangs, and to the all of the URF family. To the all of the folks in Pomona, it has been good to walk with you: the Beyers, the Drakes, the Engdahls, the Funks, Mark Gearhart, the Georges, John Guthrie, the Hsiehs, the Hwangs, the Johannsens, Mark Kim, Megan Krogh, the Manguiat family, the McKelveys, Emily Peine, the Ramos family, and the Robinsons.

It has been a blessing to be surrounded by so many family members whose lives have been woven into the fabric of ours, and thanks to the Yoo, Chung, Shin, and Lee gangs! My sister, Peggy, my brother, Eugene, and my brother-in-law, Billy, and their families have given a lot over the years for which I am grateful. So much more could be said about my parents and my in-laws, whose tangible and intangible love and support have sustained me and my family for so long, I cannot remember a time when such was not the case.

Finally, my greatest thanks are to my immediate family, to Ruth and the life we share; its unfolding has been marked by much sweetness that I hope that will extend well into our golden years. More than any other person, she has watched this book take shape, adding her own contributions in countless ways. Jonathan and Joshua have also made their mark, largely through the gift of who they are to us and many others. I give thanks that we have been on this journey together, and this book is dedicated to Ruth and our boys with much love and affection.

*Contentious Spirits*

# Introduction

Church for me as a child began well before we ever entered the sanctuary. The process of getting ready involved the entire family, rushing about in the morning, grabbing Bibles and black-leather hymnals with gold Korean lettering, and jumping into the sedan. As we pulled out of the driveway and on to the streets of southern California, we usually stopped at the local do-nut store, where my mom and I carefully piled a dozen or so warm boxes of glazed twists into the backseat. On other occasions like outdoor worship, we took large trays of deep-fried dumplings and seaweed wrapped rice. Those aromas served as a kind of incense that I associated with our weekly ritual.

The views out the car window represented a visual dimension of experience. The path to church took us by an oil refinery with its tangle of steel and smoke. We then passed under the 405 Freeway and then by the community college campus. Off in the distance lay the mammoth screen of the drive-in theater that during the week doubled as a bustling swap meet. As we neared the church, I spotted the burger shop that my friends and I sometimes went to after the service. In addition to eating snacks, we would feed quarters into the small black-and-white television mounted to the tables so that we could watch our favorite sports teams.

Our immigrant Korean Presbyterian group rarely if ever interacted with the European American Lutherans from whom we rented the space where we worshipped, despite sharing the site for many years. Except for the occasional times when we had not cleaned up sufficiently, the church seemed like it was ours—a place in which we sang and prayed and played. People often gathered in front of the long planter outside the sanctuary, greeting one another and engaging in lively conversations, including some heated arguments. By virtue of my parents' lay leadership positions, we were almost always one of the first families to arrive and among the last to leave, making most Sundays painfully long journeys. We sat through marathon-like prayers and sermons. Many of us young people struggled to contain our laughter as the old men in the front pews slept and nodded their way through much of the service, and then abruptly awoke and shouted "Amen!" like clockwork when the preacher ended his message.

On certain occasions during the year—for instance, at graduation time in June—an elderly woman in our congregation, Elder Whamok Lee, would address the youth in English and tell us not only about the Bible but also about Korea and those who had ventured to this country as immigrants. She encouraged us to study hard and never to forget our roots. I thought of Elder Lee like a grandmother, and we spent much time at her home since much of church business took place there. Only as I grew older did I realize that she was the only woman elder in the church, a fact that did not change throughout my entire childhood and youth. Elder Lee provided leadership instrumental in establishing the congregation after it had broken off from another church. Again, only with time did I learn that she had been a fiery Bible evangelist from northern Korea, where Protestant Christianity took root in the late nineteenth century.[1]

The line between church and the rest of my family's life further blurred when we hosted what seemed to me an endless stream of individuals and families from Korea. People whom my parents knew from Korea or others who had connections to us through church networks often stayed with us briefly or for extended visits. I can still recall the huge pieces of luggage and the distinctive smells that I associated with the newly arrived. These folks often looked a bit shell-shocked as they passed through our home. My parents effectively served as unofficial social workers, helping families to find work and housing, enrolling their kids in school, teaching the basics of setting up a bank account and writing checks, and even sacrificing our car for driving lessons. I benefited, though, from nice presents that grateful people gave to me as a way of thanking my parents. Church life cast a long shadow in my family's life and in the lives of those of most of the Korean Americans I grew up with.

## Legacies Explored

Although my youth within a southern California immigrant Korean Protestant church in the 1970s represents a later period than is the subject of this study, my family's experience is part of a larger story that dates back to the turn of the twentieth century and that extends forward to the present. My parents arrived in the United States after the Korean War, long after the first arrivals of Koreans in 1903, but before those who entered after the passage of the 1965 Immigration Act. The act removed long-standing discriminatory quotas that had been in place since 1924. Related race-based legislation, set into motion by the Chinese Exclusion Act of 1882, had created formidable barriers to Asian migration to the United States. Similarly, the Naturalization Act of 1790 restricted citizenship to "free white persons," profoundly affecting the life chances and the quality of life for those who did manage to get in.[2]

The people making their way through our home and church, including nearly all of my extended family, were part of a large-scale migration of Asians to the United States that has occurred since 1965.[3] Korean Americans today number approximately 1.5 million, concentrated in major urban areas like southern California.[4] Some estimates indicate that almost 80 percent of that population identifies as Christian, and in certain locales, nearly 90 percent of adherents attend services once or twice a month, with many in church once or more a week. In contrast, Buddhists account for 5 percent of the population.[5] Scholars have paid attention to the religious dimensions of this community, focusing on a range of issues such as ethnic identity formation, gender, and generation especially within the context of Protestant Christianity.[6]

It will come as no surprise to those who are familiar with post-1965 Korean America that churches form the core of these communities. Much less is known, however, about the religious experiences of Koreans in the United States in the early 1900s. *Contentious Spirits* represents the first book-length study of religion in the early history of Koreans in the United States. The narrative focuses on the greater Honolulu and Los Angeles areas during the period from the first arrivals in 1903 to end of World War II in 1945. Protestant Christianity provides the primary lens to examine the broader sweep of Korean America during this era.[7] The central argument is that religion provides the most important entry point to Korean

America history because it attended to the full range of human experience marked by complexity and contention. Churches provided an institutional structure for community and everyday life, while the sensibilities of Christianity touched upon the moral and the sacred.

The first Korean laborers contracted to work in the sugarcane plantations of Hawai'i arrived in January 1903, followed later by student-laborers, picture brides, and exiles who planted churches and formed communities in the islands and on the mainland.[8] The Korean American population during these early decades hovered around ten thousand people, and those based in the United States represented a vital link within a transnational network that spanned across the Pacific to Korea and other parts of East Asia. People, material resources, institutional networks, and ideas traversed these spaces against the backdrop of global capitalism and imperial imaginings. Protestant Christianity, moreover, facilitated much of this movement. As the study will bear out, Koreans in the United States should not be viewed simply as migrants, but also as exiles. They provided key leadership and much-needed finances for the diasporic independence movement and, in importance, far exceeded their numbers.[9]

*Contentious Spirits* is less a comprehensive history than an exploration of the structures and sensibilities of Protestant Christianity within the broader context of Korean America.[10] Institutional aspects of religion are very much a part of the stories told here, but so are religious processes not easily measured or rendered visible, which deeply affect individuals and communities. While social scientists have provided valuable insights into how religious institutions function, there is also a dimension of the religious that operates in the realm of the sacred and that shapes people's views of the world and how they live in it. The classical distinction between the functional and substantive aspects of religion, of course, speaks to the difficulties of conceptualizing, articulating, and understanding religion. To take another tack, this study aligns itself with a recent collection of essays on race, nation, and religion in which the effort is made "to blur the boundaries between religion and society without reducing either to a pale reflection of the other—to demonstrate the concrete, empirical foundations of religious discourse and experience as well as the otherworldly, metaphysical foundations of social order and identity."[11]

In addition, Robert Orsi's discussion of envisioning religion as relational is instructive. Orsi traces the relationships between humans and holy figures and the implications of those relationships for the everyday lives of American Catholics in the twentieth century. Something happens between heaven and earth as well as among human beings. Orsi reminds us that "religions are as ambiguous and ambivalent as the bonds that constitute them, and their effects cannot be generally anticipated, but known in practice and experience."[12]

*Contentious Spirits* grounds religion in Korean American history through three sets of relational themes: (1) religion & race, (2) migration & exile, and (3) colonialism & independence. These themes constitute the interpretive framework of the study. In the first theme, religion & race, religion shaped the racialization of Koreans in the United States. A shared religious tradition with the majority of Americans did not shield Koreans from being racialized in the sugarcane plantations or in the urban spaces of Honolulu and Los Angeles. At the same time, religion provided the means by which Koreans carved out and sustained their own identity as a people.

The book's second theme, migration & exile, examines how religion literally fueled the transnational migration of Koreans through European American missionary and Korean Christian networks. The introduction of Christianity in Korea set into motion both structures and sensibilities that laid the groundwork for this transnational movement. Religion informed the ways in which migration also involved exile. In the third relational theme, colonialism & independence, *Contentious Spirits* underscores how religion intertwined with the visions and activities of independence and the entanglements of colonialism. The narrative serves as a reminder that Koreans encountered the colonial not only in their homeland, but also in Hawai'i and California.

## Religion & Race

Religion and race are complicated categories in their own right, but this study holds them in creative tension with one another because they are deeply connected within the history of the United States. Constructions of religion and race have influenced one another from the very start, but the fact that they are often treated separately suggests how much of the existing literature reinforces and replicates troubling racial dynamics. That studies of American religion can segregate race by "marking" certain groups as racialized leaves unquestioned why other groups (read European Americans) remain largely unmarked and normative. At stake is the power to define what and who is central to the field (and by extension, to the nation) and, subsequently, what and who is marginal. Recent studies have attempted to address issues of race, but it continues to be largely relegated to those who study the "other" and perhaps, on occasion, to those who touch upon race relations. The scripts may vary, but the basic premise still holds: the place of race is in the margins.

More than simply questions of inclusion and exclusion, as important as those are, the stories of Korean Americans act as a reminder that the entire landscape of American religion is deeply racialized. In other words, racial constructs have been at the heart of how individual and group religious identities in the United States have been formed. Moreover, the formulation of those identities, far from being a neutral process, has involved issues of power expressed and embedded in the legal code, in the structures of education, and in popular culture. Emphasizing that all of American religion is racialized highlights the foundational and enduring legacy of race in the United States. Sociologist Howard Winant examines the impact of race on identity:

> Race must be grasped as a fundamental condition of individual and collective identity, a permanent, although tremendously flexible, dimension of the global social structure. The epochal phenomenon of race has been the basis for the most comprehensive systems of oppression and injustice ever organized, and simultaneously the foundation for every dream of liberation, at least since the inception of the modern world.[13]

For Koreans in the United States, the religious entailed the racial, beginning with their passage, often facilitated through church-related networks that continued upon their arrival. Mission structures in the islands and on the mainland helped place Koreans in jobs in which they shared the same faith with owners of plantations and farms, but this did little to blunt the workings of race in terms of housing restrictions, differential wage scales, and blatant racist encounters. Other "racialized" Christians, of course, could have warned Korean Americans of what lay in store for them. American Indians who adopted Christianity in response to mission work still suffered the dispossession of land, broken promises, and violence. African American converts found that Christian baptism did not entail freedom from bondage and, after the Civil War, from Jim Crow. Christianity did little to shield Mexican Americans from conquest. In each of these contexts, race trumped religion. These examples suggest how many European Americans utilized racialized understandings of religion to directly benefit from the status quo.[14] Indeed, the association of the United States with Christianity had been itself implicitly racial, namely, white European American Protestant Christianity, defined against these racialized "others," including coreligionists. The legacy of protest that stretches across our country's history represents alternative versions of the nation that include religion.[15]

In making a case for the centrality of race in American religion, *Contentious Spirits* also demonstrates the need for ethnic and racial studies to pay greater attention to religion. Overall, those within Asian American studies have tended to neglect religion as a serious subject of study.[16] And yet religious institutions and ideas provided individuals and communities with an important means of negotiating the circumstances of life. Churches and temples served multiple purposes, as places of worship, social gathering places, employment centers, and centers of local and transnational politics. Religious practices like reading the Bible and rituals like worship services infused imaginations, comforted souls, and provided meaning.

For many Korean Americans, religion informed the dilemma of their racial status in the United States. Some wondered how a supposed Christian nation could harbor racism toward fellow believers. At the same time, Korean Americans found that their mission and denominational connections could also be a source of acceptance and community. Simply put, the confluence of religion and race engaged the complexities and contradictions of human experience.

## Migration & Exile

The second theme fosters a rethinking of migration to the United States in its transnational and exilic elements. In placing Korean American history in conversation with modern Korean history, *Contentions Spirits* emphasizes a transnational perspective to explore how individuals and communities maintained ongoing relationships with the homeland even as they established new lives in the United States. Although the primary focus rests upon the experiences of Koreans in the United States, this study builds upon the work within the field of U.S. immigration history and its transnational turn.[17] That turn has been accompanied by efforts to situate U.S. history within a global context to counter a deeply entrenched American exceptionalism.[18] The vast social scientific literature on international migration suggests the complexities of the subject, and the narrative presented here constitutes a case study that lifts up the particular experience of Korean Americans while also pointing to its larger significance.[19] For one, as a work of history, *Contentious Spirits* illustrates that transnationalism is not a recent phenomenon instigated by airline travel and the Internet, but reaches back much further in time.[20] Asian American historians have warned of transnational excess that can mute the ongoing significance of the nation-state, but no one would dispute the importance of a transnational perspective.[21]

Religion played a major role in early migration, and an estimated 40 percent of those who left Korea identified themselves as Christians.[22] Hospitals, schools, and churches exposed Koreans in the homeland to new ideas and institutions, and missionaries sponsored men and women to study at denominational colleges and seminaries in the United States. Religious networks not only connected Korea and the United States, but also extended to China and other locales. Missionary Horace Allen, physician to the royal family, conduit for American investments, and U.S. envoy to Korea, exemplified the importance of religion for migration within the larger context of international relations and commerce.[23]

Along with its transnational nature, migration created an avenue of exile for Koreans to keep alive the vision of a free Korea.[24] Men and women through their hard-earned dollars sustained the independence movement abroad that transcended national boundaries and created a sense of diaspora among Koreans in different parts of the world.[25] Leaders called upon Christian connections to navigate their exit from Korea and subsequent survival in the United States. Korean American churches as well as the framework of Protestant Christianity brought together religion, politics, and nation for many.

Exile, moreover, counters nationalist narratives of America as a promised land. For many groups, migration to and settlement in the United States have been marked more by ambivalence than celebration. That Koreans envisioned themselves as a people without a country spoke to the annexation of Korea as well as the oppressive conditions in the United States. As exploited workers on the sugarcane plantations of Hawai'i and in the fields and streets of California, most Korean Americans faced a hardscrabble life. The fervor with which Korean Americans expressed their loyalties to Korea, in part, reflected their alienation from the United States.

The theme of exile of course has a religious genealogy. Korean American immigrant Christians could identify with the plight of Israel depicted in the Hebrew Bible. Indeed, some observers commented that Korea suffered a geopolitical fate like Israel's in which its strategic location meant that the peninsular nation had faced invasions from foreigners throughout its history. Biblical texts like Psalm 137 with reference to Israel's exile and singing the Lord's song in a foreign land resonated with Koreans in the United States and elsewhere. Protestant Christianity served as an important source of homemaking for Koreans in exile—a means by which they forged a multivalent sense of community and place marked by sustenance and hope as well as conflict and contention.[26] Koreans experienced life in this country within the context of migration & exile.

## Colonialism & Independence

The third major theme involves the relationship between colonialism and independence. Japan officially annexed Korea as a colony in 1910, but empire building had begun earlier, foreshadowed by the Sino-Japanese War of 1894–95 and the Russo-Japanese War of 1905. Japan's victories in both of these conflicts made clear their imperial designs on Korea. Those in the United States formed an important facet of the anticolonial struggle as part of larger networks in Korea and China.

Korean Americans represented a repository of Korean identity in the face of the systematic efforts by Japan to erase and absorb Korea into its empire. The Japanese colonial enterprise included the rewriting of history textbooks, the prohibition of Korean language, and the renaming of geographical places. In light of such measures, Korean Americans viewed their role as preserving Korea as a distinct people and nation through a community of memory.[27] At the same time, Koreans in the United States underwent major changes, reflected most visibly in their children, many of them U.S. citizens by birth. Nevertheless, the ways Koreans in the United States envisioned and worked toward a liberated homeland formed part of an expansive nationalism and sense of peoplehood that resonates with Gi-Wook Shin's examination of the embedded, contingent, and contested dimensions of ethnic nationalism in Korea and its complicated relationship with modernity.[28] Another study has pointed out that Koreans shifted the meaning and even the future of the nation outside Korea itself to places like California, beyond the direct bounds of Japanese colonialism.[29]

In focusing on Japan as the colonizer, it is easy to overlook U.S. colonialism. Scholars such as Oscar Campomanes have written about how the portrayal of the United States as a nation of immigrants whose supposed melting pot has created an egalitarian society has fostered a denial about how the United States has engaged in imperial projects at home and abroad. Campomanes has called for the contextualization of U.S. racial domination as part of a "world historical drama in which the white West via its culture, economic system, and political power has spread virtually throughout the globe."[30] The growing scholarship on the United States as empire serves as a corrective to the amnesia deeply embedded in the historiographical literature and in much of the American psyche.[31] In a pioneering essay, sociologists Edna Bonacich and Lucie Cheng laid a theoretical foundation for pre–World War II migration of Asians to the United States, not as distinct and unrelated factors in the sending and host countries, but as part of an interconnected world capitalist system.[32]

Religion in Korean American history makes these points plain in several respects, beginning with the intersection of this history with the Hawaiian Islands. Physically removed from the continental United States, Hawai'i is often forgotten altogether or added as an afterthought in national histories. The tourist industry also has generated a kind of erasure that has run roughshod over historical realities and the contemporary Hawaiian sovereignty movement. Reorienting our perspective cannot help but reveal the fingerprints of the United States upon this territory and peoples. Protestant missionaries, moreover, are heavily implicated in the creation of an American colony that dates to the early nineteenth century. The European American oligarchy of the islands in the nineteenth and twentieth centuries reads like a who's who of Congregational missionary families. Korean Americans entered the islands to labor in the sugarcane plantations under the control of these families in conjunction with the U.S. government. In this sense, colonialism is very much a part of the history of American religion.[33]

As Wayne Patterson has noted, American recruiters seeking Korean labor for Hawai'i met with success largely because of their connections to Protestant missionaries who urged their new parishioners to leave their homeland for the promise of a land under the influence of Christianity.[34] Mission work, foreign and domestic, that took place in Korea, Hawai'i, and California reflected comity agreements by denominations that designated which parts of the nation and foreign lands would go to which religious groups. These Protestant designs suggest a troubling parallel with the United States' imperial aims at home, in East Asia, and other parts of the world.[35]

Koreans on the mainland encountered a different version of colonialism than that which operated in Hawai'i, since they inherited a structure marked by enslavement, subjugation, conquest, and exclusion. Robert Blauner's now classic model of internal colonialism challenged the presumption of an immigrant/assimilation model for racialized groups such as Asians. Blauner argued for a linkage between what he called the third world abroad and the third world at home.[36] A recent study has also picked up on the connections within and beyond the United States in the racial formations of Latinas/Latinos and Asians (and Latin America and Asia itself). The designation of these two diverse groupings of peoples as perennial outsiders or foreigners has been an important component of U.S. nation-state formation and empire-building that reaffirms the normativity of white America.[37]

The past and present come together in the colonial experiences of Korean Americans, as a recent study has suggested that Korean immigrants in the post-1965 period have carried with them a U.S. imperial legacy in Korea that can be traced to the end of World War II.[38] In fact, that legacy is more properly located in the late nineteenth century, when Americans, primarily Protestant missionaries, first arrived in Korea. The religiously framed ideas and institutions that they introduced profoundly affected Korea's encounter with colonial modernity.[39] Because Japan colonized Korea, it is easy to overlook the imperial seeds sown by the United States much earlier than 1945. There is little doubt that Protestant Christianity served as a means for the planting of those seeds. The workings of empire, moreover, extended to those Koreans who migrated to the United States in the early decades of the twentieth century, even as that legacy has continued to the very present.

Colonialism of course is never simply a one-way process, and the experiences of Korean Americans spawned visions of independence. Plantation and other laborers barely able to make ends meet sacrificed their time and monies to support efforts within their communities and overseas. While religion could serve the purposes of colonialism, it also fueled independence through the messages found in the Bible about liberation and freedom. Religion acted as a double-edged sword that cut in paradoxical directions.

The widespread zeal of Koreans for the independence of their homeland lent itself to conflict. Religious institutions and affiliated organizations bore the brunt of much of the internal strife within Korean American communities in the islands and on the mainland. The contention stemmed from competing visions as well as clashing personalities. The independence movement came with no instruction manuals, and given the limited resources and the geopolitics of the day, independence represented a lofty goal perched upon a precarious foundation.

Conflict also arose because where some saw a clear dividing line between politics and religion, others did not. The ensuing fissures affected individuals who fought for their views, and congregations that struggled with this issue sometimes split apart. In at least one instance, a church organized that broke completely from the denominational mission structure in place. Hence, some Korean Americans interpreted the move away from missionary control and oversight to independent status as a faithful expression of the kind of freedom envisioned for Korea. In other words, Korean Americans exercised the kind of leadership and tried to live out the independence that they sought for their homeland.

## Fields of Study

The three relational themes outlined above—race & religion, migration & exile, and colonialism & independence—point to the complex and layered nature of religion in Korean American history. They speak to the fields of American religion and racial and ethnic studies (Asian American Studies).

The Korean American case suggests how all of American religion is racialized; in sum, racial constructs have deeply informed religious identity for individuals, communities, and the nation. On the flip side, if the study of Asian Americans has attended to race, then religion has often been left out of the picture. Migration & exile as a theme not only reinforces the transnational turn among scholars who study immigration to the United States, but adds an exilic dimension. Finally, Korean American religious history adds important insights into the workings of an American empire and into movements of independence within and beyond the borders of the nation-state. Exceptionalism and denial notwithstanding, the United States has been a colonial power to be reckoned with for quite some time. The manifestations of empire have generated visions of independence that for Korean Americans drew upon their engagement with Protestant Christianity.

*Contentious Spirits* also asks those who study American religion and racial & ethnic studies to rethink other categories that have long held sway in these and related fields. For instance, Koreans in Hawai'i and California challenge the black/white binary that has shaped so much of our collective thinking about race in the United States. While there is good reason for this frame given our history, race has been multifaceted from the very beginning. The black/white paradigm masks important regional differences and privileges some areas of the country while rendering others as exceptional and less important. Such designations contribute to an impoverished understanding of race in the United States. What does it mean for race in America that Asian Americans have long represented the majority of the population in Hawai'i? Likewise, how does one interpret California's multiracial past (and present) and the fact that the state today is by far the most populous in the nation when addressing issues of race across the nation?[40] The relational themes that guide this study say something of the larger issues and significance embedded in Korean American history.

## Chapter Summaries

Given the important linkages between Korean America and Korea in the late nineteenth and early twentieth centuries, Chapter 1 provides a brief overview of Protestant Christianity in modern Korean history. In particular, the chapter attempts an answer to the question of why Protestant

Christianity made significant inroads into Korean society. The arrival of American missionaries in 1884 accompanied the forcible "opening" of Korea to the international stage. Japan, the United States, China, and Russia each had its sights on the peninsular nation while rulers of Chosŏn Korea (1392–1910) fought to maintain sovereignty. The influence of Protestant Christianity reached elites, who saw in Christianity elements of reform, and extended to women and the lower classes, who gained access to education and social mobility.

Religion proved instrumental in the course of events that led Koreans to depart from their homeland, and Chapter 2 discusses the migration and settlement of Koreans in Hawai'i through the framework of Protestant Christianity. Clergy and lay leaders established churches on the sugarcane plantations throughout the islands. Methodist missions created a network linking the work in Hawai'i to people and structures in the homeland. Koreans shaped and guided their faith and community within the larger context of events that they faced in moving from one colonial setting to another.

Chapter 3 tells the story of the Korean Christian Church of Honolulu, founded in 1918, and how its origins represent a legacy of independence and also a practice of religious nationalism. Syngman Rhee, best known as the first president of the Republic of Korea (South Korea), looms large as the founder of the church, having come to Hawai'i through Methodist connections. The controversial patriot parted company with the missionaries in Hawai'i to form the nondenominational Korean Christian Church with his followers. The ensuing divide between Korean Americans in the Methodist camp versus the independent Korean Christian Church shaped local politics in Hawai'i for decades. The beginnings of the church and its presence in the lives of Korean Americans reflected a religious nationalism that integrated faith and politics.

In shifting focus from Hawai'i to the mainland, Chapter 4 examines the contours of Korean American experience through the Korean Methodist Church of Los Angeles. The church served as a way station and hub, and its history in many ways reflected the larger community. For instance, the migratory hardships of the population found expression in the frequent church moves that gave some indication of the challenges of the congregation to survive in the first decades of its existence. Evident in the congregation's history are the relational themes that structure the narrative.

Chapter 5 extends the history of the Korean Methodist Church to the period from 1930 to 1945—an era marked by the Great Depression and World War II. The extraordinary times called upon Koreans to negotiate difficult circumstances on a new level, and the church served its constituency. The second generation began to come of age, and an influx of students from Korea breathed new life into the congregation and community. Of interest is how the Korean Methodist Church served as a haven for the more politically progressive.

A remarkable publication called the *Korean Student Bulletin* (*KSB*) is the subject of Chapter 6. Associated with the YMCA in the United States, the bulletin created an outlet for Korean international and Korean American college students to find their voices on a range of issues. The publication's explicitly religious (Christian) orientation provides access to the thoughts of men and women in their own words. The relational themes guide the analysis of the bulletin, and while national and international in scope, the *KSB* also addressed concerns within Korean American communities in Hawai'i and California.

## A Note on Sources and Name/Place Citations

*Contentious Spirits* relies on primary source materials not easily found. Such is the challenge of studying people whose lives allowed little time for documentation or record keeping. The various churches that appear in these pages—Methodist, Episcopal, Korean Christian, and Presbyterian—kept some materials that proved valuable, as did missionary and denominational records. Personal papers of long-time members and oral history interviews also helped piece together the past. University-based archives and state and local historical societies in Hawai'i and California helped fill out the larger context. Newspapers, journals, and newsletters provided a voice for Korean Americans that did not readily appear elsewhere. Similarly, autobiographical writings as well as literary works about Korean America allowed insight into experiences and perspectives. The secondary literature on Korea and the Korean American community proved invaluable, providing general background and serving as a guide to other sources.

In general, I have tried to follow the McCune-Reischauer Romanization System for Korean words, but there are a number of exceptions. In some cases, individual names that appeared in sources (published and unpublished) did not contain Korean-language characters, making it impossible to know with certainty how the name might be romanized. At other points, I have retained certain English spellings of names or places to match spellings in source materials. Overall, I have aimed for consistency and placed explanations into the notes at various points throughout the book to provide some guidance to the reader.

## A Particular Past

This introduction opened with recollections from my family's experiences during the 1960s and 1970s within the immigrant Korean American community in southern California. In part, I wanted to stress the resonances of this period with an earlier era as well as the present. The church of my youth, for instance, split off from the Los Angeles Korean Presbyterian Church founded in 1906; this historic congregation continues its ministry today near the campus of the University of Southern California. Next to the church, not coincidentally, is the building that housed the Korean National Association, a key organization of the independence movement. The intertwining of politics and religion, marked by colonialism, migration, racism, and sheer survival engendered much contention within and among Korean Americans—alluded to in the title, *Contentious Spirits*.

My discussion of the personal also provides an opportunity to acknowledge the issue of subjectivity. As a Korean American and Protestant Christian, I am very much a part of the tradition that is the focus of the narrative, though filtered through my own lenses and across the span of time that both connects and divides the present from the past. In addition, my views have been shaped by the study of United States history and Asian American studies. All perspectives, of course, obscure as much as they reveal, and *Contentious Spirits* is merely one of many religious histories of Korean America that could be told. This introduction and its various components provide some indication of the particulars. The telling that unfolds in the pages to follow is an offering of sorts, given in gratitude and with respect for those Koreans who first made their way to the United States and who kept the faith.

# ONE

# God's Chosŏn People

Peter Hyun recalled that time in the winter of 1919, when he and his seven brothers and sisters accompanied their mother and father to the South Gate railway station in Seoul. Church business had often taken Peter's father, the Reverend Soon Hyun (Hyŏn Sun), to different parts of the country. What struck the young Peter was that his father had come and gone on many such trips, but never before had the whole family, including his invalid sister, Soon-Ok, been assembled to bid him farewell. Only later would Peter and the other children learn that their father was fleeing the country to work in China for Korea's liberation. It would be a year before Maria Hyun somehow snuck herself and her children across the border to join her husband and other Koreans who had set up the provisional Korean government, exiled in the French Quarter of Shanghai.[1]

According to Peter Hyun, his father used his position as a leading Methodist minister to take part in the planning of a national uprising that galvanized the independence movement in Korea and abroad. On 1 March 1919, Koreans declared their independence through the rallying cry *Manse!* [Long live Korea!] and the display of Korean flags in a massive, well-planned, and peaceful demonstration that caught the Japanese colonial government by surprise.[2] Peter Hyun remembered: "THE AWESOME CHANTS of the surging crowd still ring in my ears. It was Seoul, Korea, March 1, 1919; I was twelve years old. Countless thousands of Koreans—men and women, young and old, defying the Japanese police—poured out onto the streets of Seoul and shouting and dancing, proclaimed their national independence."[3] Hyun did not heed his mother's orders to stay indoors and once outside got swept up into the streets by demonstrators. They passed by the Methodist church that Peter's father had served and the American Tennis Club where he had seen people play the strange-looking game. He walked with a group of women students from Ewha, the Protestant missionary college for women. Thousands of people had gathered in the city, taking part in the display of nationalism. Hyun's pride quickly turned to horror when he saw the Japanese mounted marines repeatedly charge into the crowd with sabers slashing to and fro. Hyun managed to get to the fringes and ran as fast as his feet could carry him until he reached his home—physically and emotionally shaken by what he had witnessed. He worried about the college students he had walked with and wondered about the fate of so many who had joined forces.[4]

Choy Hai-Arm, a foreign student in the United States writing in 1937 and 1938, chronicled his participation in the events of 1 March 1919. He had finished at a public middle school in 1918 under the supervision of Japanese teachers and then started junior high at a private Korean Christian school in northern Korea. The change in schools took some adjustment, as he soon discovered that he had entered another world. His fluency and skill in the Japanese language earned him no points from his teachers, and his peers teased him on the playground for not speaking Korean. In class, he heard stories about Korea's past for the first time. Over the course of a year, Choy commented that he had become a Korean boy again.[5]

On that fateful day, under clear blue skies, Choy and other students went to the auditorium for a brief chapel service. Afterward, a teacher told them that they would be joining Koreans throughout the country in making a nonviolent statement for Korea's freedom. Students were instructed to remove the flags from their coats at the signal and to shout "Manse!" After a brief ceremony noting the passing of the Korean king, Kojong, a pastor rose at the podium and began to read the Declaration of Independence. Two large silk Korean flags hung along both sides of the platform, and people stood out of pride and respect. Choy recalled:

> Japanese detectives tried to stop the reading, but quailed before the fearsome shouts of the crowd. When the reading was ended, the pastor cried

aloud, "This is our resurrection day. For nine long years we suffered the loss of our freedom which our forefathers had enjoyed for more than four thousand years. Today is the reviving day of our nation." We shouted "Mansae" aloud as vocal capacity allowed, following our leader's direction. Oh! What a sight it was!

After circling the city, the people gathered in front of the police headquarters and demanded the release of the imprisoned leaders. Police called upon the firemen to spray water to control the crowd, but this only angered those gathered. Screams and chaos followed the gunshots as people ran into the side streets carrying the wounded.[6]

These two eyewitness accounts of the momentous events of March First contain clues about the nature of religion in Korean American history. The first has to do with the theme of migration & exile. Peter Hyun and his family left Korea for China and then Hawai'i. Peter, however, had already traveled with his family across the Pacific and back by the time he was twelve and took part in the events of March First. Born in 1906 on the island of Kauai in the U.S. Territory of Hawai'i, Peter may have been the first Korean male born on the island. The Reverend Hyun and his wife, Maria, arrived in Hawai'i in 1903 and helped establish churches there. His work in Methodist missionary circles enabled Reverend Hyun to accompany Koreans to Hawai'i and eventually led him back to Korea, but he returned to the islands again and spent a good portion of his ministerial career serving churches in Hawai'i. Much less is known about Choy Hai-Arm, the international student who authored the two-part article that appeared in the *Korean Student Bulletin*.[7] Choy and Hyun's experiences suggest something of the relational theme of migration & exile.

Religion is another key element that emerges from these stories. The church-based school of Choy Hai-Arm helped shape his identity formation as a Korean under Japanese colonial rule. Protestant Christianity directly influenced his sense of nationalism, from the use of Korean language to the framing of March 1 in the language of the resurrection. In addition, Christians accounted for sixteen of the thirty-three signers of the Korean Declaration of Independence. Choy's connections to missionaries and the church probably enabled him to study in the United States. Many Koreans who studied abroad returned to Korea to assume prominent positions in education, church work, and other fields.

Peter Hyun's experiences also indicate how religion infused the lives of the Hyun family. The Reverend Hyun traveled throughout Korea, China, and the United States, laboring for the church and his homeland. His position as the superintendent of Methodist Sunday Schools in Korea allowed him to canvas the country in support of the church's mission and cultivate networks to mobilize the uprising. Leaders had organized directly under the noses of Japanese authorities and also without the knowledge of American missionaries.

Along with migration & exile and religion & race, the relational theme of colonialism & independence is evident in the very fiber of the events described by Hyun and Choy. March First stands as the symbolic marker for modern Korean independence against Japanese colonialism; it set into motion a greater sense of nationhood among Koreans in Korea and those outside the peninsula. The Hyun family's transpacific crossings reveal the machinations of American capital in search of cheap labor as Soon and Maria Hyun accompanied workers to the sugarcane plantations of Hawai'i. The industrialists of the American colony, fittingly, called upon American missionaries in Korea to help them entice workers to leave their homeland, even as they were the descendants of the first missionaries who represented the chief architects of the overthrow of the Hawaiian monarchy and annexation by the United States.

While these major themes provide a backdrop, this chapter focuses on the legacy of Protestant Christianity in Korea in the late nineteenth and early twentieth centuries. An understanding of the nature, development, and particular historical context of this religious tradition is critical because Korean American Protestants embodied, adapted, and extended this legacy beyond the boundaries of the homeland. The journeys of Peter Hyun and Choy Hai-Arm illustrate how religion linked people, institutions, and even nation-states across time and space. Although Protestant Christianity represented only one element during this cataclysmic period, it proved to be very significant for the nation and for many of those who left for the United States.

Of particular interest is unpacking how Protestant Christianity managed to exert considerable influence in Korean society so quickly from the time of its introduction in the 1880s. As with most questions of historical causality, there is no single, neatly defined answer, but rather a set of interlocking factors that together begin to approximate an explanation. There is some credence to the suggestion that the religious foundations of Korean society aligned with aspects of Protestant Christianity such as belief in a supreme being and the afterlife. Missionary strategies, moreover, stressed the need for Korean leadership in the propagation of the faith, and an indigenization of Christianity took root early. Protestant Christianity also introduced new concepts and institutions that meshed with nationalist efforts in Korea. A crumbling nation-state and the rise of a Japanese empire enabled Christians to position themselves in a manner that helped them address the needs of Koreans at this juncture in the nation's history. According to historian Chung-Shin Park, "The history of the remarkable growth of Protestantism in modern Korea is a history of the metamorphosis of the religion from a foreign, Western faith to an accepted Korean religion."[8]

## The State of Religion

Given the focus on Protestant Christianity, it is easy to overlook the deep and diverse religious foundations of the nation.[9] One study of Protestantism and nationalism in Korea reminds us that in Chosŏn Korea (1392–1910) no clear lines separated philosophy, religion, and state ideology. By the late nineteenth century, Protestantism entered a conversation that was well under way.[10] The earliest traces of Christianity in Korea date to the sixteenth century, when Korean envoys to China encountered Europeans, including Roman Catholic priests and religious tracts. In addition, some three hundred Koreans who had been taken back to Japan with the Hideyoshi invasion reportedly received instruction in Catholic doctrine in 1596. In the last quarter of the eighteenth century, Catholicism began to spread among the population in Korea, first among elites and then among the general population. By 1785, the state banned Christianity—seen as a threat to the Confucian state—and growing repression drove the church underground. Approximately eight thousand martyrs died in the Great Persecution (1866–71), about half of the entire Catholic population.[11]

Catholicism also influenced other movements, including Silhak, or empirical study, in which scholars opposed what they considered the extreme metaphysical speculation of the official neo-Confucian orthodoxy. Kenneth Wells points out that these scholars responded to peasant unrest in rural

Korea in the eighteenth century and the strain this put on the existing feudal structure. Some of the key proponents of Silhak were either Catholics or those who had attempted to fuse Catholic theological teachings and science with Confucianism in an effort to revise existing economic and political structures. Proponents were not successful in gaining tolerance from the court, and Silhak was suppressed.[12]

Throughout the Chosŏn era Buddhism was disfavored in the effort to construct a Confucian state. By the nineteenth century, Buddhism was suffering from a long period of decline in which its infrastructure, organization, and influence had deteriorated. Cut off from major political and economic institutions, Buddhism had been sidelined as a major social force as Korea was pulled onto the international stage. Korea's diplomatic and trade contacts with the outside world, however, brought a respite from official suppression of Buddhism. The presence of Protestant Christianity also sparked some of the more progressive elements within Korean Buddhism to action. With colonial rule, Japan sought to bring its institutional structure of Buddhism as part of its efforts to absorb Korea into its empire. Though such efforts met with mixed reception, the strong influence of Buddhism in Japan brought a measure of protection to Buddhism in Korea, even if only for Japan's own political agenda.[13]

If Catholicism and Buddhism suffered at the end of the nineteenth century, such was not the case for a conservative, millennial religious movement called Tonghak (Eastern Learning) that surfaced in the 1860s. Ch'oe Che-u began teaching peasants a millennial blending of Confucianism, Buddhism, and Taoism to help Korea ward off the evils of Western learning, especially Catholicism, though Ch'oe himself had been influenced by it. The primary teaching stressed the unity of heaven and humanity and the equality of all people. Tonghak rode the wave of peasant unrest borne of long-standing and increasing agrarian distress caused by onerous taxation policies. It adopted the slogan "Drive out the Japanese dwarfs and the Western barbarians, and praise righteousness." The movement gathered strength in the southwestern farming regions, and a number of armed victories alarmed those in Seoul. By 1894, nearly a thousand soldiers left the capital garrison to quell the rebellion, but half deserted and Tonghaks routed the other half. King Kojong called for help from China, and soon Japanese troops followed, setting into motion the Sino-Japanese War of 1894–95 in which Japan soundly defeated

China. A suppressed Tonghak resurfaced as Ch'ŏndogyo (Religion of the Heavenly Way). The movement emphasized a supreme being and curative magic, and it formed part of the growing nationalism during this era.[14]

The Sino-Japanese War signaled the demise not only of the Tonghaks, but also of Korea's long-standing Sinocentric orientation. The existing order was plunged into greater crisis, the court managing its tenuous sovereignty through a strategy of checks and balances with the foreign powers involved in Korea. Playing one imperial power against another was a tricky business, especially for a hermit kingdom only recently forced out of its isolation. For Protestant Christianity, linked primarily to the United States, the turn of events at the tail end of the nineteenth century created opportunities for its influence in ways that would have been unthinkable a few decades earlier during the Great Persecution of Catholics.

## Religious Affinities

While the social and political realities of a severely weakened nation-state undoubtedly created an opening for Protestant Christianity in Korea, the question remains why people gravitated toward this religious tradition. One theory is that the religious foundations of Korea, rooted in the cult or myth of Tan'gun and the notion of a monotheistic supreme being, helped missionaries to find some common ground on which to stand with Koreans. The supreme deity known as Hwanin, or Hanŭnim, the Heavenly One, was equated with the God of the Bible. Missionaries and early converts made the association between the two to stress monotheism. And yet polytheism and pantheism operated widely in Korean religious and folk culture. This worldview has sometimes been labeled as Shamanism, one in which individual spirits existed in all natural, material, and animate phenomena. Nevertheless, the appeal to the Heavenly Being served its purpose of suggesting a connectedness between the new religion and the religious sensibilities of the Korean people.[15]

Similarly, others have suggested that the layers of religious development in Korea over a long period of time and their commingling resulted in a receptivity to Protestant Christianity. Religious studies scholar David Chung has suggested that the attempts by the Chosŏn rulers to create a pure Confucian state constituted an ideal more than a reality. Despite severe suppression, Buddhism continued to be part of the cosmology of Koreans, addressing issues of life and death that Confucianism did not. Moreover, Taoism, though never a dominant religion in Korea, did influence philosophical thought and some ritual practices. And, as mentioned earlier, an indigenous religious tradition served as a foundation of religion in Korea.[16]

Chung speculates that Protestant Christianity enjoyed tremendous growth because of what he has termed congenial aspects of Korea's existing religious traditions to its central tenets. In short, the groundwork had already been laid, and missionaries and early converts built on that religious foundation. Chung suggests that, along with monotheism, other elements, such as the longing for salvation that is part of the Pure Land Buddhist tradition, worked well with Christianity's message. Messianic hope and the idea of an afterlife provided further points of contact.[17]

In the end, of course, proving such causal linkages is next to impossible, but perhaps it is enough to say that as foreign as Christianity might have appeared in Korea at the outset, there may have been more affinities with Protestantism than expected. Missionaries and Korean Christians, then and now, have seen such signs as providential, even as others might chalk them up to coincidence. To that end, one observer has noted that in modern Korea it is not uncommon for people to be Confucianists, Buddhists, and Christians at the same time.[18]

## Missions and Indigenization

Many people have noted that Christianity has been Koreanized, meaning that over the course of time Koreans have made Christianity their own.[19] Such a claim ought not to be surprising given the global extension of Christianity to all parts of the world. With new converts overwhelmingly in places like Asia, South America, and Africa, Christianity is hardly the preserve of Europe and North America. Christianity, properly understood, is not Western, but a world religion.[20] Korean Christianity clearly has helped shape a global Christianity.[21]

While numbers never tell the whole story, they do say something when one in a thousand Koreans was Christian in 1890, one in fifty in the 1930s, one in twenty in 1955, and now one in four.[22] One reason for Protestantism's advance may have been the religious predisposition of Koreans, but another important element in the story involved missionary strategy and the zeal of Korean converts to make the faith an indigenous one. Much has been attributed to the Nevius Plan, so named for a Protestant missionary to China. Ironically, the plan seemed not to have made much headway in China, but it did meet with success in Korea. The Nevius Plan had four main goals for Christian converts: (1) to be an individual worker for Christ, living out one's beliefs in one's own neighborhood and supporting oneself through a trade; (2) to develop methods and machinery only as much as the native church could manage; (3) to set aside individuals in the native church to do evangelistic work among neighbors; and (4) to let natives provide their own church buildings. In short, Korean churches were to be self-supporting, self-propagating, and self-governing. L. George Paik, a leading church historian writing in the 1920s, also noted that Protestantism benefited from additional methods such as itinerancy, the distribution of Christian literature, and street preaching.[23] The fact that 186 out of 188 Presbyterian churches in Korea achieved self-supporting status by 1908 suggests something of the embrace and effect of these methods.[24]

Bible translation work spearheaded by missionaries and their Korean counterparts also aided the growth of Protestantism. In particular, the decision to translate the Bible into the vernacular, *han'gŭl*, rather than Chinese characters, made the text far more accessible.[25] Despite the real tensions among missionaries and converts alike, the agreement on a single translation of the Bible and a common hymnal contributed to a shared sense of Christian community.[26] The efforts by missionaries to offer education to the masses of Koreans meant that reading the Bible led directly to rising literacy rates. The power of the written word came in large part in the form of biblical stories and references. And like converts everywhere, but especially for those in the throes of oppression, Koreans found in the Bible a message of liberation that differed from that of the missionaries. Once unleashed, texts carried messages beyond the control of any particular group.

In addition to using method and text, Protestants gained ground through building institutions, primarily hospitals and schools, which became a very potent means of influencing Korean society and culture. Early on, these institutions served as primary sites of interaction between missionaries and Koreans, allowing exchanges to take place, care to be offered, and impressions made. Under unusual circumstances that will be discussed later in the chapter, the king authorized a Western medical hospital under the direction of the American missionary Horace Allen.[27] As early as 1892, mission hospitals treated nearly ten thousand patients, from the royal family to the most disenfranchised.[28]

Schools also drew pupils from all walks of life, and the traditional Confucian educational and examination system no longer held a monopoly on the aspirations of the Korean population. Mission schools exposed students to a different kind of learning, one associated with the United States and the West. That knowledge had enabled the United States to prosper and to gain international standing. European learning, filtered through China, had also given Korean elites some sense of science and cartography that differed from their own. Upper-class conservatives may have shunned the ways of the foreign barbarians, but others from privileged backgrounds passed through mission schools and served as a bridge of sorts from the classical Chinese-based education to the newfangled ideas presented in Protestant schools. Likewise, through the schools commoners gained access to education that was otherwise out of their reach. For this stratum of society, the mission schools fostered social mobility during a time of tremendous flux. By 1910, over eight hundred Presbyterian and Methodist educational institutions operated in Korea.[29]

The changes taking place in medicine and education signaled both loss and change on a massive scale. Paik characterized Koreans as a people full of despair and with hatred toward the colonizing enemy, and he sensed that these issues evinced a spiritual need that sowed the seeds of the Great Revival of 1907. What began in the north during the annual Bible Training Class spread quickly throughout the peninsula. The distinctive practice of loud unison prayer marked the revival. Paik commented that "public confession of sins determined the extent of the revival and the fervor of the prayer in unison proved the depth of the spiritual experience."[30]

The genuineness of the revival could be seen in the fact that the Korean Christian church had come into its own. Paik indicated that the revival set the Korean church on its own spiritual path, one distinct from that of the missionaries. Korean Christians kept the faith in the face of the hardships and trials that followed the revival as Japan tightened its grip on Korea and viewed Christians especially with suspicion. The indigenization fostered by the revival also meant that Korean believers realized that the missionaries "were not altogether saints." A fuller sense of missionary humanity emerged, for better and for worse. All in all, according to Paik, by the late 1920s Korean Christians were already looking at the Great Revival as the source of their spiritual life.[31]

Revival had not been so much about a flood of new converts as the bolstering of those already in the faith, but Paik recognized the connection between revival and evangelism.[32] In the short span from 1905 to 1907, the number of churches had grown by 200 percent (to a total of 642). The number of baptized adherents had increased by nearly the same percentage (9,761 in 1905 to 18,964 in 1907). Those who had entered the churches but had not yet been baptized—probationers—jumped nearly 350 percent, numbering almost one hundred thousand.[33] In 1910, two hundred thousand believers represented less than 2 percent of the total population.[34] At the same time, Christianity's influence went beyond the numbers; while American missionaries took some credit for this, events like the Great Revival of 1907 cast Protestant Christianity in a Korean mold.

## Reform and the Nation

Along with religious predispositions, missionary strategies, and growing indigenization, the reform elements of Protestant Christianity were mixed in the crucible of nationalist sentiments and movements in Korea. Women and working-class Koreans found in Protestant Christianity a social and spiritual world more egalitarian than the Confucian order they had known for so long. If greater equality and democracy appealed to those who had been on the margins of Chosŏn Korea, then these notions also appealed to elites who saw in Christianity a means of reforming an ailing nation. Koreans differed of course how they applied their faith, but in the era prior to 1 March 1919, Protestantism exerted a significant influence on nationalist politics.

Protestant mission work in Korea, according to Paik, could hardly be called uniform. Nine different mission groups from four denominations (Anglican, Baptist, Methodist, and Presbyterian) had entered Korea in the last two decades of the nineteenth century.[35] Comity agreements attempted to carve out respective areas of the peninsula, but such agreements could not erase the real differences that split denominations like the American

Presbyterians and Methodists into northern and southern branches.[36] Nevertheless, some general policies had implications for the class and gender structures of Korean society. One principle stated that, when possible, missionary work should be directed to the working classes. Another principle involved the conversion of women and the training of Christian girls, since mothers exerted great influence over future generations.[37]

Such an approach made sense, given that the disenfranchised had the least to lose and the most to gain from this new religion. Conversion could bring ostracism from family and fellow villagers, but it also opened avenues for education and church life that pulled believers into a new universe of ideas, institutions, and activities. Paik recounted the conversions of a significant number of butchers, reported to be about thirty thousand. Considered cruel, perhaps because of the nature of their occupation, butchers could not marry outside their caste, and to say that a man behaved as a butcher constituted a terrible insult. Protestantism empowered butchers to work for reform, petitioning the government and winning from it concessions in terms of their treatment in society.[38]

Women believers also spoke about a newfound sense of humanity, and many availed themselves of an opportunity to go to school and to gain skills that had been denied to most women. Perhaps it is not surprising, then, that Christian women were some of Korea's strongest proponents of women's rights, becoming nationalist leaders and activists. Prominent patriots such as Maria Kim, Esther Hwang, and Yu Kwan-Su were all Christians. Many of these women, moreover, defied missionary strictures in their nationalist activities, seeing congruence between their politics and faith where others saw incompatibility.[39]

The complicated relationship between Protestantism and politics drew all ranks of Korean society within the orbit of the church and its related institutions. New ideas and learning fueled hopes of reform for Korea in the face of growing imperial threats. According to Chung-Shin Park, during the early colonial years, "Almost all nationalist activities occurred in and around the Protestant religious community, and most of the major personalities behind these movements, whether moderate culturalists or militant socialists, were members of the Protestant church or products of this religious community."[40]

Protestantism occupied an exceptional place in the time from 1884 to

1919 in that it continued to operate when other political and social groups had been shut down. Religion provided spaces in which political debate, leadership training, and information sharing could take place. Park underscores that the close working relationship between nationalists fighting for independence and those in the churches manifested itself in events such as the March First Movement.[41]

Two other points about Protestantism and its relation to the nation merit mention. The first, alluded to earlier, is that the national network of information, people, and institutions connected to the church in turn enabled the work of nationalism to take place. Despite surveillance and pressures, the umbrella of Christianity provided a means of maneuverability for those under it and associated with it. Until Japanese colonial policies shifted in the aftermath of 1919, which allowed other avenues of nationalist activity to develop, Protestant Christianity occupied an unrivaled position in terms of Korean nationalism.[42]

Nationalist activities under the aegis of Christianity clearly concerned many of the American missionaries, and as stated earlier, tensions did arise between Koreans and missionaries. The Nevius Plan may have worked too well, and as the church experienced robust growth, missionaries could not control the directions that churches and related institutions took.[43] Many Korean Christians interpreted their situation in the light of the biblical story of God's deliverance of the Jews from slavery in Egypt. The fact that the massive March First Movement caught the missionaries unawares is especially telling given the prominent place of Korean Protestant Christians in the uprising.[44] National identity formed the core of the history of the Protestant church in Korea.[45]

The second point is that Protestant Christianity, arguably more than any other influence, helped ease the historic divisions between the classes. Conversion by no means magically dissolved the real differences that existed between elites and commoners, nor did it automatically elevate women from their subordinated position. And yet, as one insightful study emphasizes, the teachings of Protestant Christianity did not privilege those of high social standing, and notions of equality as sinners before the Lord provided a framework for reform. The Great Revival of 1907 highlighted the basic principle of personal renewal that knew no bounds.[46] Christianity did offer believers a sense of shared community and the theological notion of the body of Christ. That sense of belonging, while not a charm to ward off the schisms and divisions within Korean Christianity (mirrored among missionaries), still fueled a sense of collectivity. For many Korean Christians, the bonds of fellowship as believers also included the bonds of nation.

## Timing and Happenstance

In the effort to explain the growth and development of Protestant Christianity, several interlocking factors have been identified. The particular timing of Protestantism's introduction to Korea as well as unforeseen opportunities it enjoyed also need to be taken into account. By the late nineteenth century, the demise of the Chosŏn dynasty coincided with the entry of various nation-states, including the United States. In the midst of these events, a failed coup provided an early medical missionary a major entry point into the graces of the royal family. Finally, Japan emerged as the colonial force to be reckoned with.

Korea's tributary relationship with China and the balance of power between the monarchy and aristocrats had created a relatively homogenous society whose stability had helped the Chosŏn dynasty to rule since 1392. Korean leaders knew something of the changes taking place in the nineteenth century in East Asia, but the status quo became a stumbling block in terms of navigating the tremendous changes in store. Efforts at reform mobilized conservative forces that sought to maintain the old order, and those decisions maintaining the status quo often undermined Korea's ability to adjust to changing realities. The defeat of China in the Sino-Japanese War of 1894–95 placed Korea in a very vulnerable position.[47]

It is perhaps not surprising that Protestantism's real growth began after 1894.[48] In part, this timing had to do with the events described, but it also took time to establish institutions and to allow programs to have some effect. Korea's weakness allowed Protestantism to operate more freely than would have been the case under different circumstances. State weakness coupled with Protestantism's contributions in envisioning a different kind of state and nationalist activities all served its influence and growth.[49]

One incident in the early fortunes of Protestantism in Korea illustrates how the events of history can turn on the most unexpected of circumstances. Horace N. Allen, a Presbyterian medical missionary, arrived in Korea in

September 1884. Given Korea's hostility to foreigners and their ways, Allen kept his missionary intentions quiet; his presence in Korea was ostensibly to serve as physician to the American legation. The failed coup by radical reformers in December 1884 left Prince Min, the powerful queen's nephew, on the brink of death. Allen successfully treated the prince, and in so doing, he forged a strong relationship with the royal family. He became the court physician, and the king granted the establishment of the Korean Government Hospital with Allen in charge. Allen became the secretary of the American legation, advancing missionary and state interests of the United States in Korea over the course of the next decade.[50]

The introduction of Protestantism to Korea benefited not only from Korea's weakened state and from an unusual opportunity to forge close personal ties to the royal family, but also from the looming presence of Japan as a colonizing power. From the end of the Sino-Japanese War in 1895, and with the defeat of Russia in the Russo-Japanese War a decade later, Japan followed through with its plan for annexation, which officially took place in August 1910. Earlier efforts at national reform shifted to the cause of Korean independence. Korean Protestants participated in the thick of nationalist activities playing out in the early years of the colonial period. The centrality of the Christian networks, leadership, and religious meanings, varied as they were, enabled Protestantism to deflect charges of foreign imperialism. The Japanese represented the enemy, and its colonial rule drove many into the Christian fold.[51]

## Conclusion

Although only a brief overview, this chapter has suggested that the growth and presence of Protestant Christianity stemmed from a number of related factors rather than any single cause. The state of more established religions like Buddhism as well as the rise of other religions like Tonghak (Eastern Learning) in their own ways created space for the introduction of Protestant Christianity. The existing religious context, including what might be termed favorable religious predispositions to tenets within Christianity, may have fostered receptivity. Others have pointed to a long history of religious syncretism that now included Protestant Christianity.

One certainly has to acknowledge the role that Protestant missionaries played, especially in their basic strategy of empowering Korean Christian churches to govern and support themselves and propagate their faith. No doubt Korean zeal and leadership among the faithful also allowed Christianity to mature and to grow, as evidenced in the Great Revival of 1907. The process of indigenization also meant that Korean Protestants took responsibility for their faith. Though varied in their views, Christians took an active role in nationalist activities in the face of encroaching Japanese colonialism.

Those activities had their roots in earlier progressive reform efforts, and in the years leading up to 1919, no other element in Korean society arguably had a greater effect on Korean nationalism than Protestant Christianity. Issues of timing also helped Protestantism, as it was introduced when the nation was in a weakened state and when people were more open to moving beyond the status quo. Personal relationships at the highest levels, tied to Western medicine, added a bit of luck or providence, depending on one's view. With Japan as the colonial oppressor, Koreans could look to Protestant Christianity for direction in the quest for independence.

The establishment of Protestant Christianity in Korea in the late nineteenth and early twentieth centuries makes for a fascinating and layered narrative replete with a cast of missionaries, royalty, and converts on an international stage. Religion proved to be a powerful force for change during an especially volatile period of modern Korean history marked by dynastic deterioration and colonialism. Korean Christians played a pivotal role in these events, making the religious tradition their own in the midst of the religious pluralism that had been a part of Korean society and culture for many centuries. The specter of race appeared not only in the contact and exchange with foreign missionaries, but in the racialized ways that the Japanese sought to absorb Korea.

Korean American adherents of the faith of course represented the migrant and exilic elements of Protestant Christianity, as the churches and religious networks in Korea and abroad bound people to one another. The events discussed here set the stage for the movement of people not only across spatial expanse, but also in the cause of the nation. Religion clearly fueled visions of independence, even as colonialism became an ever growing reality in turn-of-the-century Korea. Christianity played a major role in the diasporic politics of independence.

As a young boy, Peter Hyun probably gave such issues little thought while demonstrating for Korea in March 1919. The entire Hyun family returned in 1924 to Peter's birthplace in Hawai'i so that his father could resume serving migrants and exiles there. This suggests something of the threads that connect religion in Korean American history. Only later would time and perspective allow Hyun to reflect upon the legacy of his family and the land of his ancestry.

The religious legacy of Korean Americans can in part be traced to the genealogy of the religious imaginations, institutions, and historical circumstances of Protestant Christianity in Korea. We now move to Hawai'i to follow how that legacy played out in the lives of Koreans in a territorial outpost of the American empire.

# Paradise Bound

Soon and Maria Hyun said their good-byes to family and friends in February 1903 and boarded the Japanese liner docked at the port in Chemulp'o (Inch'ŏn).[1] The Hyuns and about 120 other Koreans were headed to Hawai'i courtesy of the American sugar industry. The group arrived in Honolulu around 20 February and headed by train to the Kahuku Sugar Plantation. In his autobiography, the Reverend Hyun noted: "Almost all of my fellow Koreans were discouraged to live in such a terrible camp and work so hard in the sugar cane field."[2] Despite and perhaps because of the backbreaking work, Koreans organized English language classes, a Christian church, and a mutual association.[3]

Hyun played a major role among Koreans in Hawai'i as an interpreter, a leading figure in the fight for Korean independence, and a Methodist minister. Born on 21 March 1879 and growing up near Seoul in the last decades of the nineteenth century, Hyun learned the Chinese classics.[4] His education, however, also included English and American influences through formal schooling as well as public lectures. Hyun's formative years coincided with the beginnings of modern Korean history. During the final and turbulent years of the Chosŏn era (1392–1910), foreigners such as American Protestant missionaries introduced new ideas and institutions.[5] Hyun learned about a Protestant Christianity closely identified with reform and nationalistic fervor, and he converted in 1901.[6] His connection to Christianity proved important for Hyun's future in ways that would have been difficult for him to envision.

Hyun's remarkable life journey underscores the centrality of Protestant Christianity within Korean American history, and this chapter examines the expansive ways that religion unfolded in Hawai'i during the first half of the twentieth century. The relational themes of religion & race, migration & exile, and colonialism & independence are nested within a framework that presents Protestant Christianity as implicated in the racialization and exploitation of Korean laborers within transnational colonial contexts. At the same time, religion also provided a measure of spiritual, intellectual, and physical space that helped Korean Americans negotiate harsh conditions. Too often scholars have reduced religion to an apparatus of oppression and cultural domination that obscures its multivalent nature. Consequently, the discussion of religion that follows highlights the entanglements of religion as a source of resistance, agency, and community. Primacy is given to the lives of historical agents for whom religious ideas, practices, faith, and institutions have encompassed the fullness of humanity and divinity.

Issues of religion & race deeply informed the migration of Koreans to Hawai'i at the turn of the twentieth century. The annexation of Korea by Japan created a very real sense of exile for those who lamented the loss of their homeland even as they resolved to fight for its independence. Koreans in Hawai'i may have been concerned about colonialism in Korea, but an American version of empire had brought them to the plantations as part of an international workforce. Protestant Christianity made its presence felt from the Bible studies and prayer groups of Koreans scattered throughout the islands to the missionary networks that linked both Koreans and European Americans to the Korean peninsula, the continental United States, and other parts of the world such as China. Inasmuch as plantation owners looked to religion as a means to control and harness labor, Koreans had other ideas about how to live out their religious convictions.

## Religion, Race, and Sugar

Any discussion of the history of Koreans in Hawai'i necessarily must begin by asking how that history intertwined with a political economy in the islands shaped by race and sugar. Recruiters sent to Korea by American sugar plantation owners not only sought cheap labor, but also wanted to offset the growing dominance of Japanese workers in Hawai'i. A combination of Hawaiian and U.S. government restrictions, including the Chinese Exclusion Act of 1882, limited the growers' access to Chinese labor and resulted in the turn to Japan. By the turn of the century, owners sought to take advantage of the historic animosities between Korea and Japan. In fact, by recruiting Korean laborers, the growers practiced divide-and-rule within the specific racial politics of Hawai'i.[7]

The transnational reach of race and sugar extended to the Korean peninsula, but religion holds the key to understanding the movement of men and women to Hawai'i. Historian Wayne Patterson has noted the difficulties of David Deshler, who on behalf of plantation owners set up an early version of a multinational corporation designed to recruit, process, and deliver laborers. Few Koreans wanted to leave their families and their homeland. The advocacy of the Methodist minister Reverend George Heber Jones broke the ice for the first group to depart for Hawai'i in late 1902. The charismatic minister, fluent in the Korean language, spoke of the scenery and weather, but he emphasized to his parishioners that Koreans would be able to evangelize and enjoy religious freedom to exercise their newfound faith. Over half of those who boarded the Genkai Maru on 22 December 1902 came from Jones's church.[8]

Recruiters hoped that enticing a first group would set a pattern for migration. Over eight thousand Koreans followed from 1900 to 1915, most of whom were men (84 percent) who came to labor on the plantations, along with women (10 percent) and children (6 percent). The numbers likely would have been higher, but potential Korean emigrants found themselves caught in competing colonial interests. American sugar companies desired more laborers, but Japan's victory in the Russo-Japanese War in 1905 meant that Japan had eliminated the competition for Korea. The imposition of lopsided treaties and protectorate status meant that Japan increasingly controlled much of the politics in Korea. The Japanese had a hand in the decree issued by the Korean government in April 1905 that stopped further emigration abroad. While some picture brides and students-laborers-exiles trickled in, the main flow of Koreans to Hawai'i had been shut down. As a rising empire, Japan monitored its citizens abroad, conscious of how their fate reflected upon their international standing. Hence, the Japanese government viewed Koreans in Hawai'i as competition for its own emigrants.[9]

In the thick of these events appeared Soon Hyun, in the employ of David Deshler and also a regular worshipper at the Methodist church pastored by Jones. Hyun found out about the East-West Development Company through a newspaper ad, and Deshler hired Hyun as an interpreter.[10] It is not clear whether Hyun's religious affiliation helped him get the job, but many of Deshler's Korean employees were Christians. Recruiting efforts targeted Christians, and given the ties that bound religion, commerce, and the state among Americans in Korea, it is not surprising that missionaries like Jones lent aid to the plantation owners.[11] The growers themselves of course had their own missionary connections, with many of the leading commercial families tracing their roots to the American Protestant missionaries who had set sail for Hawai'i in the early part of the nineteenth century.[12]

The larger context of Korean American religious history in Hawai'i is a reminder that the men and women who lived in the islands in the early decades of the twentieth century moved from the grasp of one emerging empire (Japan) to another (the United States). The annexation of Hawai'i in 1898 and its designation as a territory two years later by the United States represented the culmination of a long process by which European Americans had set their sights on the island kingdom. One study noted that in the 1840s, American missionaries pushed for the implementation of private property as a means of purportedly developing thrift and industry among commoners. The appointment of a Board of Land Commissioners in 1846 provided Americans access to governance over land claims and the settlement of land disputes. Not long after the creation of the board did it institute the Great Mahele of 1848, which fundamentally altered the system of landownership in the islands. Soon afterward, foreigners could acquire lands, and land speculation by European Americans and the manipulation of deeds and taxes resulted in non-Hawaiians and their corporations owning three out of every four acres of privately owned land by 1890.[13]

The altered landscape enabled European Americans to amass large enough holdings to sustain a plantation economy. The passage of the Reciprocity Treaty in 1875 allowed Hawai'i to ship its sugar to the American market duty-free. Growers aggressively pushed the demand for sugar initially sparked by the California gold rush and the Civil War. Profits increased and created a colonial oligarchy in Hawai'i that effectively displaced the native royalty.[14]

Jonathan Kay Kamakawiwo'ole Osorio's study confirms the influential role that Protestant missionaries played in persuading Hawaiian leaders to institute new laws and a Western economic system that had such damaging effects upon the land and Hawaiian nationhood. Laws criminalized sexual relations outside of marriage and the nonobservance of the Sabbath. In addition to shaping everyday behavior, legal codes undermined the cultural foundations of Hawaiian society in areas such as the regulation of hula. Osorio makes a compelling case that the laws created a deep fissure between the ruling class and the people of the land that neither could control and that intruded into family and other sets of relationships. The upheaval of these legal changes must also be placed within the context of the devastating effects of disease and death that by the end of the nineteenth century had reduced the native population of the islands to somewhere between five hundred thousand and eight hundred thousand people—a loss of between 92 and 95 percent.[15]

Despite these formidable circumstances, the Hawaiian people struggled against the colonialism. Scholars such as Osorio and Noenoe Silva have helped to shed light on these movements. Silva, for instance, has documented how Hawaiians utilized the print media to ensure that their stories would be preserved and passed down to future generations. The fact that these stories have been neglected and suppressed underscores Silva's point that Hawai'i is not a postcolonial state, but a neocolonial one in which the contemporary sovereignty movement is the inheritor of this legacy of oppression and resistance.[16] Many Hawaiians did adopt Christianity, but they did so by incorporating it into their existing religious milieu.[17] Evidence of this is found in the attempts by missionaries to control and shape the religious practices and beliefs of converts, but also in the obvious fact that religious systems are constantly in flux, especially at points of contact and exchange, and that adoption entails a complicated process of negotiation.[18] By the beginning of the twentieth century, plantation colonialism fueled the need for cheap labor that Korean Americans helped to fulfill. The path of virtually all Koreans in Hawai'i crossed the sugarcane and pineapple plantations. In the grueling and dehumanizing context of plantation life, these men and women received a quick introduction to their racialization as unskilled labor in an American colony. Koreans represented 11 percent of the workforce in 1905, the peak year of Korean presence on the plantations. A typical workday ran from the shrill wake-up bell at 4:30 AM until 4:30 PM with only a half-hour break for lunch, six days a week, for sixteen dollars a month.[19] Men and women were referred to by the number on the identification tag issued to them by the plantation, and they lived in crude, unsanitary, and overcrowded shacks. In the fields, laborers not only faced long, hot days, but battled the razor sharp stalks of cane that towered over them, cutting off sunshine and creating a finely granulated dust from the red dirt that got into workers' lungs and nostrils. The work truly broke backs, as so much time was spent bent over, weeding or hoeing or harvesting.

Anna Choi recalled that the reality of Hawai'i stood in stark contrast to the stories she had heard in Korea about a tropical paradise. The acres upon acres of sugarcane brought aches and pains: "Sometimes I wished I was a dwarf so that I would not need to bend down so constantly."[20] Laborers literally built the sugarcane industry from the ground up as they cleared and planted fields and built the plantation infrastructure to process the harvest.[21] Women faced even tougher conditions, as some who worked in the fields also had domestic duties to tend to before and after work. For those women who did not work in the fields, the day could begin as early as 3:30 AM with food preparation and stretch until well into the evening with the washing of dishes and clothes and preparations for the next day for as many as two dozen people.[22]

Korean Americans, along with members of thirty-three other racial-ethnic groups, faced harsh conditions on the plantations, but within these confines, laborers exercised an agency that took various forms of resistance.[23] The physical violence that some *lunas* (overseers) meted out swung back around through violent attacks on them. Some workers produced counterfeit plantation script to undercut the monopoly of the company-owned store. Setting cane fires, engaging in work slowdowns, and withholding labor through strikes and organized efforts all represented efforts to improve conditions.[24]

If laborers found some common ground in their efforts to better their circumstances, then strikes highlighted the way transnational ties competed with life on the plantation. Owners sought to take advantage of Korean animosity toward Japanese colonization. Toward that end, owners brought in Koreans and other groups as strikebreakers. Gary Pak captures this tension between class and ethnic solidarity in his historical novel *A Ricepaper Air-*

*plane.* In one scene, Sung Wha, a main character, carries on a conversation with Cho, another Korean laborer, underscoring how the hostility toward Japan is pitted against the common plight of workers on the plantation. It is a quandary not easily resolved, and the dialogue poignantly describes the dilemmas that Koreans faced in Hawai'i:

> "Ah! This sun is too cruel—beating my back like lashings from my step-mother!"
> "I hope those Japanese dogs lose whatever they're fighting for!"
> "We should not work. Japanese, Filipino, Korean . . . we're all the same."
> "Japanese are bastard pigs! Don't you know what they're doing to our country?"
> "The white bosses are bastard pigs!"

As Brenda Kwon points out in her analysis of the text, Sung Wha identifies with his compatriots from Korea in their nationalism expressed in the strikebreaking, but he also distinguishes what is happening in Hawai'i as a classic divide and rule strategy of the owners.[25]

If language, homeland politics, and their relatively small numbers worked against the Koreans' ability to forge a deeper sense of community with their fellow laborers, then their Protestant Christianity also set them apart. The faith and religious legacy that many Koreans brought with them found expression through plantation religious life that made the worship services a central part of the one day off from work. In her pioneering master's thesis on Koreans in Hawai'i, Bernice Kim noted that by 1905 a network of churches had been established throughout the islands with over thirty mission stations, ten evangelists, and four teachers. Religious leaders knew some English and also helped Koreans on the plantations as interpreters and mediators on a wide range of matters. As spiritual guides and social workers, these evangelists and teachers gave dedicated service to their community.[26]

Soon and Maria Hyun and their growing family ministered to the needs of Koreans on Oahu and eventually on Kauai. Maria Hyun extended hospitality and care for Korean individuals and families. After church services, Soon Hyun shared news from Korea and other world events and collected offerings for the work of the church and for the independence movement. The conditions for these early Korean religious leaders, despite Methodist support, proved difficult, and at one point Hyun considered switching his denominational affiliation to the Episcopal Church because he was offered housing and better pay. Superintendent John Wadman convinced Hyun to stay, and he had two separate stints of ministry in Hawai'i.[27]

On the island of Hawai'i, the Reverend Cho Wan See, a missionary from Korea, oversaw the ministry among Koreans on the big island. Much of the activity centered around the Olaa Plantation, and by 1910 the Hilo Korean Methodist Church had been established. Exhorter S. H. Sim traveled much of the island in service of the mission, and while many of the lay leaders did not have much formal education, such was the case for many of the Methodist circuit riders who had found their calling on the mainland in earlier eras.[28] Religion provided Korean Americans important spaces—to gather together, to punctuate the workweek, and to affirm the humanity of its practitioners. According to one study, within a few years of their arrival, Koreans organized thirty-six makeshift churches.[29] One estimate suggests that Christians accounted for more than two-thirds of the first wave of Korean immigrants.[30]

The issue of power and control entered into the relationships of those who worked and lived on the plantations. Owners looked to organized religion to promote a more stable and productive workforce. Given the grueling conditions, many workers drank and gambled into the night. It was hoped that Christianity would keep workers sober and encourage hard work and responsible behavior. Whether or not organized religion played such a role is difficult to discern, but it is striking that Koreans were arguably the most religiously active of the various groups on the plantations and proportionately one of the fastest to leave the fields.[31]

In 1906, Koreans accounted for 10 percent of the plantation workforce, slightly ahead of the Chinese (9 percent) and substantially less than the Japanese (66 percent). Just two years later, Koreans represented approximately 4 percent of the workforce, and as historian Wayne Patterson has pointed out, had it not been for the strike in 1909, those percentages would have dropped even further. Sugar producers worried about this rapid departure of Koreans from the plantations, not only because of the need for labor, but also because of their strikebreaking potential. Accordingly, owners welcomed the work of the Methodist missions.[32]

Korean Christians forged their understanding of religion within the context of plantation and mission, but from the very start, they exercised an ownership of the faith that expressed both clerical and lay leadership and independence. Well before official mission work began, Koreans had met for worship and Bible study.[33] Mission money and denominational structure provided support and educational opportunities, but Koreans directed the practice and shaping of religious life. This fact is evident in the fervent religious nationalism of Korean Christians that often disturbed missionaries.

Congregational life remained largely the purview of Koreans themselves, but a larger mission structure did create a layer of support and supervision. In addition to the ministry within a given denomination and its various populations, several Christians groups set up shop on the islands. Some of the first arrivals had ties to the Church of England in Korea, and they formed a small, religiously based mutual association. In 1907, Isaiah Ik Sung Kim started services at St. Elizabeth's Church and developed a sustained relationship with the Episcopal Church in Hawai'i. A year later, Kim launched a Korean Language School in which students learned Korean, Chinese characters, and other subjects.[34] Kim's lay efforts supplemented the ministry of John S. Pahk, who attended divinity school in California and in 1916 became the first ordained Korean Priest in the Episcopal Church in the United States.[35]

St. Luke's Korean Mission relied upon the support of St. Elizabeth's in the early decades, but the members exerted an independence over the ministry of the mission. Church members coordinated classes for children and women's groups, as well as English language classes for adults. In the fall of 1924, Noah K. Cho arrived from Korea, having been ordained by the Episcopal Church in 1928; he provided able leadership until his retirement from St. Luke's in 1950. Lay leaders helped the congregation realize the long-held vision of moving St. Luke's into its own church structure. No strangers to sacrifice, the members raised three thousand dollars for a building fund by 1924. As with nearly all the Koreans in the islands, members of St. Luke's supported those in Korea, and in the midst of the building fund, they diverted hard-earned money to an orphanage in Korea.

In May 1925, St. Luke's dedicated a new building.[36] The chapel on the grounds of St. Elizabeth's had served the congregation well, and yet many felt that St. Luke's deserved its own site, as a statement of maturity. Between 1938 and 1951, this small group collected fifteen thousand dollars, and by 1951 many of the original immigrants had grown old. After working all day, many women came to the church in the evenings to prepare foods that could be sold at fund-raisers on the weekends and throughout the community. The young people offered their assistance by helping to cook and to serve meals purchased by friends and members of St. Luke's. C. H. Hong captured the spirit of giving when he presented his donation to Father Noah Cho: "You know me, lame man, also I'm under *kokua* (charity). You see, me no *kaukau* (eat) and save my God's money and give it to God's new house." Apparently, Hong had limited himself to one very humble meal of rice per day in order to save the $450.00 he donated. Leaders used the funds to purchase the church bell, and St. Luke's moved into its own building on Judd Street, where the church still stands today.[37]

The pews in the sanctuary of St. Luke's today are worn, a visible reminder of its long history within the Korean American community in Honolulu. The parish hall floor and kitchen bear the marks of time, but also of the obvious care and maintenance that the church has invested in the structure. There is a peacefulness on the well-maintained campus. Michael Kim, treasurer and unofficial caretaker of the church, shared stories with me about St. Luke's history, suggesting that part of its longevity may have been that it steered clear of the factional politics and religious nationalism that involved Korean leaders in Hawai'i. Kim indicated that members supported the independence movement but never aligned with either of the two main groups represented by the Korean Methodist Church and the Korean Christian Church. "It probably helped that we were always a pretty small church," said Kim. Peak membership numbers in the 1950s were about 125 persons (85 adults in mass and about 40 in the church school).[38]

## Methodist Missions

If St. Luke's represented a small but steady presence within the Korean American community, then the Methodist missions dominated the religious landscape in Hawai'i especially in the early years of migration. The prominent role of Methodists derived in part from the transnational networks that linked Christians in the islands to Korea. The Hawaiian Mission of the Methodist Episcopal Church held its first session in December 1905 and reported on three language groups: English, Japanese, and Korean. The Reverend Hyun served as the secretary for the Korean work, and the Reverend John Wadman, the superintendent, oversaw the operations as a whole.[39]

The mission notes provide an overview of the Methodist mission, and the picture that emerges is one of an extremely active mission, supported by the denominational structure, but run largely by Koreans. In part, this had to do with language, but it was also a result of the remote and scattered nature of the population. Hong Chi Pum (Hong Ch'i-bŏm), a tireless religious leader assigned to Maui, for instance, made his way across the expanse of the island not by car, but by horseback.[40] Fortunately, Hong had use of two horses since he often spoke multiple times on any given Sunday to parishioners spread out far and wide.[41]

By the early 1910s, Methodists alone accounted for nearly twenty-five churches and about seventy-five mission stations. While reports tracked the role of Korean leaders under the Methodist watch, other local preachers and exhorters worked not with the denominational mission, but rather under a loose confederation of Korean leadership. Oversight proved minimal because of the nature of plantation life and limited modes of communication. Hence, a more independent form of Christianity developed that allowed space for concerns such as the events taking place in Korea and the fight for independence. Missionaries questioned the political ties Koreans had to their homeland and their bearing upon the work of the ministry in the islands.[42]

Church-based schooling served as a key site for the religious life of Korean Americans, who wanted their children to receive an education and an opportunity to have a future not bound to the plantations. Despite their poverty, Koreans directed thousands of hard-earned dollars to the support of the Korean Compound School that got its start in 1906. Young boys and girls came from plantations throughout the islands, and the boys boarded at the compound campus that at various points consisted of a dormitory, classrooms, a dining hall, and a chapel. The number of students grew steadily over the years, with early classes numbering in the twenties, but by 1915, the school had almost eighty boys. In addition, nearly fifty girls, housed elsewhere, ate lunch and took classes at the compound school. Total enrollment at the school approached 160 (including day-only students) with tuition set at sixty dollars per year.[43]

Stella Haan remembered leaving her parents when she was six years old; together with her older brother she was headed to Honolulu to attend the Compound School. Her parents worked on a sugarcane plantation in Kauai, where she was born. "I cried for two years because I was so homesick," she recalled, "but there was not much I could do." She attended the school for eight years, and she remembered that the students did a lot of the chores at the school, including the cleaning of the dorms and the grounds and helping prepare the meals. Students attended chapel on Wednesday nights and services on Sunday. In looking back, Haan appreciated the chance to get an education. She paid her way through public high school and college by working as a nanny for an Australian family and had a long career as a public school teacher in Hawai'i.[44]

The Reverend Min Chan-ho (Min Ch'an-ho) of the Korean Methodist Church helped Stella Haan find the placement with the Australian family, and Haan also recalled the presence of Korean teachers throughout her education. She mentioned that Syngman Rhee represented an important figure within the community, and she remembered him as being especially kind to the students.[45] The mission reports indicate that European Americans served as the principals of the schools (with the exception of Syngman Rhee), but that Korean teachers served on staff from the founding of the Compound School.[46] The controversy surrounding the Compound School and Rhee's leadership led to divisions between some Koreans and the Methodist missions and also within the Korean American community itself. These events will be taken up in the next chapter, but on one level, the controversy related to the tensions that some Korean Americans had with mission oversight.

## The Korean Methodist Church

As Koreans moved from the plantations to the city, the Korean Methodist Church in Honolulu served as an early and ongoing center for religious life. The congregation's history encompasses much of the overall history of Korean Americans in Hawai'i. Although sources are fragmentary, glimpses emerge of the religious life of the congregation and how it intertwined with other dimensions of the community. Furthermore, the church served as an alternative space in which to navigate the missionary and colonial dimensions of life in Hawai'i and to forge a sense of independence.

The beginnings of the church date to the very first arrivals of Koreans to the islands and to early gatherings in private homes for Bible study and prayer.

In November 1903, a group led by Ahn Chung-Soo (An Chông-su) and U Pyong-gil (Yun Pyŏng-gu) began to hold services in a rented home. This group prefigured the Korean church formally recognized by the Methodist Episcopal denomination in April 1905.[47] Transnationalism came in the form of pastoral leadership, as Methodists in Korea sent Hong Sung-ha (Hong Sŭng-ha) and, later, Min Chan-ho to oversee the congregation in Honolulu.[48] As a measure of the church's place within the Korean American community, the Sunday School population grew to 605 children by 1905, a mere two years after the first major arrivals. Koreans far outnumbered Japanese Americans and European Americans, who had 276 and 64 children respectively.[49]

### Religion and Politics

Although mission supervisors wanted to downplay the politics of independence, Korean American church members clearly differed in their orientation to events taking place in their homeland. Missionaries preferred a path of separation, but Koreans often saw the two intimately connected, providing further insight into the theme of colonialism & independence. The course of politics took some important turns in the decade following the establishment of the church in Honolulu. The first incident, which occurred in 1912, involved Superintendent John Wadman's acceptance of funds from the Japanese consulate to be used for work among the Koreans. Wadman had been a long-term missionary in Japan, and his pro-Japanese sentiments bothered church members. The acceptance of these funds ignited a controversy in which Koreans demanded that Wadman return the money. They also insisted that Wadman cease working with Koreans and depart from the islands. Japan's annexation of Korea in 1910 weighed heavily on many within the congregation, and the funds rubbed salt in the wounds of nationalist pride.[50]

### The Contours of Religious Life

In 1915, independence politics within the Korean American community affected the Methodist Church in Honolulu. Two pivotal leaders, Syngman Rhee and Pak Yong-man, had once shared a jail cell in Korea, both incarcerated for their reform efforts, but they split over their vision of how best to work for Korea's freedom. Those differing visions, Rhee's rooted in diplomacy and Pak's in a military approach, found expression in competition over control of the Korean National Association (KNA), which was created in 1909 by Korean Americans to spearhead the work of independence. After violent encounters and some legal wrangling, Rhee's faction gained control of the KNA. These events created a bitter long-term divide that affected the church community, as Rhee and his supporters broke with the Methodist missions and the Korean Methodist Church to start an independent religious organization. Other Korean Americans, disillusioned with the infighting, also left the Korean Methodist Church; by 1920, membership had declined by some 60 percent.[51] Reverend Min and his wife, Mollie, became important religious and community leaders in Hawai'i; they also held the distinction of serving in key positions both in the Korean Methodist Church and in its rival, the Korean Christian Church, established by Rhee and his followers.[52]

In 1921, the Korean Methodist Church purchased a new property on Fort Street in Honolulu, and despite the fallout from independence politics, the church continued to be a mainstay within the community. By 1928, the membership of adults and children had grown to over four hundred. Pastoral leadership during this period included the Reverend Hyun, who had returned from a stint in Korea and China to begin a second and longer tenure of ministry in the islands. E. S., a student at the University of Hawai'i, provided an overview of the church and its surroundings in a paper written for a sociology class in 1928. The student described a neighborhood of small cottages occupied by Chinese, Japanese, Hawaiians, and Koreans, with the Koreans representing the majority group. According to this account, the various nationalities did not mix very much, except for the children who played and occasionally fought at a nearby park. Most of the residents worked as store clerks, in furniture factories, as housemaids, and in a range of unskilled labor positions. In contrast, the church membership represented the upwardly mobile in the Korean American community, with some teachers, doctors, and small business owners. The majority of the Korean students at the University of Hawai'i had ties to the Korean Methodist Church.[53]

Adults and youth arrived at the grayish-yellow church building and campus at a quarter to ten to attend Sunday school classes, in which the first fifteen minutes were spent singing, followed by a short anecdote related to the upcoming lesson given by the superintendent of the Sunday school. Accompanied by music from the pianist, church members then departed the meeting area for their individual classes. At the conclusion of classes, people made their way to the sanctuary for services that began at eleven o'clock. Music filled the worship space, from congregational hymns as well as a robust choir that offered songs in Korean and, on occasion, in English. Along with the sermon and prayers, voices could be heard in the neighborhood reciting the Apostles' Creed and the Lord's Prayer. As the services ended, members and guests spilled out into the campus to greet one another and to catch up on news. While some went off to share meals, others stayed for church committee meetings, such as those of the Women's Relief Society, an important organization of Korean American women that provided social services to community members in Hawai'i and also raised support for families in Korea.[54]

## Ladies and Leadership

Hee Kyung Lee, a stalwart member of the congregation, emerged as one of the leaders of the Relief Society. Lee's story has been told by her daughter, Margaret Pai, who wrote of her family's experiences in the book *The Dreams of Two Yi-Min*.[55] As an eighteen-year-old picture bride, Lee arrived in Honolulu in 1914 to meet her future husband, Do In Kwon, a twenty-four-year-old laborer for a prominent businessman. Kwon came from a farming family, and with no chance to go to college because of a lack of funding, he opted to go to Hawai'i. He had arrived in 1905. Lee, like so many other picture brides, cried upon the realization of their new lives in a harsh land, which was very different from the visions of education and other hopes pinned to her decision to leave Korea.[56]

As a Christian and part of the Methodist Church in Korea, Lee turned to the church in Honolulu:

> But Sunday was the special day that she looked forward to. Her husband took her to worship at the Korean Methodist Church. She put on her prettiest *cho-gori* and *chi-ma*, and he wore his only suit. They walked down Punchbowl Street . . . [and] mingled with other picture brides who wore their colorful native dress. Like her new friends, she found immense comfort and solace in the Methodist Church. She believed her religion survived well the transplanting process.[57]

The mix of religion and politics captured the sentiments of many Korean women in Hawai'i. One article noted how the Methodist Church provided an organization base and leadership experience that fueled women's participation in the independence movement.[58] In the summer of 1918, the Woman's Club, the forerunner of the Relief Society, raised funds to send Lee and her daughter, Chung Sook, to Korea to help the cause of independence.[59] After spending time with her family and getting treatments for Chung Sook, who had battled whooping cough, Lee set out for Seoul, where she enrolled as a college student at Ewha, the Methodist college for women. Ewha became a stronghold of nationalist activity, and Lee and her classmates played an important part in the events that led to the demonstration and declaration of independence that took place on 1 March 1919. For her part in the uprising, Lee was imprisoned by the Japanese for ten months, as were many others. Harassment and delays from the Japanese authorities would not allow Lee and her daughter to leave Korea until August 1921, and once again Lee was detained by the Japanese in Yokohama before they were able to make it back to Honolulu.[60]

Upon returning to the Korean American community in Honolulu, Lee and her daughter discovered the corrosive effects of the internal fighting that Pak Yong-man and Syngman Rhee and their followers had become embroiled in. One of Lee's friends said to her: "Hee Kyung, you must feel that all you did was in vain. We're sorry. I wish we could think of a way to unify the factions and bring the two churches together." Pai lamented the split in politics and, even more so, the fallout that resulted in two rival churches. In her portrayal, irrespective of her family's church loyalties, Pai questioned the Methodist mission leadership and their unwillingness to work with Syngman Rhee in his efforts to extend education to Korean girls.[61]

As a charter member of the church, Dora Moon advocated for women's advancement, and she continued to do so after her official appointment as a local preacher by the Methodist mission in 1931. Moon converted to Christianity in northern Korea while attending a Methodist school. Her father-in-law at the time strongly disapproved of her conversion and demanded that she leave the church, but instead Moon left her husband's household with her daughter and enrolled at Ewha Womans College. She then boarded one of the early ships leaving Korea for Hawai'i because American missionaries had asked her to accompany laborers to Hawai'i. Within a year of her arrival in 1903, she had married Hong Suk Moon. With him she had five more children while also working alongside him on the plantations.[62]

Like many other Koreans, the Moons decided to leave the plantation for the city, where they hoped to find better economic opportunities and to be closer to the church. Moon started the Korean Women's Club, and after 1 March 1919, she worked with other Korean women to form the Women's Relief Society. At the heart of her activities, however, Moon dedicated her energies to the life of the church and to ministering to others.[63] In 1932, Moon started the Korean Missionary Society, which assisted church work and families of those engaged in ministry. For over forty years, Moon raised funds to send to Korea, and her efforts represented a full circle in which she lent aid to the Protestant church in Korea that had given Moon her start.[64]

Moon's granddaughter recalled: "[My grandmother] was such a strong person. In church you could see her standing with the men. They respected her convictions." Her recognition by the mission authorities gave Moon official standing in the church community, but accounts of her fervor and passion for church work suggest that Moon would have been a force to reckon with regardless of her title. In addition to her designation as a local preacher, Moon held many other positions of leadership within the church. A lengthy illness in her eighties slowed Moon down, but her presence remained with the congregation even beyond her death in 1971 at age ninety-three.[65]

## Faith for the Generations

In his discussion of the Korean American church in Honolulu in the 1920s and 1930s, historian Yŏng-ho Ch'oe describes a situation in which the growing second generation represented a constituency with particular needs in the area of language. The leaders of the church requested that the district superintendent seek out a pastor with formal education in the United States who possessed strong bilingual ability. In 1930, the Reverend Fritz Pyen arrived in Honolulu, having graduated with a Bachelor of Divinity and a Ph.D. from the Methodist-affiliated Drew University in New Jersey. Reverend Pyen delivered sermons in both Korean and English and represented a new kind of leadership able to attract young people to the congregation.[66]

In a periodical called *The American Korean*, an editorial published in the

2 June 1929 issue commented upon the expectations that young people in Hawai'i had of the Christian church. The unidentified writer acknowledged the central place of the church, even while underscoring the second-generation critique of the deep factionalism they had witnessed while growing up. The editorial suggested that churches needed to work with young people to make the connection between the spiritual and moral concerns of Christianity and the everyday concerns of the second generation. The writer pointed to the need to make the immigrant church a more hospitable place for young people, since they recognized the importance of faith in their lives. The editorial emphasized that religion addressed the totality of one's life.[67]

Second-generation connections to the churches initially came through parents, but as young people came of age, other influences began to shape their views. Public schools and other spaces introduced American-born Koreans to issues and perspectives outside the sphere of family and church. If language served as a barrier between immigrant groups in Hawai'i, then English in its standardized and pidgin forms provided the second generation some common ground for communication. Accounts vary as to how much actual mixing took place, and some suggested that segregation by ethnic groups still predominated campuses and other social settings. And yet, there is no doubt that Korean Americans lived and moved in a multiethnic and multiracial setting. Wayne Patterson's study noted the range of experiences that Korean Americans had with the various groups in the islands, such as discrimination from European Americans and Japanese Americans to the relatively amicable relations with Chinese Americans, with whom they shared negative views of Japanese Americans because of events in Asia. Ironically, Korean Americans often replicated stereotypes and prejudices against African Americans, Filipinos, and Puerto Ricans despite their own racialization. Within these complex racial dynamics in the islands, about 25 percent of males and approximately 40 percent of females of second-generation Korean Americans married outside of their group in the 1930s. In part, this had to do with the fact that Koreans constituted such a small percentage (1–2 percent) of the total population in the territory.[68]

As the United States moved toward war, the wider world of the second generation included experiences with the military, and these experiences for some increased the relevance of the church and religious faith. The attack on Pearl Harbor in December 1941 pulled the United States into the global conflict and ushered in a period of hope, frustration, and sacrifice. The news of war between the United States and Japan breathed new life into the independence movement that had fallen on hard times in the years before the war. Many members of the church at the forefront of nationalist activities saw new hope that their homeland would be freed. At the same time, because of their status as aliens ineligible for citizenship, Korean immigrants resented having the same classification as the enemy Japanese.[69] Given their long history of independence efforts, the U.S. Department of Justice lifted the designation of Korean Americans as enemy aliens in 1942, but the military governor in Hawai'i was slow in removing restrictions such as curfews.[70]

Despite these setbacks, members of the congregation sacrificed much during the war, from sending their sons into the military to buying bonds and conducting hospital visitations. The church held special services to pray for those involved in the war effort. Eighty-one young men from the church joined the armed forces. The news of the death of George S. H. Lee, who had been killed while serving with the U.S. Army in Europe in January 1945, shook the congregation.[71] In the church files, correspondence between the Reverend Lim Doo Hwa (Im Tu-hwa) and young men from the congregation serving in the war portrayed the ties that bound the men to the church and community. In a letter in June 1944, not long after the invasion of Normandy, the Reverend Lim wrote to a "Brother Pak" providing news about the youth fellowship. In addition to reporting about a wedding of some friends in the fellowship, the Reverend Lim wrote with pride about the women's contribution to the war in preparing surgical dressings for the Red Cross.[72] In another letter, Soon Chun, a member of the U.S. Navy and a radio operator stationed on Midway Island, wrote to the Reverend Lim in November 1944 with news of his assignment in the Pacific. Chun noted with thanksgiving that his younger brother attended the Korean Methodist Church more regularly. If more people like his brother devoted themselves to the church, then the Korean American community might experience greater unity.[73]

John Pai, a sergeant in the U.S. Army stationed in England, wrote to tell his pastor that he worshiped in tent church at his camp. He explained the special place of the Scriptures: "I have a New Testament and keeping it right in my pocket of my shirt next to my heart, every time when I'm lonely or in truble [*sic*] I'll read my bible to keep me from truble [*sic*], in other words the bible is my closest friend were [*sic*] ever I go, and it is my guid [*sic*] with your help, Father Lim."[74]

Writing from "Somewhere in France," Thomas Park wrote to Reverend Lim to thank him for sending along an inspirational book. In an understated manner, Park stressed the importance of spiritual need on the front lines of battle. He sensed the closeness of God, and prayer had become a staple of his tenuous existence. He told his pastor: "I have seen friends of mine, sleeping near me, getting hit by fragments from enemy shells. So far I have been very fortunate." Park prayed to God from his fox hole at night, and added: "I like, millions of other people, all over the world, wish that this ghastly war would come to an end soon."[75]

The close of World War II in 1945 ushered in a number of changes for the church and its membership, including returning young men from the military and expanded economic opportunities related to the war in areas such as boarding homes and apartment complexes. By 1940, the church had outgrown its space on Fort Street and had begun planning for a new site, but it had placed many of these plans on hold because of the war. Those plans were resumed, and in 1947 the church purchased land on Keeaumoku Street in the Makiki neighborhood—twice the size of the former location.[76] Both the Korean Methodist Church and the Korean Christian Church had approximately a thousand members each, representing the two largest Korean American congregations in Hawai'i. By comparison, a survey reported only thirty Korean American Buddhists in the islands.[77]

## Full Circle

In 1940, after many years of service, Soon and Maria Hyun retired from a vibrant ministry that had taken them from Korea to Hawai'i to Korea to China and back to Hawai'i. In 1907, Hyun met with the Reverend George Heber Jones during Jones's visit to Hawai'i to check on the parishioners he had encouraged to leave Korea for the islands. Jones asked Hyun and his family to return to their homeland to assist in the work of the church there. The fluidity of the ministry between Methodism in Hawai'i and Korea as well as Hyun's zeal for his homeland pulled him and his family back across the Pacific. Similarly, the call to ministry and the welfare of Koreans had been the impetus for the Hyuns to accompany migrants heading in the other direction in 1903. In May 1907, Soon and Maria Hyun, along with their three Hawaiian-born children, Alice, Elizabeth, and baby Peter, departed from Honolulu for Korea.[78]

Reverend Hyun served in various capacities within Methodist ministries throughout the Korean peninsula, and at the same time, he served the cause of Korean independence. His movement between such work and the connections between them demonstrate the nature of religious transnationalism. Hyun's involvement with the 1 March 1919 declaration of independence precipitated his departure on the eve of that historic event.[79] Maria Hyun's even more remarkable escape with eight children, ranging in ages from one to seventeen, suggests something of the strength of character and determination within the Hyun household.[80]

In his writings about his family, Peter Hyun described his father's Christianity as one that mixed a genuine faith with visions of Korea's freedom. That blending often entered into Hyun's sermons and teachings. Hyun apparently had chosen Jesus over Buddha because of his militancy.[81] That militancy took Hyun as part of the provisional government across the United States to Washington, D.C., in 1920. But as Hyun settled in to the American capital, he discovered that he had been dismissed by Syngman Rhee as part of the Korean Commission office based there. Hyun did not provide much detail about the dismissal, after which he returned to China, where he faced real financial hardship. With the need to provide for his family, Hyun welcomed the call in 1923 to take the post of minister at the Korean Methodist Church in Honolulu. In three stages, the entire Hyun family relocated to Hawai'i between 1923 and 1925. Hyun served the church in Honolulu from 1923 to 1926, after which the mission assigned him to Kauai, where he had begun his ministry twenty years earlier.[82]

The relocation to the island of Kauai represented a homecoming of sorts for Peter, who had been born there but had been raised in Korea and China.[83] Life in Kauai provided the Hyun family a serenity and stability they had not known for much of Peter's first seventeen years of life, and his memoirs provide a rare glimpse into the life of a Korean American pastor and patriot and his family. On Sunday mornings, the family packed into the Ford that Peter drove as the Hyun family made its rounds to the various Korean families and communities on the island to hold worship services and to check in on people:

All of the services were held in little plantation houses where the Korean laborers lived. The shiny wooden floors where we sat showed much wear from constant scrubbing and mopping. The services were very brief, but Father's deep feelings never failed to move me. Part of the time was devoted to the weekly news. . . . Father was especially happy to dispense news of the Korean independence movement that he received from Kim Koo, the Korean patriot. . . . They would respond to Pap's sermon by dropping a few coins into a little basket. Papa would save these for a month and then send the money to Kim Koo in Shanghai.[84]

Peter and his siblings looked forward to the last service of the day, since it meant eating a meal consisting of: "freshly cooked steaming white rice, a bowl of seaweed soup in broth made with meat bones discarded by the butcher, and slices of abalone, the family treasure, dipped in soy and vinegar sauce. . . . We ate with much relish and gratitude."[85]

On alternating weekends, the Hyun family moved between the "wet" and "dry" sides of Kauai, and the main stop on the "wet" side was Kapaa, where families gathered at an actual church sanctuary. The worship service consisted of many hymns and a fuller sermon along with news of local events and events taking place in Korea. After the service, the Hyun family called on those families too far out to attend services on that side of the island, including a fisherman who lived in cove near Kilauea. Peter recalled having to climb down steep cliffs to visit the fisherman, who had married a native Hawaiian and had two sons. As his father's chauffer and eldest son, Peter accompanied his father on many pastoral visits. The phone would ring day and night for needs like a ride to the doctor or translation help or supplies such as firewood and kerosene. The needs never seemed to end, and Peter marveled at how his family survived on their father's sixty dollars per month provided by the Methodist missions.[86]

As had been the case for so many Korean plantation workers, one by one the Hyun children migrated to Honolulu for school and for better economic opportunities. After fourteen years of ministry on Kauai, Soon and Maria Hyun retired from ministry in 1940 and followed their children to Honolulu. The elderly couple leased a plot of land on which they raised carnations and cucumbers to sell locally. With the entrance of the United States in World War II, Reverend Hyun and some of his children found work with the military to aid the war effort.[87]

## Conclusion

Soon and Maria Hyun and their family's journeys provide a good entry point to the three relational themes of religion & race, migration & exile, and colonialism & independence that guide this study. Although Reverend Hyun's story is not typical of those who came to labor on sugarcane and pineapple plantations, he did accompany them from Korea as a translator and spiritual leader. His work for recruiters hired by plantation owners linked his religious convictions as a Christian with missionary networks that spanned both sides of the Pacific. In the employ of the Methodist missions in Hawai'i, Hyun served and lived among his fellow Koreans and established a ministry in association with, but largely outside of, the confines of mission control.

Not only did Hyun leave Korea for Hawai'i with an early group of migrants, but religious connections to Korea took him back to his homeland to work for the church, and that eventually led to his exile to Shanghai as a member of the Korean Provisional Government. Hyun's political activity directly related to his role as a religious leader, since his post provided a national network and the means for him to travel the country in support of Korea's independence. His work in China and his brief stint in Washington, D.C., underscore his migratory and exilic existence. Migration continued as Hyun left China for his second tour of ministry in Honolulu and then back to the island of Kauai that brought him and his family full circle. Despite the stability this period provided, Hyun and his wife and children had all been deeply shaped by transnationalism of the body, mind, and spirit.

Colonialism permeated the various settings, from the Japanese takeover of Korea to the European foreign quarters in Shanghai and the American empire in Hawai'i. The presence and legacy of American Protestant Christianity and its missionary enterprise in East Asia and the Pacific formed layers within and among these nation-based colonialisms. At the same time, Koreans fought for the independence of their homeland, remembering and keeping hope alive for Korea's sovereignty. The struggle to see Korea free constituted an integral part of the faith of leadership and laypeople in the churches. The men and women who had ventured far from their birthplace, moreover, sought a measure of dignity and livelihood against the backdrop of grueling and dehumanizing work conditions that they encountered. A shared Protestant faith did little to thwart the racialization of Koreans by the European Americans who ran Hawai'i. Nevertheless, religion provided many Koreans a bulwark against the effects of white supremacy.

Within all of these overlapping and interlocking contexts, Korean Americans looked to their faith and to the religious communities they formed for guidance and strength, even if religion also proved to be the site of internal contention and strife. Religion thus represented a double-edged sword of sorts—all the more so when it came to the issue of religious nationalism in Hawai'i, to which we will now turn.

# THREE

# Practicing Religious Nationalism

Two elements of the architecture of the Korean Christian Church in the Liliha Street neighborhood of Honolulu stand out for their nationalistic symbolism.[1] The first is the entrance to the sanctuary itself, a facade that is a replica of an ancient palace gate in Seoul. This ornate and brightly colored passageway into the church was the pride of the congregation when it was dedicated in 1938. The distinctive style of the church acted as a marker in the neighborhood, testifying to the presence of the congregation as a place of faith and racial-ethnic identity. Although somewhat faded by the years and the elements, the gateway stood the test of time until 2000, when the entire building was demolished as a result of structural problems.[2]

The second architectural feature, a statue of Syngman Rhee, stands in the center of the campus. The plaque accompanying the imposing figure of Rhee identifies him as the father of South Korea and the founder of the Korean Christian Church. Rhee is best known as the first president of the Republic of Korea (South Korea), but he spent more than forty years in the United States as a student, exile, and leader within the Korean American community. Hawai'i proved to be an important base for Rhee's activities, even as he also spent time in China, Europe, and on the mainland. As alluded to earlier in the study, it is difficult to underestimate the role of Protestant Christianity in Rhee's career, from his Western education and relationships with American missionaries in Korea to how those influences

Korean Christian Church. Photo by Ruth H. Chung.

paved the way for Rhee's experience in the United States. Rhee and the Korean Christian Church both served as important if controversial anchors within the immigrant community in the islands and throughout the Korean diaspora.

The facade of the sanctuary, the statue of Rhee, and other elements of the history of the Korean Christian Church richly illustrate how the relational themes of religion & race, migration & exile, and colonialism & independence found expression in the context of Korean American experience in Honolulu during the first half of the twentieth century. In particular, this chapter argues that religious nationalism functioned as a Christian practice. The examination of religious nationalism reveals how this practice served as a conduit of exchange with society and culture and involved issues of power, negotiation, and resistance. Moreover, the sensibilities and dispositions that informed the practices associated with the church provide insight into how religious nationalism was part of the lived religion of Korean Americans in Hawai'i.[3] For the men and women of the congregation, practicing religious nationalism meant embodying the independence that they sought for their homeland, even as they sought to make their way in an often inhospitable new land. Although the church proved to be many things to many people within the community, there is no doubt that the founding and the ongoing mission of the Korean Christian Church enabled expressions of religious nationalism that stressed agency and sovereignty.

Korean Americans in Hawai'i represented a transnational community with important ongoing ties to people, institutions, and events in Korea. At the same time, those in Hawai'i were fashioning a new life within the territorial context of the United States. While Koreans in Hawai'i encountered a context in which power rested disproportionately in the hands of European Americans, the history of the church accentuates how a group of men and women made their own history even as they contended with circumstances often beyond their control. In keeping with the relational themes of the study, the analysis of religious nationalism as a Christian practice demonstrates the entanglements, for instance, of colonialism & independence.

By focusing on the practice of religious nationalism, the story presented here invokes a rich and varied legacy within United States. Often discussed within the context of an American civil religion, the subject of religious nationalism has most often signaled an understanding of the United States as a nation destined to fulfill its destiny as God's New Israel.[4] Providential destiny, however, has been open to multiple interpretations from the very beginning. As Albert Raboteau has pointed out, the very meaning of the nation itself could vary radically depending upon one's circumstances. What British colonists heralded as the New Israel constituted for African slaves the New Egypt.[5] Korean Americans, along with many others who would venture to these shores, shaped and defined their experiences in the United States through religious traditions and institutions that they transplanted and made anew. Like African Americans, most Korean Americans claimed a Protestant Christianity that set them within the dominant religious tradition of the nation. Yet, by virtue of race, they were set apart from their European American counterparts.[6]

The case of the Korean Christian Church in Hawai'i, then, reminds us that practices such as religious nationalism have been influenced by constructs of race. It is not simply the case that certain groups have been marked as religious and racial others, but that the very categories of difference have been instrumental to unmarked, normative, and European American understandings of the United States. Consequently, the case of the Korean Christian Church highlights at least three interrelated dimensions of race. The first is that Koreans in Hawai'i saw themselves as literally embodying and preserving the people (and perhaps nation) of Korea in the face of pernicious Japanese colonialism in the homeland.[7] At the same time, Korean Americans in Hawai'i underwent a process in which they inherited a racial legacy in the United States that lumped them with other Asians and extended discriminatory policies and stereotypes to them. Finally, Korean Americans faced the enduring racial markers that have been reserved largely for Native Americans, African Americans, and Latinos.[8] These racial formations reflected the ways in which Korean Americans in Hawai'i represented both a migrant and exile community.

If the history of the Korean Christian Church illustrates how practices are racialized, then also evident is the politicization of Christian practices that spanned an expansive geographic and imaginative landscape. The religious nationalism that took shape in Hawai'i brought together Protestantism and politics in ever widening circles, ranging from the local to the international and the intricate webs that connected those transnational contexts. The practice of religious nationalism entered into the local politics of Korean Americans in Honolulu and the Methodist missions in the islands. Furthermore, many Korean Americans had strong ties to American Protestant missions in Korea and the important role such missions played (and continued to play) in the development of modern Korea. Finally, the practice of religious nationalism formed an integral part of a diasporic independence movement that not only spoke to the efforts to free Korea from Japanese colonial rule, but also involved an American empire with vital interests in East Asia as well as the Hawaiian islands.

By pointing to religious nationalism as a Christian practice, the question remains: what identifiable forms did the practice take? Four subpractices collectively suggest how religious nationalism took shape in this context: self-determination, education, social services, and the nationalist marking of the physical landscape. Self-determination, a concept that gained wide currency in President Woodrow Wilson's Fourteen Points speech in 1918, stressed the sovereignty of nations.[9] As a practice, self-determination was reflected in a sensibility, or worldview, that was rooted in a legacy of Protestant nationalism in Korea and that made its way to Hawai'i through the migration of Korean Americans. Along with this sensibility, self-determination lay behind the tensions between Syngman Rhee and his compatriots and the Methodist missions in Hawai'i. The eventual break with the Methodists and the formation of the Korean Christian Church as an independent congregation represented a foundational practice of self-determination that girded the religious nationalism of the congregation. Self-determination, in its conceptual and practical dimensions, profoundly shaped the religious nationalism within this community.

Church-related education also emerged as an important locus for the practice of religious nationalism. The church-sponsored private schools for boys and girls through the Korean Christian Institute indicated the importance placed upon the training of Christian nationalists. The Korean Christian Institute put into practice Rhee's vision of inculcating future Christian leaders, reflecting how his own education in Korea and the United States had shaped his views of religion and self-determination. Thus, in this chapter, the parameters of Christian practice are expanded to incorporate the founding of church institutions and the teaching of certain curricula.

Furthermore, in its social services, the church also cultivated a religious nationalism. The Korean Christian Church established the Korean Old Men's Home to care for aging men who had long labored in the sugarcane plantations. Religious nationalism in the form of racial pride and religious convictions prompted the church to take care of its own. The Korean Christian Church also provided key leadership to the Women's Relief Society, a social service collective in the islands with strong church ties. The Relief Society enabled many of the women of the congregation to work for the local community and their homeland in the name of God. As mentioned earlier, the specific architectural choice manifested in the church facade and in the statue of Syngman Rhee also illustrates the practice of religious nationalism on the physical landscape. In both examples, members of the church gave physical expression to the religious nationalism that they embodied and sought to live out.

An examination of the Korean Christian Church enables us to enter relatively uncharted territory in the study of American religion. The locale of Hawai'i removes us from typical narrative landscapes. How many histories of American religion account for territorial experience? If the story of such a singular church pushes us deep into the local, then the geography and cultural identity of that church moves this narrative outward into the transnational. Most of the Koreans who left their homeland were part of a global movement of individuals sought out for their labor. The first stop on their route was at the sugar plantations covering the islands. Along with these laborers came Korean ministers, who not only helped establish churches but also had denominational ties to American Protestant missionaries and organizations. Korean laborers in Hawai'i thereby entered a nexus of peoples, institutions, and ideas that facilitated the transition from the United States to Korea and back again. Telling this story of Christian practice will necessarily press us beyond obvious regional borders and postcolonial presumption.

## Protestant Nationalism in Korea

The practice of religious nationalism among Korean Americans, especially in the areas of self-determination and education, was an adaptation of Protestant nationalism in Korea. Historian James Grayson has suggested that Protestant Christianity has been among the most important influences on Korean history in the last century along with Japanese colonial rule (1910–45).[10] That the two were so intricately intertwined during the early twentieth century says much about the rise of Protestant nationalism in Korea. The contact and exchange that took place between Koreans and Americans in the peninsular nation set the groundwork, particularly in terms of sensibility, or worldview, for the religious nationalism practiced by Korean Americans in Hawai'i. Relationships forged between missionaries and the royal family in Korea enabled Americans to establish schools, hospitals, and churches that provided structures for interaction between Koreans and Americans. At these sites, Koreans were directed in practices of learning that would form the basis for how they envisioned and lived out their religious nationalism. The intermingling of Western medicine and an American educational curriculum under the larger rubric of the Christian faith meant that Korean Protestants assembled elements of a new worldview that would help them interpret and navigate the tumultuous change and loss unfolding before them. Ideas of reform, democracy, and liberation animated the education received and the biblical texts studied. By going to school and church, then, many Koreans forged a Protestant nationalism.

The American Protestant missionary strategy to educate both the elite and nonelite segments of the Korean population meant that a wide range of people were brought into the sphere of educational influence. The emphasis on teaching nonelites in the vernacular Korean script or alphabet stood in stark contrast to the long-standing classical Chinese education reserved for the upper class. This decision not only provided access to education to those traditionally excluded, but also inculcated in many new converts and students a democratic impulse that fueled religious nationalism and influenced views about the role of women in society.[11] This impulse clearly carried over into the Korean American community in Hawai'i, including a strong penchant by plantation laborers to seek education for their children, male and female. Education in Hawai'i initially took place under the Methodist missionary educational system, which mirrored the kind of schools that Americans had established in Korea. The educational practices of the Korean Christian Church, while representing a break and divergence from the Methodist missions, nevertheless, borrowed from them.

For elites like Syngman Rhee and other nationalist leaders, the educational experiences with missionaries at places such as the Methodist Paejae School in Seoul spawned a religious nationalism that advocated widespread societal reforms and spiritual renewal as critical for the future of their beleaguered homeland. The Independence Club, established in 1896 by former and current students at the Paejae School, served as an important forum for the religious nationalism brewing at the turn of the century. Philip Jaisohn (Sŏ Chaep'il), a convert to Christianity and eventual expatriate physician in Philadelphia, was a key figure in the club. He and others expressed their views through publications and discussion groups that proved formative to many future Korean American leaders in their efforts to envision and live out their religious nationalism.[12]

Within this environment, various strands of nationalism took root in Korea, some of which identified closely with a Protestant Christianity that had both indigenous and foreign elements.[13] Many Korean Christian nationalists, by virtue of their ties to American missionaries, found a measure of maneuverability within a domestic context in which Japan fended off other rival powers, like China and Russia, and positioned itself to annex Korea in 1910. Influenced in part by American Christian resistance to Japanese colonialism, many Korean leaders and nonelites shaped their understandings of nation and God together.[14] How Korean Christians made sense of their nationalism varied. Some leaders found in the Bible a message of liberation that fostered a religiously based form of nationalism and activity that they viewed as consistent with claims of Christian faith upon all of the created order. The combination of religion and nationalism, according to Wi Jo Kang, could result in radical thinking and action, including the use of violence.[15] Other Christian leaders in Korea, however, began to separate out the affairs of state from religion as a means of preserving the church's ability to continue its work, especially as Japan began to tighten its imperial grip over Korea. According to one study, a strain of Protestant-influenced nationalism stressed the internal, spiritual renewal of the Korean people as critical for independence and self-rule. Such a notion resonated with the Confucian heritage of Korean leading thinkers and gave Christianity an influence that extended beyond those who became converts.[16]

One finds in Korea during this tumultuous period, then, multiple views of how Christians related to their times. Protestant Christianity, reflected in its ideas, texts, and institutions, became an important means by which some Korean converts and leading thinkers envisioned reform for their homeland and, in the aftermath of annexation, independence. The directions that Christianity took in Korea influenced how Koreans understood both their faith and the appropriate relation of church and state. Understanding the varied nature of Protestant nationalism in Korea underscores its vitality, but also its ability to divide as well as to unite. For better or worse, religious nationalism in Hawai'i would suffer from a internal major split. Different visions, each with antecedents in strains of Korean Protestant nationalism, would result in deep antagonisms that polarized the Korean American community. One faction was led by Syngman Rhee and based at the Korean Christian Church, while the other group was led by patriot and Christian Pak Yong-man and tied to the Korean Methodist Church. In many ways, the two groups and churches shared similar practices and sensibilities when it came to their religious nationalism, but issues of personalities and particular strategies of implementing religious nationalism drove a wedge between the groups.[17]

The religious nationalism practiced in Hawai'i by Korean Americans owed much to the specific history of Protestant nationalism in Korea, as well as ongoing connections to it. The role of education in fostering a religious nationalism for both elites and nonelites in Korea was reflected across the spectrum of the Korean American population in the islands. Those practices would be configured to take into account local concerns, but the ties to Korea fostered a nationalist sensibility and provided structure for the practices themselves. For some men and women, as discussed in the previous chapter, the decision to migrate to Hawai'i was literally influenced by missionary encouragement to venture forth. Others, especially Korean students, attended colleges and seminaries in the United States with direct sponsorship by missionaries to denominational colleges, universities, and seminaries. After their arrival in Hawai'i, most Koreans encountered a version of the missions that they had left in their homeland. Moreover, the theme of independence encompassed events taking place in Korea as well as in Hawai'i. On multiple levels, then, Koreans left one colonial setting for another.

### Koreans in Paradise

Although the reasons why people choose to migrate from their homeland to another place are complex, religious nationalism certainly shaped the journeys of Koreans to Hawai'i at the turn of the twentieth century. European American owners of the plantations hoped to tap into the nationalism of Koreans to offset the growing labor monopoly that Japanese workers represented in Hawai'i.[18] In addition to the elements of religion and nationalism evident in the process of Korean migration, leaders like Syngman Rhee chafing under Japanese surveillance and harassment also made Hawai'i a destination of exile. Ironically, the departure from Korea for many of these leaders was also made possible through the sponsorship of American Protestant missionaries who not only helped the captains of industry in Hawai'i find their laborers, but also aided the interests of the United States by their presence on the peninsula.

In the islands, church-sponsored education played an important role in the religious nationalism among Korean Americans, even if such sensibilities and practices were not the intended outcome of mission educators. The Compound School, founded in 1906 by the Methodist mission, established a boarding school for Korean boys and offered a primary education through the eighth grade in English as well as in Korean. Many students who otherwise would have had difficulty acquiring an education benefited from the school. A number of the graduates went on to public and private high schools in Honolulu, and some continued their studies at the College of Hawai'i and on the mainland.[19] The school also provided an opportunity for students from different islands to share a common experience and to develop a sense of community.[20] A product of this educational process was a heightened sense of being Korean, in part fostered by immigrant parents and churches concerned about events in the homeland, but also reinforced by the treatment and status of Koreans as laborers and merchants struggling to survive in an often hostile setting. The issue of religious nationalism itself would become a point of controversy within the structure of the Methodist missions.

## School Controversy and Syngman Rhee

The arrival and looming presence of Syngman Rhee and the events surrounding the Compound School controversies, mentioned in the previous chapter, illustrate the ways in which the sensibility and practice of religious nationalism took place among Korean American Protestants in Hawai'i. The ongoing presence of the homeland and events taking place in Korea for this transnational community sparked a heated and hostile reaction from Korean Americans in protest over the use of Japanese consulate funds for the work of Methodist missions on the islands that included Koreans. Syngman Rhee's entry into this debate in 1913 and to the islands via Methodist missionary channels added another layer to the practice of religious nationalism. The person of Rhee represented a convergence—not only in the actions that he took as a leading figure within the community, but also in how his life journey embodied the religious nationalism that he advocated. Education and self-determination as religious nationalism led to the severing of ties with the Compound School and the establishment of the Korean Christian Institute, the educational wing of what would become the Korean Christian Church.

The religious politics of Korea followed the women and men who left their homeland for Hawai'i. Prior to Rhee's arrival, the Reverend John Wadman, superintendent of the Hawai'i Mission of the Methodist Episcopal Mission, received funds from the Japanese consul in Hawai'i for mission work that included the Korean Compound School. When news of the source of the funds circulated, angry Koreans disavowed the money as add-ing insult to injury, given the recent annexation of Korea by Japan in 1910. Wadman must have been concerned about offending the Japanese consul-ate as well as the substantial Japanese population that was also part of the Methodist missions in Hawai'i. Perhaps for this reason and perhaps to ex-ert mission authority and discipline, Wadman stated that the donation had been given in good faith and that it was indeed appropriate to apply such funds for the Compound School. Many of the students went on strike and refused to attend the school. Wadman, who had been aware of Rhee's stand-ing among missionaries in Korea, sought out Rhee's assistance and later asked him to become the principal of the Compound School.[21]

Rhee's entry into the life of the Korean American community in Hawai'i in 1913 would have major implications for the nurturing and exercise of reli-gious nationalism. The timing worked well for Rhee, who had been looking for an opportunity to get back to the United States after a brief stint as the general secretary of the Korean YMCA. Japan had annexed Korea a few months prior to Rhee's return to Korea, and as might be expected, Japanese control had grown considerably since he had departed in 1904 to study in the United States. Rhee came to believe that he could do more for Korea in exile than at home. After attending a Methodist conference on the main-land, Rhee arrived in Hawai'i and helped to diffuse the controversy over the funds.[22]

Rhee's involvement with the school and eventual falling out with the Methodists is an important part of the story of religious nationalism among Korean Americans in Hawai'i, but it is also critical to recognize the fusing of religious nationalism in the person and life of Syngman Rhee. The exiled leader represented a transitional figure in modern Korean history. Trained in the Chinese classics, Rhee also studied in Methodist mission schools. His education brought him into contact with reformers like Philip Jaisohn and introduced him to a worldview steeped in religious nationalism. His exer-cise of that religious nationalism through the Independence Club and in other venues ran afoul of the royal court, and in 1899 Rhee was jailed under a life sentence for sedition. American missionaries who had tutored Rhee called upon their contacts and influence to try to protect and free their for-mer student, and these efforts along with changes in the political climate in Korea led to Rhee's release in 1904.[23]

Rhee read widely and also wrote while in prison, and he embraced his religious convictions through a conversion to Christianity. His major prison writing, *The Spirit of Independence: A Primer of Korean Modernization and Reform* (1910), is largely focused on the need for reform in turn-of-the-century Korea. Though the text does not address religion in much detail, there is a telling passage near the end of the document. Rhee makes a case that the nation of Korea must be founded on Christianity: "We must adopt this religion as the basis of everything."[24] One hears in these words the stirrings of a religious nationalism that would soon gather momentum.

Education would be a major catalyst of that momentum as missionaries arranged for Rhee to leave for the United States soon after his release from prison. Rhee earned three degrees: Bachelor of Arts (George Washington University), Master of Arts (Harvard University), and Doctor of Philosophy (Princeton University). Rhee was the first Korean to receive an American Ph.D. (Politics, 1910).[25] It seems plausible that Rhee further developed his views on religious nationalism during these years, since he was often invited to the home of Woodrow Wilson and may have learned something of the future president's stance on self-determination. In addition to politics, Rhee studied Christian theology at Princeton Seminary, living in seminary housing and learning from prominent Christian leaders such as Charles Erdman, while working toward his Ph.D. in politics.[26]

Given his credentials as a Christian, a highly educated man, and one who had suffered hardships for his homeland, Rhee assumed a position of leadership within the Korean American community in Hawai'i from the outset. His presence may have helped calm the controversy over the Japanese consulate funds, but it was not long before his religious nationalism, mixed in with his authoritative style, would embroil the Methodists missions and the Korean American community in further controversy. As the Compound School principal, Rhee had the means to assess the conditions of the Korean immigrant communities throughout Hawai'i. He discovered that many Korean girls received an inadequate education and proceeded to recruit them to board at the Methodist-run Susanna Wesley Home. Rhee intended to instruct them together with the boys at the Compound School, but the Methodists questioned the wisdom of coeducation. Those in charge of the Wesley Home blocked the girls from attending, and the first signs of strain emerged.[27]

A change in leadership among the Methodist missions added to the troubles, as the Reverend Wadman had been replaced by the Reverend William Fry in 1914. Rhee and Fry clashed over the mission of the Compound School beyond the issue of coeducation. Fry objected to use of the school and the church for what he considered political purposes.[28] Rhee and other Korean Americans, however, saw their nationalist activities as part and parcel of their Christian faith. While Rhee had enjoyed the support and guidance of many American missionaries and educational institutions, he also represented in his religious nationalism a movement that often placed Korean Protestants in tension with their missionary counterparts. Perhaps the most compelling example is the fact that American missionaries were caught completely unaware (along with Japanese authorities) by the massive, nonviolent declaration of independence in Korea on 1 March 1919. Korean Protestant clergy were prominent signers of the declaration, and it is unlikely that the event could have occurred without the church institutions and networks that coordinated the uprising.[29]

The conflict over the proper place of politics gave rise to the practice of self-determination as Rhee urged Koreans to take a strong stand for complete autonomy. Apart from the criticism of the nationalistic education of the Compound School, Rhee and others resented the fact that the Compound School and the Korean Methodist Church, supported by hard-earned dollars from the Koreans themselves, were owned and controlled by the missions. Management of funds proved to be another sore point, as Rhee had also raised funds for students during a tour throughout the islands but met with mission disapproval for not having received proper authorization from the Methodists.[30] Given the resistance of the Susanna Wesley Home to educate Korean American girls, Rhee circumvented the mission schools by starting the Korean Girls' Home, which would become the Korean Girls' Seminary in 1915. Rhee resigned his position as principal of the Compound School the following year and then helped to establish the Korean Christian Institute.

As a move of self-determination, the founding of the Korean Christian Institute also marked the key place of education within the religious nationalism of Korean Americans in Hawai'i. The very naming of the Institute as Korean Christian underscores the linkage between religion and nation. The curriculum, teachers, and classroom spaces reflected the fact that education, nationalism, and the church went hand in hand for many Korean American youth. Children learned Korean language, history, and patriotic songs, but they also sang Christian hymns. Often their teachers were lay evangelists and pastors. Much of the instruction that students received would take place in Sunday School classrooms and church sanctuaries. Korean American–run schools nurtured patriotism not only in the students but also in the parents and other adults who formed the audiences for oratory contests held throughout the islands.[31]

The Korean Christian Institute became the educational framework for Rhee and his followers to practice a religious nationalism free from the constraints of missionaries who in their admonishments against politics and faith conveniently overlooked the pro-Japanese stance of some missionaries who tacitly approved of the annexation of Korea and the racialization of Koreans as an inferior people. The institute, in contrast, was to be a vanguard for the new Korea, and Rhee instructed his students: "You are Americans by birth, but you are Koreans by blood. Someday you will be builders of new Korea. Mingle yourselves with Korean boys and girls. Study hard the Korean language and Korean history if you truly love your fatherland. Do not marry foreigners."[32] A proper education would produce the kinds of women and men needed to lead Korea in the future.

Perhaps Rhee had these students in mind when he helped launch a separate political organization in Hawai'i called the Comrade Society (Tongjihoe) in the early 1920s. Rhee believed that the well-established Korean National Association had outlived its purpose after the creation of the Korean Provisional Government in the aftermath of 1 March 1919. As with all of the organizations connected to Rhee, the Comrade Society's members pledged fierce loyalty to their leader. Chapters sprung up on the mainland, but Honolulu remained the stronghold of the organization.[33]

The efforts of Rhee as principal of the Compound School and then as leading figure behind the organizations like the Korean Christian Institute and the Comrade Society, however, did not win the approval of all Korean Americans in the islands. As much as some men and women were drawn to the authoritarian patriot, others who remained within the Methodist fold clearly did not agree with his style of leadership even if they were largely sympathetic to the religious nationalism that he stood for. The controversies surrounding Rhee would create deep fissures within the Korean American community. The religious nationalism that precipitated the break with the Methodists and the beginnings of the Korean Christian Institute would have further consequences for religious life in Honolulu through the creation of the Korean Christian Church.

## The Korean Christian Church

As vital as the Korean Christian Institute was in its educational endeavors, it was the establishment and the subsequent life of the Korean Christian Church that gave the fullest expression for the practice of religious nationalism. At first glance, the origins of the church can be attributed to the controversies and clashes with the Methodist missions. And yet the creation of the Korean Christian Church can also be viewed as the outgrowth of a religious nationalism that began in Korea and that underwent adaptation to the particular circumstances that Korean Americans encountered in Hawai'i. As such, the organization of the congregation itself was a foundational practice of religious nationalism—a case in which sensibility and legacy coalesced in the decision to start a church without ties to the missionaries who had introduced them to the Christian faith. In turn, the congregation served as an umbrella for other practices reflected in the social services and physical landscape of the Korean Christian Church.[34]

The tensions and fundamental disagreements over issues such as educational mission, funding, and religious nationalism led to the departure of Rhee and some eighty Korean Americans from the Korean Methodist Church, and this group began to meet together in the fall of 1916. The New Church people, as they were known, formed the Central Korean Christian Church in December 1918.[35] The Reverend Min Chan-ho, former pastor of the Korean Methodist Church in Honolulu, took up the duties as the founding pastor. Min received the call in Los Angeles, where he had gone for graduate study at the University of Southern California. He and his family arrived in the early part of 1919, and for ten years Min and his wife, Mollie, helped set the foundations for the church in Honolulu as well as the branches in Oahu, Maui, and Hawai'i. Eventually, Korean Christian Churches would also be established in Los Angeles and in Korea. An administrative umbrella organization, the Korean Missions Incorporated, guided the work of the church, including the ordination of ministers. As more and more immigrants left the plantations for the city, churches in the outer areas faded accordingly.[36]

In addition to the events and milieu surrounding the establishment of the Korean Christian Institute and the Korean Christian Church, the social services sponsored by the congregation exemplified its religious nationalism. A case in point is the Korean Old Men's Home founded in 1929 to serve the growing number of elderly men who had long labored on the sugarcane plantations. Young and hopeful when they arrived in the islands, these men over time had borne in their bodies the years of grueling labor and in their spirit the effects of unfulfilled dreams. Biblical injunctions to care for the elderly meshed with Confucian notions of filial piety. The men were given housing and limited board and health care oversight. The care was humble by modern standards, but significant since many of these men had no other means of support.

In caring for these old-timers, church members also exhibited a pride that melded religion and nation. The church sponsored dinners and other events such as pioneer recognition ceremonies to honor the sacrifices that these men had made in Hawai'i. Despite the meager wages they earned, these men demonstrated their faithfulness to the church through their service as well as patriotism for their homeland by sending funds to support the Korean independence movement. The practices of religious nationalism associated with the Korean Old Men's Home sought to reclaim the past but also instructed the younger generation about how Korean Americans in Hawai'i might live out their convictions.

It comes as no surprise that women were active in nearly every aspect of social service in the congregation; this included local needs of the church in its many functions within the community. Many Korean Christian Church women, furthermore, took part in and provided key leadership for larger efforts such as the Korean Women's Relief Society. Although the society attracted women throughout the Korean American community in Hawai'i, church-related women played a major role in the activities of the organization. The society gave women a means of providing leadership for their respective congregations and for the larger Korean American community in Hawai'i.

In March 1919, forty-one representatives of the Korean women's societies throughout the islands met in Honolulu to merge their efforts into a single organization that would eventually become known as the Relief Society. The events of 1 March 1919 created a ripple effect across the sea to Koreans abroad. Although the primary aim of the organization was to provide support for women and children in Korea, the society operated as a broader vehicle for Korean American women to engage a range of political, educational, and religious issues in Hawai'i. The society was an ardent supporter of the provisional government in Shanghai as well as other political activities in the United States and Europe pertaining to Korean independence.[37]

The Relief Society also took an interest in the needs of local Korean American communities. Helen Chung, a stalwart member of the Korean Christian Church, remembered her mother and other ladies who helped other needy families in Honolulu. Chung remembered her days as a young girl:

> There was such a spirit of giving back then, and my mom and the others worked hard all day and then came to the church at night to make kimchee and other food to sell so that they could raise funds for the church and for Korea. People would come by the church all the time, not just on Sundays, and whenever you needed to find someone, you usually could find them there.[38]

Evident in Chung's memories is the devotion to the homeland that the church inculcated through everyday practices such as making food and raising funds. In 1946, despite the aftermath of World War II, the Relief Society managed to send over seven hundred tons of goods to Korea.[39] The rendering of social services through the Korean Old Men's Home and the Women's Relief Society illustrate how the Korean Christian Church put its religious nationalism into practice.

Religious nationalism also manifested itself in the lives of church members like Nodie Kimhaikim Sohn, who emerged as a key leader within the immigrant community in Hawai'i. Her activities and loyalties, in particular, were closely tied to Rhee and the constellation of organizations he helped to establish. Sohn came to the islands with her family at the age of seven in 1905, and a series of migrations and misfortunes left Sohn and her mother alone to fend for themselves. Rhee took an interest in Sohn, helping her to continue her education in Hawai'i and then arranging for her to attend the Wooster Academy and Oberlin College in Ohio. Sohn graduated in 1922 with a B.A. in Political Science from Oberlin and returned to Hawai'i to take the post of superintendent of the Korean Christian Institute.

The work with the institute marked the beginning of a string of leadership positions for Sohn that extended her influence throughout the Korean American community. While she held top spots in gender-specific organizations such as chairwoman of the Relief Society, she also served as a trustee of the Korean Christian Church, an officer of the independence movement organization, Comrade Society, and as superintendent of the Korean Old Men's Home.[40] In her social service and leadership, Sohn epitomized the sensibility and practice of religious nationalism within the context of the Korean Christian Church.

## Landscaping Practices

This chapter opened with a discussion of the religious nationalism expressed in the physical landscape of the Korean Christian Church. Given the history of this congregation, it seems fitting that the architecture and campus have borne witness to these concerns and commitments. Particularly striking is the gateway to the main sanctuary that replicated the entry to an ancient palace in Seoul. The facade was clearly a sign of national pride and paid tribute to the long and rich history of Korea. The gateway, however, did more than reference the past, since it physically and symbolically combined religion and nation by serving as the primary entryway into the worship sanctuary. As members and visitors made their way into the church, the architecture symbolized the ties that bound them by faith and ancestry to Korea. The very existence of the church and its ministries proclaimed that God was on the side of the oppressed and disenfranchised. The message of liberation in the exodus story was very much alive in the hopes that the men and women of the church had for their homeland. In the early years of the church, the gateway also stood as a reminder that Korean Americans in Hawai'i were torchbearers for their homeland as Japan sought to absorb and erase Korea into its empire.

Although it is unclear whether a connection existed, two other prominent churches in Honolulu, one Japanese American and the other Chinese American, also reflected traditional architecture from their respective homelands.[41] The Makiki Christian Church, founded in 1904 and led by the Rev-

Korean Christian Church facade. Photo by Ruth H. Chung.

erend Takie Okumura, undertook fund-raising and construction during the Great Depression. Although some wondered about the timing, the church dedicated its sanctuary in 1932, loosely modeled after a castle from Okumura's hometown of Kochi, Japan.[42] The First Chinese Church of Christ dates to 1879, and during the late 1920s the church embarked on the construction of a new church building that incorporated design styles from China, including a distinctive pagoda-styled bell tower. The pagoda stood for a place where evil spirits never dwell.[43] It is safe to assume that the structures functioned as a display of ethnic pride, but given the growing tensions in East Asia, it seems plausible to think of these churches as also embodying a nationalism evident in the Korean Christian Church.

Scanning the details from the printed program of the dedication service for the Korean Christian Church gateway and sanctuary in April 1938 as well as coverage from the Honolulu press makes clear that the occasion was marked with considerable fanfare. Members sent a message that the experiment of creating an independent church had proved viable. The congregation dedicated its new building that had cost the impressive sum of nearly forty-five thousand dollars.[44] While members scraped together their funds, the building also benefited from donations by wealthy friends, contacts credited to Rhee. Apparently, the break with Methodists in forming the Korean Christian Church earned Rhee and his compatriots the favor of the elite network of Congregational ministers and missionaries such as the Yale-trained W. D. Westervelt.[45]

Amid the celebration, the gateway also spoke to the fact that the liberating message of religious nationalism of Korean Americans had run up against resistance and indifference in the halls of the United States government. By the late 1930s, morale had waned. The accomplishment of dedicating a new church building and its gateway must have buoyed the spirits of those involved. In multiple ways, the gateway provided physical and spiritual expression of the religious nationalism of the Korean Christian Church.

The other feature of the church landscape mentioned earlier is the statue of Syngman Rhee placed high on a granite pedestal near the fellowship hall named in his honor. Dressed in traditional Korean clothing, Rhee holds what might be an open Bible in his left hand with his right arm raised and extended as if to bless those in sight of the statue. Unlike the gateway, the statue was dedicated more recently in a ceremony, fittingly, on 15 August 1985, forty years to the day that marked the end of Japanese colonial rule in Korea. Like the gateway, religion and nation are bound together, but in this case, within an individual, and the statue is a literal embodiment in stone. The plaque on the statue identifies Rhee both as the father of the Republic of Korea (South Korea) and as the founder of the Korean Christian Church in Hawai'i.[46]

Further evidence of the religious nationalism on display can be found near the base of the statue. Engraved in stone is text taken from the Letter to the Galatians: "For freedom Christ has set us free; stand fast, therefore, and do not submit again to a yoke of slavery." Korea was no longer under the yoke of the Japanese, and church leaders seemed to be sending a message that Christ was to be credited for this liberation. By virtue of the subject of the statue, however, the church also emphasized that God had used servant Syngman Rhee as a principal agent of this freedom.

As might be expected, church members basked in the limelight of the Rhee presidency, but they sought in their commemoration to serve notice that the nationalism of their leader was steeped in Protestant Christianity. One can

Syngman Rhee Statue.
Photo by Ruth H.
Chung.

read the statue as a tribute to the man whose leadership of the organizations and activities affiliated with the Korean Christian Church represented a microcosm of the religious nationalist vision he had for Korea itself. The statue referenced that what had begun in Honolulu had extended across the Pacific to the Korean peninsula. The ascendancy of Rhee to the presidency could be considered the fruit of decades of practicing a religious nationalism in the context of the Korean American community. It is as if the statue physically confirmed what Rhee had written in prison about Christianity—that the religion must be adopted as a foundation of reform in Korea.

The church building and the Rhee statue capture in wood, steel, and stone the religious nationalism that enlivened the dispositions and actions of Korean American Protestants in Hawai'i associated with the Korean Christian Church. The landscape of the church campus has served as a reminder to members and those passing by of a historic and enduring religious nationalism.

## Expanding Horizons

The migration and exile of Koreans to Hawai'i and the events connected to the founding and history of the Korean Christian Church demonstrate the inner workings and the practice of religious nationalism. Instrumental to this discussion has been an understanding of Christian practice as sensibility and as lived religion. Korean Americans gave expression to their religious nationalism in the islands as an adaptation of the Protestant nationalism forged in Korea under the religious, racial, and political pressures of a nation undergoing colonization by Japan. American Protestant missionaries and the institutions and ideas they introduced would provide much of the material for a Protestant nationalism that stressed self-determination, education, social services, and the physical landscape. Figures like Syngman Rhee embodied and envisioned the practice of religious nationalism in Hawai'i. The contentious circumstances surrounding the creation of the Korean Christian Church involved controversy and tensions not only with Methodist missionaries but also with other Korean Americans. The founding of an independent congregation itself constituted a practice representing an important exercise of religious nationalism.

The case of Korean American Protestants and their practices in the islands provides an opportunity to draw out some potential lessons for the larger significance of the study of American religion and Asian American history and studies. First of all, located far from the North American continent, the territory of Hawai'i and its modern history underscore the fact that colonialism is very much part of the nation's past. The United States not only laid claim to Hawai'i, but extended its reach throughout the Pacific to the Philippines and to East Asia. In underscoring the colonial, independence as part of the overall relational theme reminds us that embedded in colonialism are stories of people who worked against its effects at the individual and community level as evidenced in the case of the Korean Christian Church.

The story of religious nationalism presented here also complicates standard dichotomies along the lines of race and geography. The practices of these men and women addressed intra-Asian (Korea and Japan) race relations with roots in East Asia as well as an American territorial colonialism in the islands. The racial dynamics of a black/white divide, while not completely absent, prove less helpful in deciphering the racial formations that emerged in Hawai'i. Majority and minority racial labels have been inverted in the islands, where Asians have been the most populous group.[47] In terms of geography, the Korean American case moves us off the mainland but also contributes to the effort to reclaim a religious legacy in the U.S. West, a region generally portrayed as devoid of religion.[48] Another dimension of geography is how the story of Korean Americans blurs the divide between East and West. American missionaries in Korea helped to set in motion an indigenous Protestant nationalism that then moved and adapted to local conditions on the fringes of the United States.

Like the binaries of black/white and East/West, the practices presented here call into question the assumptions underlying the term *American.* Koreans in Hawai'i occupied a profoundly ambivalent place in their relationship to the United States because the islands themselves occupied a liminal space in relation to the nation. On one level, religious nationalism was directed toward Korea; on another level, some of the fervor Korean Americans felt for their homeland was in response to the legal and extralegal forms of marginalization and dehumanization they experienced in the United States.

The case of Korean Americans provides an immigrant link to the racial legacy of the United States in which certain groups (namely, Native Americans, African Americans, and Latinos) have been used to differentiate those who are and are not normatively Americans. Religion, moreover, and Christianity in particular, has often served as a marker of difference. That marker most often has been framed as a Christian/non-Christian divide. That process of "othering," however, has also applied to those under the umbrella of Christianity (Protestant or Catholic) and, in the case of Koreans, to those within the Protestant fold, and even within the same denominations. These realities point to the salience of religion & race in the United States as they relate to one another.

Many groups, of course, have resisted and have staked their own claims as Americans despite the barriers they have faced. The practice of self-determination that resulted in the formation of the independent Korean Chris tian Church, for instance, not only resisted Methodist control but also represented an alternative version of religion, race, and politics in the United States to those of missionaries and plantation owners.[49]

## Time Passages

By the time of World War II, the Korean Christian Church was clearly one of two major Korean American churches in Hawai'i along with the rival Korean Methodist Church. The close identification of the Korean Christian Church with Syngman Rhee has been perhaps the most commonly referenced aspect of the congregation, though the stories told here suggest that there was more than that to the church's place within the community and its ongoing legacy that stretches into the present. The educational and social services of the church, for instance, provided much for Korean Americans. The war marked the ending of an era, as the fight for independence gave way to the tragic division of Korea, civil war, and as more and more of the early immigrants began to pass on.

A student at the University of Hawai'i, Manoa, in 1965 wrote an essay for a sociology course on the topic of the Korean Christian Church and its current situation. The student knew the church well as a member, Sunday School teacher, and church organist. As part of the essay, she provided a historical overview of the congregation that included some general history of Koreans in Hawai'i. In much of the paper, the author identified issues such as intergenerational tensions and how in the current (1965) climate of the times, some young people questioned the relevance of the church. Nevertheless, what emerges from the paper is an appreciation for the congregation's role within the Korean American community. Despite controversies and ups and downs, "the Korean Christian Church became deeply involved with the various movements and reflected the aspirations and hopes of the Koreans."[50]

The student's paper further highlighted themes that have been important to the discussion of the church. For one, the author commented on how the Korean Christian Church was one that ministered to a racial minority. That status was not lost on the church's members, who decided to remove themselves from the mission context of the Methodists. Not surprisingly, the relationship between politics and religion also emerged as an important dimension of the church's history. The student recalled from her own experience and from her parents' recollections that the church was *the* gathering place for Koreans for a wide range of activities. There was a sense of loss as an era had passed, but the church would continue and indeed, the church has continued to minister to the Korean American community in Honolulu to the very present.[51]

The relational themes of race & religion, migration & exile, and colonialism & independence imbued the events surrounding the origins and early history of the Korean Christian Church. The case for religious nationalism as a Christian practice has enabled an examination of a transnational space that held together the precarious position occupied by Koreans in Hawai'i during the decades of the twentieth century up to World War II. Those men and women associated with the Korean Christian Church took part in the practice of a religious nationalism that enabled them to give meaning and direction to their lives. Although not without differences, Korean Americans on the mainland also wrestled with many of the same issues as their counterparts in Hawai'i, and we now cross the Pacific once again to explore the theme of religion among Korean Americans in Los Angeles.

# FOUR

# City of Angels

Susan Ahn Cuddy, daughter of the renowned patriot Ahn Chang-ho (An Ch'ang-ho), recalled her youth, when those who had attended services at the Korean Methodist Church of Los Angeles (KMCLA) gathered at her parents' home afterward.[1] The Ahn home and the church served as way stations for many Koreans who lived migratory lives on the mainland, and they must have seen the Ahn children as angels sent to minister to them. The animated conversations over a simple but plentiful meal of rice, spicy pickled cabbage, and salted herring no doubt included updates and inquiries about the comings and goings of those who sat around the tables and about events unfolding in places like Honolulu, Seoul, and Shanghai.[2] Protestant churches connected Koreans in all of these locales, and the story of the Korean Methodist Church in Los Angeles provides a loose framework for extending the story of Korean Americans from Hawai'i to the mainland.

From its beginnings of as a fledgling mission in 1904 to its subsequent development over the years into a more established church during the World War II period, the early history of the KMCLA is the main narrative thread throughout this chapter and the next.[3] It is not difficult to find the relational themes of religion & race, migration & exile, and colonialism & independence deeply intertwined in the life of this historic congregation. Church networks brought student-laborers to the region, and in some cases, what took place in Los Angeles represented a continuation of the contact and exchange that had initially taken place in Korea under Methodist missionary auspices.[4] Moreover, figures like the Reverend Min Ch'an-ho underscored the linkages between Hawai'i and the mainland. Other Koreans left the racialized and colonial setting of the islands to seek their fortunes on the mainland. Hugh Heung-wo Cynn (Shin Hŭngu) represented transnational leadership embodying a religiously based nationalism that fostered the work for Korean independence.

Those gathered at the Ahn table of fellowship after Sunday services reflected the migratory nature of the Korean American community and its exilic existence. Wherever Koreans went, moreover, thoughts of their homeland under colonial rule went with them, as did visions of independence. Those on the mainland may have been freed from the tight grasp of the ruling American elite in Hawai'i, but they still encountered an internal colonial model that stretched and expanded to include them as racialized "others" to be exploited.[5] Those who left the mountains surrounding Seoul or the tropical setting of Honolulu for the desert basin of Los Angeles may have been impressed by the change in landscape, but social realities tied these places to one another and to the role of religion in Korean American history. Over the course of this chapter and the next, the KMCLA provides an opportunity not only to document a particular institution, but also to explore the broader contours of community formation in California and events that extended far beyond local confines.

The religious context of California stood in stark contrast to the power and control of Protestant missionary–descended families in Hawai'i. Historians Eldon Ernst and Michael Engh have both commented on the lack of a religious establishment in California that fostered greater interreligious harmony than in other parts of the nation. In fact, Ernst notes that the lack of a clear dominant religious tradition mistakenly has been interpreted as irreligion or the lack of religion. Unfortunately, religious cooperation did not translate into racial cooperation. The racial hostility vented toward Asian Americans, Latinos, and Native Americans certainly contributed to the relatively peaceful religious coexistence of Protestants, Catholics, and Jews in California. As a kind of shorthand, one might think of the racialization of certain groups as underwriting a religious tolerance that made California distinctive from other parts of the nation. One scholar has termed the golden state a fragmented dream because of European Americans' inability to understand and accept a multicultural and multiracial society.[6]

The charged racial climate in California did not exempt African American and Korean American Protestants by virtue of their religion. Sandra Sizer Frankiel's study points to the fact that while both groups increasingly made their way to southern California after 1900, European American Protestants largely avoided them.[7] Although some racial mixing took place, one can also point to the lack of sustained relations between groups due to residential segregation and the growing geographical expanse of southern California.[8] Leaders of the KMCLA, for instance, had some contact with their European American Methodist counterparts, but by and large the two communities lived independently of one another.[9]

The breaking of bread at the Ahn household also suggests something of the transnational nature of the Korean American community on the mainland. Koreans headed to the continental United States in search of higher wages, a chance to further their education, and as part of an exiled leadership in pursuit of Korean independence. Early estimates are that about fifteen hundred Koreans had made their way to the mainland by 1910, with the vast majority of the population scattered throughout California. Koreans worked in agriculture, following seasonal crops and also engaged in truck farming in rural and semirural settings. Student-laborers found work as domestics and in a range of small businesses such as laundries.[10] As in the case of Hawai'i, an urbanization took place among Koreans with southern California emerging as the center for Koreans on the mainland by the 1930s.[11] Given the restrictions on Korean migration discussed earlier, the mainland population in the first decades of the twentieth century remained small; the 1930 census listed the population in California at about eleven hundred Koreans with fairly even numbers of males and females (687 males and 410 females).[12]

## Transpacific Links

Just as the linkages to missionaries in Korea opened up movement to Hawai'i, those same connections brought Koreans to the Korean Methodist Episcopal Mission of Los Angeles run by Florence M. Sherman. Sherman and her physician husband, Harry C. Sherman, had served as Methodist medical missionaries in Korea at the turn of the twentieth century. Born in Iowa in 1869, Harry Sherman had been raised by grandparents and other relatives after the death of his father when Harry was only two years old.

Sherman joined the United States Army as a musician at age fourteen and soon afterward received a honorable discharge because of his age. After a migratory existence, Sherman entered the Methodist Episcopal fold in Redlands, California, and his conversion to Christianity in 1890 led him to medical school at the University of Southern California and the decision to become a medical missionary. Sherman attended the First Methodist Episcopal Church of Los Angeles while at school and there met Florence Mills, who worked as a dressmaker and music teacher.[13]

A native of Ontario, Canada, Mills had grown up within a Methodist home from birth, and as a teen visiting her older brothers in Pasadena, California, she enjoyed the weather and landscape so much that she decided to stay. She joined the church in 1894 and had been an active member in the congregation when she and Sherman had been drawn to each other by mutual faith and a shared love of music. They married in August 1896, and Harry graduated about a year later. The Shermans set sail with their infant son, Mills, from San Francisco on 28 December 1897 and arrived in Seoul on 14 February 1898.[14]

Assigned to the Talsung Church, Harry worked at the church's hospital, and in just five months he had treated nearly sixteen hundred patients.[15] At the same time, Florence Sherman joined the young women's branch of the church's ministries, serving as an assistant in the Sunday school program. She quickly earned the trust and admiration of her supervisors.[16] The Reverend George Heber Jones noted the dedication of the Shermans and also indicated that Harry had hoped to help train Korean physicians who could then serve their own people.[17]

During their time in Korea (1898–1900), the Shermans made friendships with a number of Koreans who later assumed prominent leadership positions as reformers in Korea and abroad. Two people in particular, Hugh Cynn and Syngman Rhee, developed close relationships with the Shermans. Cynn became a key leader in the Korean YMCA movement. Harry Sherman identified Cynn as a young man of great promise and hoped he might also become a medical missionary. This friendship played an important role in the early work of the Korean mission in Los Angeles.[18]

Cynn's compatriot and fellow reformer Syngman Rhee also knew the Shermans, and in January 1899, Sherman asked Rhee to accompany him to see a patient. Rhee had been given sanctuary at the Methodist-run missionary Paejae School, but he had grown weary of his confinement and gladly went with Sherman. As the two men approached the Japanese consulate, police rushed in and arrested Rhee. Harry Sherman asked the American minister, fellow medical missionary Horace Allen, to work for Rhee's release. Allen submitted an official request on the grounds that Rhee had been asked to serve as an interpreter in the care of a Korean patient. Americans paid frequent visits to Rhee to ensure that he received decent treatment in jail, and Harry Sherman likely checked on him as well. Because of Allen's close relationship with the royal family, Rhee might have been released, but a botched escape attempt resulted in a lengthy imprisonment for Rhee of nearly six years (from January 1899 until August 1904). In 1904, Rhee received amnesty on his sentence of life imprisonment and soon thereafter left for schooling in the United States.[19]

As Harry Sherman continued in his mission service, the long hours in treating patients as well as his efforts to learn the Korean language and to partake in the evangelistic work of the Methodist missions all took their toll. Sherman's health deteriorated, and he contracted tuberculosis. Already quite ill, Harry, accompanied by Florence, arrived in San Francisco in June 1900 with the hope that the milder and arid climate in southern California might help ease the effects of the disease. Unfortunately, six weeks later, Harry Sherman died in Los Angeles at age thirty-one, leaving behind Florence and two boys, ages four and three months.[20]

## Mission Stateside

Despite the difficulties of her circumstances, Florence Sherman wanted to continue her mission work, and she served as the catalyst behind the founding of the Korean mission in March 1904. If she could no longer minister in Korea, the mission could relocate to Los Angeles. The new venture on 1519 South Hill Street started with about twenty-five men, largely students and laborers. A report indicated that most of the Koreans identified themselves as Christians:

> [They are] the fruit of our workers [American Methodist missionaries] who are spending their lives there [in Korea]. . . . The aim of this mission is to get hold of these young men when they first come here, before the evil influence in the city shall have had a chance to destroy the good work done among them in their own country and to help educate and train them for the Lord.[21]

The mission intended to establish an employment agency so that Koreans could find work to support their education. While the mission sought to help Korean Christians in the United States, the ministry in Los Angeles took place within the larger context of mission work overseas.[22]

Koreans formed part of a larger home missionary movement at the turn of twentieth century, and especially in the U.S. West, large Asian and Latino populations represented potentially fertile ground for converts. In the case of Asia, many of those involved in Protestant home missions hoped that work within the United States might provide access to the countries of origin themselves.[23] This is reflected in the blurred lines between foreign and home mission boards and in the efforts of institutions like the First Methodist Episcopal Church of Los Angeles, which supported ministries through multiple local and denominational channels. A racialization took place in which European Americans relegated Koreans (and other Asians) to perpetual foreigner status, regardless of how long they had resided in the United States.[24] One reason for this stemmed from the fact that the Naturalization Act of 1790 barred Asian immigrants from citizenship. Irrespective of the law, missionaries also had a difficult time looking beyond the "foreignness" of Koreans because their vantage point remained fixed across the Pacific Ocean in East Asia.

The mission structure itself replicated the imperial geopolitics of the era. Comity agreements in Asia and the United States meant that the northern and southern branches of the Methodist Episcopal Church and Presbyterians negotiated and parceled out mission work in different regions. The intermixing of work among Japanese and Koreans may have made sense to denominational administrators, but it could be the source of tensions, especially after Japan imposed protectorate status on Korea in 1905 and outright annexation in 1910. The Taft-Katsura Agreement in 1905, a secret memorandum between representatives of the United States and Japanese governments, recognized the respective claims to the Philippines and Korea. One of the consequences of this agreement classified Koreans in the United States as Japanese subjects. The tacit and sometimes explicit pro-Japanese stance held by American denomination officials represented a source of frustration and resentment among Koreans.[25]

Despite the machinations of governments and denominations, the Korean mission served its constituency, and though information is scarce in terms of its internal workings, two supervisor reports by Florence Sherman in 1908 and 1910 give a general picture of the mission. In her 1908 report Sherman noted a regular Sunday service in Korean, a Sunday school, and other programs such as a Bible class. In addition, the mission offered a day school in English language and grammar. The goal of establishing an employment referral service had been realized, and apartments in the mission provided needed housing. The political situation in Korea, according to Sherman, weighed heavily upon those at the mission as they went about their business as laborers and students. Rental fees and staff salaries accounted for the bulk of the annual budget of $756.00. The mission was supported by piecemeal funding from groups like the Los Angeles City Union, a coalition of Christian churches engaged in a variety of missions.[26]

In 1910, the mission encountered financial pressures, requiring it to find cheaper rents farther from downtown. Nevertheless, Sherman recorded that the work continued and held more significance than providing a few students and laborers with a place to sleep: "Our aim is to help prepare and train Christian workers who will, in all probability, hold important positions in their homeland. . . . What is the value of a soul?" Apparently Sherman's plea fell on deaf ears, as the City Union did not make up the difference from the decrease in support from other funders. One bright spot in the mission remained the faithful and dedicated service of the pastor, Hugh Cynn.[27]

## Pastor and Student: Hugh Heung-wo Cynn

The predictions that students from the Los Angeles mission would go on to important positions in Korea certainly held true for the well-known reformer Hugh Cynn, who served as the pastor of the mission from 1904 to 1911. Cynn's tenure at the mission illustrated the role that religion played in the process of migratory exile set against the relational theme of colonialism & independence. Given their work together in Korea, Florence Sherman thought of Cynn when she set out to establish the Los Angeles mission. As plans began to take shape, Sherman told members about Cynn, and the congregation sponsored Cynn and his wife, Elaine. The church also supported Cynn's college education at the University of Southern California, Harry Sherman's alma mater.[28]

As had been the case for many of the reformers, Cynn had come under the influence of the Paejae School for Boys in Seoul that traced its roots to 1885 and the work of American Methodist missionary Henry Appenzeller, the school's founder and first principal. The patriot and physician Philip Jaisohn (Sŏ Chaep'il) had delivered influential lectures that led to the formation of the Independence Club. The club's forums and publications became hotbeds for reformist thought and activity, and Cynn made the linkage between Christianity and democracy:

> When it is said that Christianity has furthered the democratic principles, it means that the democratic ideals are so allied to the Christian teaching and that the democratic institutions are so linked with Christian usages that they inseparable. . . . This is the true explanation of the reason why the rise and fall in the curve of the growth of Christianity have maintained such a remarkable parallelism with that of the democratic movement in Korea.[29]

Imprisoned for his activities in Korea, Cynn served time in the same facility as Syngman Rhee. Both participated in the tutoring of minors in the prison, with Cynn teaching the youngsters arithmetic and geography. He also oversaw the jail's small library. Soon after his release from prison in 1903, Cynn migrated to Los Angeles to work with the Korean mission and to continue his education.[30] From Florence Sherman's reports, it is clear that Cynn played a major role in the mission as its pastor: "We owe much to him, and appreciate the sacrifices that he, and others, have made for our work."[31]

Although there are no transcripts of Cynn's sermons during his years as mission pastor, his other writings such as *The Rebirth of Korea,* published in 1920, provide some insights into his thinking. The book responded to the declaration of independence on 1 March 1919 and the subsequent movement that continued for several months despite harsh reprisals from the Japanese colonial government. As noted earlier, Protestant Christians played a major role in the movement that caught the Japanese and the American Protestant missionaries by surprise. The title of Cynn's book invokes the biblical notion of being reborn, and he applied this framework to the nation itself.

Presumably written for an American audience and geared toward eliciting support for the homeland, *The Rebirth of Korea* reflected Cynn's Christian nationalism. The opening pages of the book set March First against the symbolic backdrop of the crucifixion and resurrection of Jesus. The nation had been in a state of death since its annexation, but the uprising signaled Korea's being raised from the dead.[32] During the years at the mission, one can imagine that Cynn preached about the hope that his fellow Koreans could take in the message of Christianity for their own struggles and for the travails of their homeland.

## Church and Society

The Christian nationalism of Hugh Cynn suggested the integration and negotiation of religion and politics for many Korean Americans who shared Cynn's sentiments and who had been shaped by Protestant Christianity in Korea and its continuing legacy in the United States. As such, the Korean mission in Los Angeles never simply represented a religious site, but encompassed the whole of life. The churches played such a pivotal role because Korean migrants in the early decades of the twentieth century constituted a stranded people, pressed on one side by Japanese colonialization and on the other by the United States, wich excluded them from citizenship. For much of Asian American history, immigrants have fared better or worse given the international standing of their home countries in relation to the United States. Given the circumstances, Koreans by and large had no one to rely upon except themselves and whatever resources they could muster.

A case in point involved the assassination of Durham White Stevens, an American adviser to Japan in March 1908 in San Francisco. Of particular interest is how the events can be understood within a religious framework. Stevens had been employed by the Japanese government since 1885 as a foreign affairs adviser, and his public relations work included portraying a positive Japanese presence in Korea. Upon his arrival in San Francisco on 20 March 1908, Stevens issued a statement that described the Korean government as corrupt and the people as backward and unable to rule themselves. Moreover, Koreans purportedly welcomed the Japanese in their midst. The statement understandably infuriated Koreans, and the community in San Francisco sent Choy Chung-ik, Chung Chae-Kwan, Moon Yang-mok, and Yi Hak-hyun to protest the statement to Stevens.[33]

The foursome went to the Fairmont Hotel on 22 March to meet Stevens, and they asked if his statement had been accurately reported and if so, whether he stood by his comments. Stevens apparently claimed the statement, at which point the men demanded that Stevens offer a retraction. Stevens refused, and according to one report, the men grew angrier with each passing minute: "We could stand it no longer and one of us struck him and he tumbled under the chairs," said Yi Hak-hyun. "It was then we attacked him. The only thing we could use on him was the little rattan chairs." At that point Stevens cried out for help, and people at the hotel enabled the bruised diplomat to escape to his room. Yi noted with disappointment: "We are all very sorry that we did not do him more harm."[34]

Koreans in the city called a meeting, and a man named Chun Myung Woon said that he would take care of the matter but did not provide any details. Another person at the meeting, Chang In-hwan, apparently did not say anything but later secured a gun. It is not clear whether he had been in conversation with Chun. Given what took place, Stevens decided to depart the city the following morning. Koreans monitored his movements, and according to one account, a Japanese-speaking Korean found out Stevens's itinerary by calling the Japanese consulate.[35] Based upon one report, Stevens arrived at the Ferry Building in San Francisco at 9:30 AM on March 23. As Stevens emerged from a car, Chun Myung Woon ran toward Stevens with a gun concealed in a handkerchief. Apparently the pistol jammed, and Chun then struck Stevens in the face with the weapon. In the ensuing scuffle, Chang In-hwan stepped into the fray and fired his gun three times, hitting Chun in the chest with one round and Stevens in the back with the other two rounds. Stevens was rushed to a nearby hospital, and Chun later received medical attention while the police arrested Chang. Chun survived, but two days later, Stevens died from internal bleeding of the intestines punctured by one of the bullets.[36]

Relying on their own networks, Koreans in Hawai'i and on the mainland raised funds for a legal defense. The trial not only pertained to events at hand, but symbolized the larger struggle of Koreans for independence and their efforts to publicize the case of Korea to Americans. Similarly, the Japanese government also viewed the incident as a means of justifying its presence in Korea. The trial dragged on through the rest of 1908, and just before Christmas the jury found Chang In-hwan guilty of second-degree murder. Chang received a sentence of twenty-five years on 2 January 1909. He served ten years in San Quentin before being paroled for good behavior in January 1919.[37]

Anyone familiar with early Korean American history will have heard about the Stevens case, but perhaps less evident is how religion formed an integral part of the transnational events. Meetings to discuss what had happened and how to respond as well as networks for raising funds all funneled through churches in Hawai'i and the mainland. A fascinating aspect of the Stevens case is that Hugh Cynn served as the key interpreter and representative of the Korean community during the trial.[38] The *Los Angeles Times* ran a story on 25 March 1908 that reported a lengthy interview with Cynn, identified as a "latter-day Oriental of the better class—with delicate slim hands, gentle brown eyes, that burn with hatred as he talks of the horrible wrongs of his country." The article identified Cynn as a student at the University of Southern California who had been appointed to explain to the American public "why it is that your esteemed countryman, Stevens, needs killing." Cynn did not take the bait, but provided a broad-based commentary of what had happened, framing the events not in terms of individual actors, but rather in the context of the nations involved: Korea, Japan, and the United States. Stevens, according to Cynn, proved to be an affront not only to Korea, but to civilization in general, as he bore responsibility for contributing to the process by which the Korean monarch had been forced to abdicate the throne at bayonet point. Furthermore, Stevens's counsel helped shape policy that resulted in Korean farmers losing their lands to Japanese migrants.[39]

Stevens may have technically been in the employ of the Korean government, but it was no secret that he worked for the Japanese who had taken control of Korea. Cynn perceptively told his audience that Americans should also be ashamed of Stevens's actions because, as an American, Stevens's loyalties to Japan came at the expense of American companies whose legitimate commercial interests and arrangements had been voided by the naked grab of power by the Japanese. If what Stevens had done up to that point weren't bad enough, he had now come to the United States to spread lies about the situation in Korea and about the Korean people. Cynn portrayed Koreans as a peaceable people: "But there come times when a man who loves his country must kill. This is one of those times."[40]

Given the nature of his task, Cynn did not spend much time on his religious background, but religion did surface. In an implicit nod to American missionaries, Cynn claimed that Korea embraced the light brought to the nation through education. More pointedly, Cynn identified himself as a Christian and acknowledged, "My religion commands me not to kill," but he also added, "Yet, I do not believe God would forbid me to kill this wretched scoundrel."[41] It is difficult to determine the reception of Cynn's commentary, but it is remarkable in its clarity and construction, especially given the advocacy of violence and the invocation of Christianity and God. That Cynn could offer such perspectives in the role of a spokesperson also suggests something of the way Koreans interpreted the relation of religion to matters of colonialism & independence.

### Trials and Tribulations

The events surrounding the assassination of Durham White Stevens galvanized the Korean American community on the mainland and in Hawai'i, and Cynn's leadership role indicated the importance of religious spaces like the mission. And yet the Stevens affair also revealed the vulnerable economic, political, and social position that Korean Americans occupied within the United States. That vulnerability extended to organizational structures, and despite the able leadership of Hugh Cynn and support from European American Protestant churches and denominations, the Los Angeles mission faced formidable obstacles. For one, much of the Korean American population lacked stability. Students came and went, since many had to interrupt their schooling to work so that they could meet basic needs like food and housing. Koreans as farmworkers followed crops in their various seasons, and this took them throughout southern California and to other parts of the state. Mary Paik Lee, whose family left Korea when she was five years old in 1905, grew up in California; she and her family moved frequently, and this pattern continued into her adulthood. Her life journey provides a rare glimpse into how Korean Americans picked fruit in places like Riverside, hired themselves out for domestic work in communities like Claremont, farmed in central and northern California, and set up roadside and retail produce stands.[42]

Henry Chung (Chŏng Han-gyŏng), a close associate of Syngman Rhee and prolific author on the cause of Korean independence, remembered his early days in the United States as a student-laborer and, in particular, his stay at the Korean mission:

> Hugh Cynn was pastor in that mission. A returned missionary woman, Mrs. Sherman, superintendent and it was supplied more or less by the First Methodist [Episcopal] Church in Los Angeles. There wasn't much I could do so the only thing I could do was to go from this family to that family. First I tried to live with a family but it was not very successful. I didn't know a thing about American customs and had no knowledge of the language so I'd work about a month or less than that; then they would tell me, "No, we don't want you." Go[ing] back and forth, I had an awful time.[43]

Along with the constant shift in population, the mission faced financial pressures because it depended upon outside sources of funding. In 1924, the *Pacific Methodist Advocate*, the official weekly magazine of the Methodist Episcopal Church, South, reported on decisions made by Protestant denominations regarding home missions work in the American West, including Methodists and Presbyterians, that ultimately affected the ability of the Los Angeles Korean mission to function. In 1910, a collective organization called the "Oriental Home Missions" coordinated the work of home missions to try to better utilize limited resources, to avoid unnecessary duplication, and to address the less-than-spectacular results (at least in terms of sheer numbers).[44] The decision by the First Methodist Episcopal Church of Los Angeles to discontinue its financial support placed the mission in an especially precarious position.[45]

When it seemed like things could not get worse, Hugh Cynn returned to Korea in 1911 after completing his studies at the University of Southern California. His departure left a leadership void in the Methodist mission and in the Korean American community at large. Cynn felt compelled to return to Korea to work on behalf of his country. Hugh and Elaine Cynn took with them two young American-born daughters, Florence (named after Florence Sherman) and Bo Oak. Hugh Cynn went on to assume major leadership positions within church circles during the colonial period in Korea, including becoming principal of the Paejae School, the general secretary of the Young Men's Christian Association (YMCA), and a spokesperson for a Christian rural movement. Cynn ran into opposition from more conservative Korean Christians for his progressive Christian views, including the equality of the sexes.[46]

The arrival of Min Ch'an-ho in 1911 from Hawai'i extended the work of the mission, but the ministry that had begun under Methodist auspices moved in new directions that included mergers, splits, and reconfigurations over the course of the next two decades. Min and his wife, Mollie, came to Los Angeles from Honolulu so that he could study at the University of Southern California as part of his training for the ministry. For unknown reasons, Min merged the Los Angeles Methodist mission with the Korean Presbyterian mission in 1912. It is likely that lack of funding required some creative decision making on Min's part, and another contributing factor may have been that the pastor of the Presbyterian mission, Pang Wha-Jung, returned to Korea in 1912 after the death of his father.[47]

## The Korean Protestant Landscape

The fact that mission efforts moved between denominations and took various forms in the 1910s and 1920s suggests that the history of the Korean Methodist Church of Los Angeles should be cast against the backdrop of the larger Korean Protestant landscape of southern California. Two ministries, the Presbyterian Korean Mission of Los Angeles and the Claremont Clubhouse, intersected with the work of the Korean Methodist mission. An organized Korean Presbyterian presence in Los Angeles dated to 1906, when immigrants sought the assistance of the Presbyterian Missionary Extension Board, which rented a home in downtown Los Angeles in which to hold worship services. The mission stabilized under the able leadership of Pang Wha-Jung. Samuel A. Moffett, a Presbyterian missionary to Korea who had been on furlough in the United States, recommended Pang when he had learned of the needs of Koreans in Los Angeles. The Presbytery of Los Angeles appointed Pang as an evangelist and the Reverend Augustus Prichard as the administrative supervisor.[48]

Pang's leadership and concern for migrant Koreans led to the establishment of a student clubhouse in the city of Claremont in 1909, situated closer to the citrus groves where Koreans worked. The clubhouse provided room and board so that students could acquire English language skills and pursue an education. Claremont had the advantage of being both a part of the citrus industry and a college town with church roots (Congregational). The clubhouse charged minimal fees, and residents largely governed themselves, but part of the house rules included English language requirements. For instance, everyone apparently had to engage in conversational English on a daily basis except for Sundays.[49] Some of those who floated through the clubhouse in the first two decades of the twentieth century did manage to achieve their goal of getting an education. Young Kang, a graduate of Pomona College in Claremont, became a journalist in Honolulu, editing a newspaper called the *Young Korea.*[50]

Korean students and workers in the Claremont area also received assistance from a Presbyterian laywoman named Mary E. Stewart, a member of a prominent citrus family in nearby Upland. She first encountered Koreans in 1908 as laborers in her family's orchards, and she stood by the workers in the face of racial hostility and anti-Asian activity in California, which had been transferred from the Chinese to the Japanese and Koreans. As the threat of violence escalated, Stewart gave firearms to the workers and instructed them to defend themselves if attacked. In the meantime, Stewart also publicized her actions and defended the Koreans as hardworking and deserving of the same opportunities for a livelihood as anyone else. Active in Presbyterian circles, Stewart knew American missionaries in Korea, and she helped support the religious activities of Koreans throughout California; that included her home congregation, currently known as the First Presbyterian Church of Upland. A chronology of the church notes that in 1920, fifty-two Korean names were removed from the church's membership roles, since the laborers had scattered to other parts of the state. The longtime Stewart family driver, Harold Snyder, recalled that he drove the Stewarts to visit with Korean friends, and the family kept close ties to the Korean Presbyterian Church in Los Angeles.[51]

## The Sweep of World Events

Koreans struggled with local concerns involving work, church, and community, but simultaneously followed events that took place beyond their immediate surroundings. The politics of independence and the fight against colonialism as well as their migratory and exilic existence nurtured a transnational consciousness. News of Korea filtered to those in the fields and orchards and in the cities, and those in the United States keenly felt their responsibility to make the plight of Korea known. As it had been in Hawai'i, the end of World War I in 1918 and the March First Movement in 1919 set the context for activity within the Korean American community in southern California.

In 1918, World War I came to an end in November, and in its wake, President Woodrow Wilson introduced his fourteen-point plan for peace along with the ill-fated League of Nations. Korean independence leaders embraced Wilson's statement about the right of peoples to self-determination as an international mandate to help free Korea. In an effort to make a case for the homeland at the Paris Peace Conference, Koreans in the United States decided to send three representatives to France. Syngman Rhee represented Koreans in Hawai'i, and Henry Chung, then a student at the University of Illinois, would go on behalf of Koreans on the mainland. It is noteworthy that Min Ch'an-ho of Los Angeles had been chosen on behalf of Korean Christians in the United States. The three men stood on the platform of the right to self-determination that had struck a deep chord among colonized peoples in different parts of the world. Ironically the delegates never made it to the conference, because the United States denied their travel permits on the grounds that they were Japanese subjects—a cruel reminder of their fate. Attempts to get visas from other countries like Canada also failed. Frustrated by the red tape, Syngman Rhee took matters into his own hands and sent a petition to President Wilson asking the League of Nations to take trusteeship of Korea until an independent government could be established. Rhee's unilateral decision created an uproar among Korean independence leaders throughout the diaspora, but faded in light of the events around 1 March 1919.[52] The case for Korea fell on deaf ears, as Japan maneuvered to treat Korea as a domestic issue akin to the Philippines for the United States.[53]

On the heels of the activity surrounding what one scholar has called the "Wilsonian moment," news spread to Korean communities in other parts of the world about the momentous 1 March 1919 uprising in Korea.[54] The call for immediate independence and the right to self-determination may not have gained much of an international hearing, but it did awaken those inside and outside of Korea to the hope and possibility that lay in the cause. As mentioned earlier, Korean Christians used their networks to help mobilize the people, and as a result Japanese colonial forces suspected Christians as key instigators of the protest.[55]

Korea Must Be Free.
Photo courtesy of USC
Korean American Digital
Archive.

After learning of the events set into motion on 1 March, Koreans in the United States rallied to help their homeland, and one sees the influence of Protestant Christianity within these efforts. Churches took up collections, and Christian networks publicized and garnered support for the independence movement, including recognition of the newly established Korean Provisional Government in Shanghai. Ahn Chang-ho sent a letter to the Christian churches of America in which he not only invoked the right of self-determination and the optimism of a new era dawning, but framed his discussion in the context of a call to fellow believers.[56] In addition, Philip Jaisohn assembled a liberty congress in Philadelphia on 14–16 April 1919. Jaisohn made a symbolic link between the Korean and American declarations of independence. Historian Richard Kim has commented upon how the leaders of the Congress wanted to showcase an independent, democratic, and Christian Korea. Part of the rhetorical strategy included the mention of how seven of the eight members of the cabinet of the provisional government were Christians and the equating of democratic ideals with Christianity.[57]

While the use of religion might be viewed simply as a vehicle for the advancement of the political agenda of Korean independence leaders and an effort to gain the sympathy of American Christians, such a portrayal overlooks the ways that many Korean Christians interpreted their faith in a context of liberation and a religious nationalism. In general, American Protestant missionaries shied away from the mix of politics, faith, and nationalism, but many Koreans saw the relationship as a natural one. Their religious nationalism accentuated racial and political differences with European Americans. In a public speech reprinted in the *Korea Review,* Jaisohn addressed the topic directly: "Regarding this question of religion, several gentlemen have said, 'We don't want to mix religion with politics,' but this is so intermingled with politics that you cannot help it." Jaisohn went on to explain to his listeners that when Koreans became Christians, they inherently received from their faith a desire for freedom.[58] A printed prayer by Korean Americans further conveyed the sentiment expressed by Jaisohn:

> We offer our thanks to Thee for the opportunities that Thou hast afforded us to manifest our humble spirit of sacrifice for the Cause which is so dear and sacred to us. We are truly grateful for the faith in Thee and Thy Son, Jesus Christ, and the love of liberty Thou has implanted in the hearts of our people. Our hope lies in this faith and we pray that righteousness and justice will reign in our land and that we may live and die a free people.[59]

Along with the Korean Congress in Philadelphia, Christians formed the Korean Christian Association in North America, and Min Ch'an-ho served as the chairperson of the organization. In April 1919, the group printed an appeal to readers through the newspaper *New Korea (Shinhan Minbo),* aimed at reaching fellow Koreans just as the Korean Congress in Philadelphia sought to widen the circle of knowledge about Korea's situation. The language of the appeal wove together faith and nationalism, painting the Japanese not only as the enemy, but also as an evil force. Moreover, the appeal stated: "It is our holy duty to give ourselves to the cause of Korean Independence and to pray for it to our Almighty Father with out utmost sincerity." European American Christian friends had begun to pray for the Korean nation, the writer explained, and how much more should Koreans be dedicated in their prayers? Toward that end, the writer asked Koreans in the United States to stop and pray three times a day. Koreans could be assured that "God will be with us in our effort to secure freedom and life of Korea when we pray and sacrifice ourselves."[60]

For those on the mainland, a vision of self-determination and the declaration of independence in 1919 drew Koreans into the fray of transnational politics informed by Protestant Christianity. Faith guided the efforts of many migrants and exiles, fueling visions of independence in the face of colonialism in their homeland and its formations in the United States.

## Contention Continued

The turbulence of world events seemed to spill over into church and community life during the 1920s. Much of the contentiousness stemmed from a lack of resources that created stress and instability. Leadership changes accounted for some of the trials, as Min Ch'an-ho finished his studies and returned to Hawai'i to lead the newly formed Korean Christian Church begun by Syngman Rhee and his followers. The Mins would be key figures in the Korean American community in the islands for many years.[61]

Min's association with Rhee seemed unlikely given the pastor's Methodist ties, but Rhee had those same Methodist connections until he broke with them in Hawai'i. Perhaps Min saw an opportunity to exercise a degree of independence not possible under Methodist mission control. In any event, Min's departure coupled with Rhee's visit to Los Angeles resulted in a divisiveness that echoed what had happened in Honolulu. In the spring of 1924, Rhee arrived in Los Angeles to begin a campaign of support for the cause of Korean independence and, in particular, his role in that cause.[62] His stature as an exiled patriot who had been imprisoned for national reform as well as his ivy league credentials brought a prestige and presence that commanded attention within the Korean American community.

Rhee's presence apparently sparked tensions within the Presbyterian mission, and conflict escalated into pro- and anti-Rhee factions, with each vying for control of the congregation.[63] By the fall of 1924, pro-Rhee forces took control, and the other faction left and began to hold separate worship services in downtown Los Angeles on Hill Street.[64] Not without struggle, the Presbyterian mission continued its ministry and in 1928 hired a pastor from Korea, the Reverend Kim Joong Soo, who had come to Los Angeles as a delegate to the World Sunday School Convention. Kim's leadership helped the church find a measure of calm after the storm.[65]

The controversy surrounding Rhee in part took the shape of denominational splintering, and given the circumstances, it is not surprising that those in the Hill Street group approached the California Oriental Mission of the Methodist Episcopal Church, South, in 1926.[66] Moreover, the original merger in 1912 meant that some people had ties back to the Methodist mission started by Florence Sherman and Hugh Cynn. The *Pacific Methodist Advocate* noted that the denomination had received an urgent request for sponsorship.[67] The Korean immigrant press reported that in the fall of 1926 the group had received denominational support.[68] Plans to move forward, however, had to be put on hold because of mission jurisdiction issues with the Presbyterians. Caught within these denominational circumstances, the Hill Street group continued independently as the Korean Free Church and relocated to a site near the University of Southern California. The Free Church consisted of thirty Korean families and utilized its space as a community center for fellowship and a Korean language school for children of the immigrants.[69] It appears that the Methodists lent the independent congregation the services of the Reverend S. K. Hahn while officials sorted things out. Hahn worked with the congregation until he left for further theological study in Chicago in November 1927.[70]

In the fall of 1930, with the way clear, the Korean Free Church of Los Angeles dissolved and reemerged as an entity of the Methodist Episcopal Church, South. The denomination named the Reverend Whang Sa-Yong as the pastor for the new congregation.[71] An established clergyperson, Whang had extensive connections within the Korean American community in California and Hawai'i. Whang helped set the direction and tone of the church in the 1930s and served as an important leader within the Korean American community in Los Angeles. In addition to his church connections, Whang took active part in community politics, sent by the Korean National Association in 1909 to check on Koreans who had gone to Mexico as laborers.[72] In 1912, the Methodist Episcopal Church appointed Whang to the status of local preacher, and he served Koreans in northern California.[73] The road leading back to the Methodist fold had been neither simple nor straightforward and had been prompted by the divisiveness of the Los Angeles Korean American church community.

*Prospects in the City of Angels*

In his 1927 annual report, Superintendent W. A. Davis of the California Oriental Mission noted that Koreans may have had the most difficult of circumstances, because they barely earned enough to keep one step ahead of abject poverty. Moreover, having left Korea in a time of great political upheaval, they bore the burden of seeing their homeland come under foreign domination. As such, many Koreans questioned whether to return. In addition, some saw a measure of opportunity in the United States, especially for exiled leadership seeking to find allies for the homeland.[74]

By the 1920s, the Korean community in Los Angeles had undergone change. Many of the early Korean immigrants who had worked Hawai'i sugarcane plantations and then had gone to the mainland to labor in the agricultural fields began to gravitate to southern California, as they could no longer sustain such physically demanding lives as they aged. The California Anti-Alien Land Laws of 1913 and 1920 legally sanctioned discrimination against Asians and made it very difficult for those few who had resources to invest in the land and secure a livelihood. Falling prices for goods such as rice in the wake of World War I also meant that many Korean farmers faced real hardship and losses. As a result, the city represented hope for some looking to find work in small businesses and had the added attraction of having a settled Korean American community.[75]

The Gentleman's Agreement between the United States and Japan in 1907 curtailed labor migration to the mainland, but it did open a window by allowing wives of immigrants to join their husbands. Picture brides made their way to Hawai'i and the mainland, one of the few benefits of being subsumed under the category of Japanese alien until the Immigration Act of 1924 effectively shut the door to further Asian immigration. Wives and picture brides enabled families to form, resulting in the emergence of a small second generation. One study estimates that 115 women moved to the mainland from Hawai'i. The church as well as the Korean American community began to mature with the passage of time.[76]

In an effort to meet the needs of the second generation, churches set up programs for children such as Sunday schools. In addition, leaders saw the need to instill in the next generation knowledge of Korean culture and language. Like so many other groups who had come the United States, immigrant parents worried that their children might lose their sense of ethnic identity in the face of American schooling and the influence of the larger society. Not surprisingly, the churches served as the primary site for Korean language classes. While nostalgia for things Korean may have been part of the impetus for these actions, many Koreans in the United States envisioned a possible return to their homeland.

Koreans in the United States saw themselves as keepers of a Korea held hostage by a foreign power, and that responsibility extended to their children. Even for those Koreans who did not envision a return, pride of heritage sparked the drive among immigrants to ensure that their children did not lose the language of their ancestors.

The California Oriental Mission recognized the importance of language acquisition, since it intended to send converts back to Korea to serve in the mission work in Asia. According to one report,

> In addition to the customary forms of service, some of the churches maintain schools for teaching the Korean and Japanese language. This rather unusual procedure of teaching children their own language is made necessary by the fact that children frequently drop their native speech and in many cases can scarcely converse with their own parents. Since the laws and the racial consciousness prevented these people from becoming an integral part of American life, it was deemed essential that they preserve at least a part of their own heritage through their own language.[77]

Along with the second generation, the arrival of some international students in the 1920s and 1930s added new energy and a progressive perspective to matters of faith and society. These students played an important role as Sunday school and Korean language school teachers. They brought news from Korea as well as providing new ideas and perspectives. Similarly, international Christian conferences provided Korean Christians a chance to travel abroad, and some twenty delegates attended the World Sunday School Conference in Los Angeles in July 1928. In their honor, the group that would rejoin the Methodist ranks and the Korean Presbyterian Church worked together to prepare a picnic for Koreans spread throughout southern California.[78] The Korean delegates numbered among eight thousand people from some fifteen nations who attended the gathering held every four years.[79] Over a hundred local congregations hosted the convention based on the theme of Christian Brotherhood and the cultivation of an international outlook.[80] Two delegates, Kim Joong Soo, a Presbyterian pastor, and Diamond Kimm, a Methodist pastor, stayed on in Los Angeles after the conference to serve the local community. The delegates and students drew upon their work with missionaries and native church leaders in Korea to help build some infrastructure for Koreans in the United States.

## A Winding Road

At almost every turn, the institutional structure of Korean church life has borne the stresses and strains of the migratory and vulnerable existence that marked most Koreans on the mainland. And yet, given these circumstances, Korean Protestants found in their church and in their faith a thread that helped them negotiate their tenuous and contentious contexts. From the earliest foundation of the Korean Methodist mission in 1904 with Florence Sherman and Hugh Cynn to the reemergence of the Korean Methodist Church in 1930, there is ample evidence of the three relational themes of religion & race, migration & exile, and colonialism & independence.

As in Hawai'i, Koreans on the mainland simultaneously occupied migrant and exile spaces with their movement facilitated by religious and transnational connections. Churches addressed the local and daily needs of their members, who by their racialization, irrespective of their Christian faith, faced very marginal lives in the United States. While Koreans struggled with their everyday existence, they also carried with them concerns that spanned great distances as the fight for Korea's independence relied on those in the United States. The end of World War I and the declaration of independence in March 1919 against colonial Japan demonstrated the deep intertwining of religion and politics.

The Methodist mission faced financial and leadership challenges and internal factions steeped in diasporic community politics that merged and splintered congregations. Legal codes restricted Koreans' life chances as immigration laws eventually closed doors to further migration. Loopholes and church avenues opened the way for some wives and international students and travelers to come to the mainland. A small second generation followed, and all of these subgroups brought a measure of newness into church circles.

One can see the indelible marking of religion in the lives of Koreans in the United States on a comprehensive level. A European American Methodist observer noted that "Koreans in America frankly have no other religion but Christianity. All of their marriages and funerals services are conducted according to Christian rites and only by Christian ministers."[81] The report overstated its case, but the centrality of religion to the Korean American experience has been readily apparent. We now continue to explore religion in Korean American history through a congregational lens that extends from the 1930s to World War II.

# FIVE

# Enduring Faith

In extending the story of the Korean Methodist Church of Los Angeles (KMCLA) from 1930 to 1945, the relational themes of religion & race, migration & exile, and colonialism & independence continue to underscore how the structures and sensibilities of Protestant Christianity remained at the center of Korean American history.[1] The long and frustrating search for a permanent church home prior to and during this era symbolized how Koreans continued to navigate a racial hierarchy of religion. Given the pervasive reality of race in their everyday lives, Koreans had few illusions about the larger church as a radically different space. Indeed, for most members the church drew people in precisely because it provided a respite from the corrosive effects of white racism. European American denominational officials often had difficulties moving beyond their mission mind-set. As a result, members of the KMCLA endured frequent church moves within the city and a lack of resources that affected both immigrants and the emerging American-born generation.

Despite these conditions, members carved out their own religious space. In particular, the arrival of students from Korea brought energy to the ongoing fight for independence that linked Koreans throughout the diaspora. These migrants and exiles contributed to church and community in California and added a progressive element related to the anticolonial struggles taking place in the homeland. As in its earlier history, the congregation could not but be influenced by events taking place in other parts of the world, and in particular by how those events interfaced with the transnational nature of the movement to free Korea. Churchgoers kept abreast of developments such as Japan's imperial schemes in China during the 1930s, which spelled trouble for the Korean Provisional Government located there and placed even greater responsibility on the government's exiled leaders in the United States. Pearl Harbor and the United States' entry into World War II infused new life into the cause of a free homeland. Many Koreans contributed to the war effort in the United States, cognizant of how an Allied victory over Japan would hold great promise for Korean independence.

## Seeking a Church Home

The band of believers who reemerged as the KMCLA in the fall of 1930 looked for leadership in the ministry of the Reverend Whang Sa-Young, who brought both pastoral experience and community leadership to the group. In January 1931, church members elected a slate of officers.[2] The KMCLA formed part of the California Oriental Mission, a subset of the denomination's Home Missions Department that worked with populations in California.[3] Those who had experienced the lean years as an independent congregation hoped for Methodist support to ease the burdens, but the congregation continued to suffer. Mission priorities in terms of staff, funding, and attention went to the Japanese, given their larger numbers, even if Korean Christians clearly had a much greater presence within their community than did Japanese Christians in theirs.[4]

The shift from rural to urban that had begun in the 1920s among Korean Americans continued in the 1930s, with the concentration of the population largely in urban sites like greater Los Angeles. As noted earlier, the overall Korean population in California remained small, around eleven hundred, supplemented by the arrivals of student-laborers from Hawai'i and overseas. Within California, the overall general population began to shift south, and Koreans followed suit. A sociological study completed in 1939 noted that Los Angeles represented the capital of Koreans in the continental United States. The main Korean American newspaper, the *New Korea* (*Shinhan Minbo*), and its sponsoring organization, the Korean National Association, operated in Los Angeles.[5]

Building woes hounded the church as it moved approximately every three years. In response to their situation, members in 1933 decided to launch a multiyear campaign to build a modest sanctuary with a social hall in the heart of the Korean community, bounded by Vermont and Western avenues as well as Adams and Slauson.[6] Despite the financial pressures from low-income work, support of the independence movement, and the effects of the Great Depression, people had earnestly begun to collect funds for a permanent church home. Perhaps in light of this sacrificial giving, Superintendent W. A. Davis met with the church building committee in 1933 and pledged eight thousand dollars toward a church complex. By 1936, the church has raised twenty-eight hundred dollars.[7]

The various sites for the KMCLA included an African American Seventh-Day Adventist Church. The arrangement allowed the church to take advantage of the fact that the Adventists worshipped on Saturdays. Among other things, the KMCLA did not have to wait for the home congregation to clear out before it conducted its own services. The new location offered a measure of freedom and flexibility in terms of the usage of space.[8]

The shared space with African Americans illustrates another wrinkle in the theme of religion & race: the KMCLA had been forced to move out a previous location because of racial discrimination. Apparently, the KMCLA had run into zoning restrictions that operated like the restrictive housing covenants that created a segregated Los Angeles. As had been the case for many racialized persons, the KMCLA discovered that European American congregations did not welcome the prospect of renting to Asian Christians. The kindness extended to the KMCLA by the African American Adventists enabled the church to find a place of worship and stood in sharp contrast to the lack of hospitality from other Christians. Davis noted: "This experience made many of our people bitter toward [European] Americans." While the superintendent may have been surprised by such treatment, it is doubtful that Koreans would have been. In fact, Davis commented that Koreans may have been discouraged, but had not given up.[9] The report acknowledged the initiative of the church members. They had not come to the denomination with empty hands but actively raised funds.[10]

Along with building and location challenges, the church also dealt with the lack of financial support for its pastor by the denomination. Some clergy had to earn income on the side to supplement their earnings, but the denomination reduced salary allocations according to its report in 1934.[11] Pastor compensation reflected the dual wage scale that Koreans often encountered in the workplace: race translated directly into differences in pay. In order to survive, the Reverend Whang and his family operated a hand laundry.[12] To make matters worse, the Whang family had to move their residence more than once, making what must have already been an extremely difficult call to ministry that much harder.[13]

The hardships the congregation encountered with its building situation and pastor compensation left many people within the KMCLA understandably angry and frustrated. The church's situation mirrored the tenuous circumstances of most of its members, who toiled long hours to eke out a living. The economics of race, which severely limited the opportunities and options of Korean Americans, trickled down to community-based organizations like the church. The KMCLA considered the possibility of another merger with the Korean Presbyterian Church, an effort to take greater control of their religious fate.

Joint meetings and services with the Korean Presbyterian Church that took place in the 1930s fueled speculation about combining forces and had the membership on both sides talking. Missionaries and church leaders from Korea on occasion passed through Los Angeles on their way from or to the peninsular nation and provided an opportunity for both congregations to gather to hear a speaker or hold a forum. From time to time, the Methodists and Presbyterians gathered together for worship, as they did in 1933 when they held a joint outdoor service at Sycamore Park with various programs and games for about two hundred people. The two churches worked together to host the autumn harvest holiday for Koreans throughout southern California.[14] The intimate size of the Korean American community, furthermore, meant that members and leaders of both churches knew each other. Business, community events, and the politics of independence allowed for a certain familiarity.

There seemed to be some sentiment among the Presbyterian mission staff in favor of a merger to facilitate raising funds for a new sanctuary. The leaders of the Korean Presbyterian Church gathered to discuss the issue and then called for a general meeting of all church members to seek their opinions. In the end, the congregation decided to keep its denominational identity in place. At the same time, the church welcomed others to join its ranks, but as new members of the church rather than as a merged entity.[15]

On the Methodist side, District Superintendent Davis mailed out a questionnaire in 1936 to determine whether the members of the KMCLA wanted to stay or go. The issue itself seemed to have helped the KMCLA in its cause, as the Methodist Episcopal Church, South, took notice and apparently did not want to lose its ties to Korean Christians in southern California.[16] It did not hurt that each sponsoring denomination knew that one of its member churches considered joining forces with another Protestant body. As has often been true in cases of skewed power relations, those in subordinate positions have learned that exerting independence involves playing groups against one another.

A sense of competition further bolstered the case of the KMCLA when the Korean Presbyterian Church dedicated its new building in May 1938. The *Los Angeles Times* reported on 30 April 1938 that the church, located at 1374 West Jefferson Street, planned to celebrate its new sanctuary the following day during its Sunday service. The church had been valued at approximately thirty thousand dollars.[17] A number of people and groups had donated generously, including the denomination, individual supporters of the mission, and members themselves. The main sanctuary seated about 150 persons and consisted of a pipe organ, stained glass windows, and a choir loft. The Reverend Dr. Kim Sung-nak (Luke), a Ph.D. graduate of Princeton Theological Seminary, served the church during this period.[18]

The Korean Presbyterian Church did not simply create space for its own religious activities, but also housed the Korean National Association on its premises in a separate building. The coexistence of the church and the nationalist association powerfully symbolized how many Korean Americans integrated independence politics and the message of liberation found in Christianity. Located near the University of Southern California, the church created a haven for student-laborers who passed through Los Angeles. People often made the church campus their very first stop when they entered in the city.

In 1939, another congregation, the Korean Christian Church of Los Angeles, established a home for the elderly as its Hawaiian counterpart had for the community in the islands. The church's presence largely revolved around this social service dimension. The population of older men who had come as unskilled laborers and lacked family needed support.[19] The blending of religion, transnational migration, and community service suggested how Protestant Christianity spanned a range of life concerns.

All of the fanfare associated with the dedication of the Korean Presbyterian Church must have had an effect on the Methodists, because during a visit in 1938 the presiding bishop promised to help church members realize the goal of securing a church home. The KMCLA organized a building committee headed by Jacob K. Dunn.[20] Good intentions aside, the church moved once again in June 1939 to a site on 36th Place.[21]

## A New Wave

As the church continued its quest for a permanent home, newer developments took the form of a rising generation of American-born Koreans and the arrival of student-laborers from Korea. They represented a new wave that highlighted the diversity of perspectives within the KMCLA. The second generation, U.S. citizens by birth, engaged the congregation from a different vantage point and with differing needs from their parents. Another layering of migrants and exiles included some who brought progressive visions of independence based upon their experiences with colonialism in the homeland. The turbulent events taking place in East Asia during the 1930s added ferment to these developments.

Leaders of the congregation increasingly realized that their children needed to find a place in the church. Early efforts to cultivate a sense of belonging included asking the second-generation members to serve as ushers and to help announce church activities. Perhaps for the first time in the Korean American community, the second generation conducted an English-language Sunday worship service in December 1933.[22] The church also set aside special services in English to inspire the youth. Local area ministers, denomination officials, and former missionaries who had served in Asia helped conduct these services.[23]

In addition to the children who had grown up in the church, some young men and women from Hawai'i came to Los Angeles in pursuit of a college education. These students had ties to the Korean Methodist Church in Honolulu, which further illustrate the connectedness of the Korean American community across broad spaces. The second-generation members and students found a measure of fame through a church choir that performed on local radio stations.[24] The choir also made the rounds at local churches under the auspices of the Federation of Protestant Churches of Los Angeles. The singers became a source of considerable pride among members and gave the church positive exposure outside the Korean American community. Florence Ahn took her musical talents to the Julliard School of Music in New York, and Earl Kim later became a professor of music at Harvard University.[25]

By the end of the 1930s, most Korean churches held their Sunday school programs in English, and older members of the younger generation served as teachers. Mary Chun Lee served as the superintendent of the Sunday school in the latter half of the 1930s, stepping down in 1941 to take on broader responsibilities as a religious social worker helping Korean and Chinese American youth in southern California.[26] Lee likely counseled the two groups on the fate of being "in-between." The *New Korea* reprinted an article from the *California Chinese Press* that articulated the plight of the second generation. Korean Americans surely identified with the writer's words: "East is East and West is West, but in us the twain have met." The essay gave voice to the frustrations of those who faced limited futures on the basis of race despite the excellent education and training that qualified them for a range of careers.[27]

The second generation signaled the emergence of a Korean American community sinking roots into American soil, even as it was keenly aware of its exilic nature. Those transnational ties surfaced not only in the memories of individuals who had left their homeland and in the work for independence, but also in the arrival of student-laborers from Korea. One study estimates that approximately nine hundred Korean students entered the United States between 1899 and 1940.[28] These new arrivals, not surprisingly, often found their passage to the United States through Protestant missionary sponsorship. They brought with them new perspectives from their experiences in Korea, including faith-based progressive politics that drew like-minded people to the congregation. Matters of church and society, especially related to East Asia, became an important part of the life of the KMCLA.

During the 1930s, the spread of Japan's imperial reach into China as well as its ongoing colonization of Korea understandably concerned those in the United States, and student-laborers carried with them news of these developments. As things took a turn for the worse, many students debated about whether to return or to take part in the fight for independence as exiles. Students became leading voices within the churches for the cause, and the immigrant press mentioned the KMCLA's announcement in 1938 that it would hold special monthly services in support of the independence move-

ment. The service aimed to inspire as well as to education members of the
church and the larger community.[29]

If the students who remained in the United States did so for a measure
of freedom, then they faced another set of issues in their decision. Many of
these people overstayed their student visas and so had to keep a low profile
lest they run into immigration officials. The specter of detention and depor-
tation cast a shadow that has long followed Asian immigrants to the United
States since at least the Chinese Exclusion Act of 1882. Even earlier, and
just on the other side of entering nationhood, the United States through its
Naturalization Act of 1790 set a color line for citizenship that extended well
into the twentieth century. Denied access to citizenship, every Korean immigrant, to some extent, understood the biblical as well as the geopolitical
dimensions of exile courtesy of the United States government.[30]

For new arrivals and more established members, the KMCLA during this
era served as an important site for students and other progressive Christians
who related their faith to social change, reform, and independence. It is not
surprising that those coming from Korea brought news from the homeland,
but they also reflected the multiple and dynamic expressions of nationalism that had been developing in Korea since the late nineteenth century.
Christian nationalists attempted to safeguard Korean identity through the
churches and school networks, but they faced surveillance, arrests, and other
pressures from Japanese colonial forces. After the March First Movement in
1919, the Japanese suspected American Protestant missionaries and Korean
Christians of fomenting resistance and rebellion. The brutal response to the
uprising splintered the nationalist effort into those who advocated military
force and those who favored diplomacy, as well as those who turned to
socialism as a rejection of Western democracy. Some Christians looked to
education as a means of establishing an ethical and spiritual base for national sovereignty and subsequently moved nationalist efforts away from
state-centered politics. Such people drew the ire of other nationalists who
interpreted their stance as a form of compromise and collaboration.[31]

Given the turmoil, Christians interpreted their times from a variety of
theological perspectives; those perspectives influenced members and their
involvement in the Korean American community. Diamond Kimm, for instance, had developed a strong belief in the relationship between faith and
social justice. Kimm had attended the Korean Methodist Seminary in the

1920s and developed an understanding of Christianity as a religion of liberation.[32]

In 1938 the Reverend Whang offered a prayer commemoration of the March First Movement that wove together politics and faith. The independence movement had fallen on hard times, and 1 March 1919 must have seemed like a lifetime ago for some. Whang reflected such sentiments in asking the Lord not to tarry in liberating Korean from bondage. The pastor of the KMCLA recognized that a renewed zeal and courage, as well as wisdom and unity, needed to spring forth from God to sustain Koreans in their journey. Through the Lord's blessing Korea could begin to set into motion the process of restoration. Mission officials may have been concerned about the propensity to mix religion and nationalism, but Reverend Whang's petition resonated with many people in community.[33]

As the world headed toward war, Koreans in the United States kept abreast of events in Korea, but they also tracked China's fate, given that the Korean Provisional Government was situated there. Along with those in Hawai'i and the mainland, Koreans in China stood at the forefront of the fight for independence. China's struggle, therefore, indirectly became Korea's struggle. Moreover, given the precarious position that many Asian immigrants occupied in the United States, their fate in this country, in part, rested upon what happened to their homelands. As such, both Chinese and Japanese American communities rallied behind China and Japan. Leaders from both groups waged a public relations campaign that sought to win support in the United States. In the process, nationalisms among Koreans, Chinese, and Japanese Americans heightened.

The jockeying by immigrant communities regarding the events unfolding in Asia found expression in church circles. Members of the KMCLA took part in relief efforts to help Korean refugees in China displaced by the Sino-Japanese War of 1937 and also hoped to ride the growing anti-Japanese sentiment as a means of publicizing and garnering support for Korean independence. Superintendent W. A. Davis noted in his annual report for 1938 that the war in Asia had ripple effects that extended all the way to California. Japanese and Koreans followed the news in their respective newspapers, and Davis commented that in the case of the Japanese, the news was drawn heavily from Japanese sources and therefore reflected a one-sided perspective. In addition to the tensions that existed between the Japanese and Ko-

Anti-Japanese Protest. Photo courtesy of USC Korean American Digital Archive.

reans, the growing support for China within the United States did little
to help the Methodists in their Christian work, since boycotts and general
antipathy sent a negative signal to the Japanese. Although Davis made no
direct causal link between these developments, he observed that Buddhists
built impressive temples and that priests actively worked among the Japanese.[34] During the 1930s and into the war years, the writings of former missionary Pearl S. Buck and goodwill visits to the United States by Madame
Chiang Kai-shek (Soong May-ling), a Wellesley graduate and a Christian,
helped mobilize public opinion in the United States in favor of China and
against Japan.

Mary Chun Lee reported on a breakfast attended by many Protestant denominational leaders to hear a team sent by the Japanese Church of Christ.
Lee seemed skeptical at the group's suggestion that they came independent
of their government. She questioned the sincerity of the group's plea to
unity in Christ, given the persecution that Korean Christians had suffered

for many years. One sees reflected in Lee's analysis the intertwining of religion and independence politics in which a local proceeding in Los Angeles clearly had linkages to the developments unfolding in East Asia.[35]

Given its transnational orientation, the KMCLA could avoid being affected by the tumultuous developments in Asia as the decade of the 1930s came to a close. The church provided a tangible link to Asia through its membership and its commitments, and the KMCLA served as an important anchor for Korean Americans throughout southern California. Membership figures hovered around 125 people, but this number did not account for others who floated in and out of the congregation. Weekly prayer meetings continued to draw believers.[36]

The church had sought from the beginning to become self-supporting, but the vast majority of Koreans faced the harsh realities of being unskilled laborers in a workforce marked by racial hierarchy and in an economy hit by the Great Depression. Denominational officials commented on how enterprising Koreans seeking to build small businesses largely met with failure under the trying circumstances. Nevertheless, the KMCLA continued its good work among the community despite the lack of resources. In contrast to the Japanese, Koreans overwhelmingly adhered to the Christian faith.[37]

The work of the California Oriental Mission underwent some change when the northern and southern branches of the Methodist Episcopal Church reunited in 1939. The church had split in 1844 over the issue of slavery. It had taken nearly a century, but both the Methodist Episcopal Church (north) and the Methodist Episcopal Church, South, came together. Consequently, the California Oriental Mission reorganized by merging with the work taking place among the Chinese and Filipinos.[38]

In the transition to the 1940s, the KMCLA faced the entrance of the United States into World War II and its implications for Korean Americans. Many members of the second generation from the church, and for that matter, from all the churches on the mainland and in Hawai'i joined the military as part of the war effort. For Korean migrant families, the sacrifices of war carried the hope of Korean independence. As a congregation, the KMCLA's long-held dream of its own church would finally bear fruit near the end of the war. In addition, a number of pastoral changes took place that would set up a time of transition into the postwar period.

## A World at War

On the morning of 7 December 1941, Korean Americans in Hawai'i and on the mainland awoke to the news of the bombing of Pearl Harbor. Emotions ran high. Sadness for the lives lost and the soberness of a nation at war mixed with hope rekindled for Korean independence. Korean migrants and exiles scattered in sites across the globe realized that a significant opportunity had arisen. In a publication called *Voice of Korea*, an editorial marking the first anniversary of the bombing noted that Korea had a key role to play in establishing a just and lasting peace in East Asia. Pearl Harbor stood as a symbol of freedom for Koreans in that it ushered in an era conducive to the survival of small but strategically important nations like Korea. The editorial invoked the religious term *resurrection* to indicate the dawning of this new world order. If many Americans in wartime encouraged each other with the words, "Remember Pearl Harbor," then Korean Americans added, "When you remember Pearl Harbor, remember Korea!"[39]

As they always had, the churches served as gathering places for Koreans. Racial classification took on immediate significance, because Korean migrants in the United States found themselves in the unenviable position of being "Japanese" in the eyes of federal officials, despite their long-standing and vocal campaign against Japan. They fought long and hard against their status as enemy aliens and won some concessions, but they suffered, especially in Hawai'i, under a host of restrictions and curfews for the Japanese that only gradually and slowly lifted for Koreans.[40]

Furthermore, by virtue of physical appearance, Koreans might be mistaken for Japanese, adding insult to injury. The infamous *Time* article that ran shortly after Pearl Harbor (22 December 1941) instructed readers on how to tell the difference between the friendly Chinese and the fiendish Japanese with no mention of Koreans. Taking matters into their own hands, Koreans issued "I AM KOREAN" buttons to help offset cases of mistaken identity and misplaced hostility. Apparently, some Japanese wore counterfeit buttons, and the *New Korea* issued a warning to its readers that they should be on the lookout.[41]

Along with the buttons, Protestant Christianity and ties to the larger Methodist denomination provided another means of trying to prevent Koreans from being identified as Japanese. Koreans in subtle and not-so-subtle ways invoked their identification as Christians and the dominant role of the religious tradition within the community as a means of distinguishing

Korean Unit, California National Guard, 1942. Photo courtesy of USC Korean American Digital Archive.

themselves. More importantly, however, the long years spent trying to publicize and work for Korean independence had laid a formidable foundation in letting the larger society know how forcefully Koreans did not identify with nor wish to be associated with Japan. Congregations like the KMCLA were important centers of such activity.

The war provided an outlet for the second generation to work indirectly for Korea through service in the United States military. In Los Angeles, fifty-five young men enlisted in the California State Guard in January 1942, the first group of Koreans from the local area to volunteer. Noteworthy in the reporting of these events is the dual nature of the allegiances of the volunteers. Based in Washington, D.C., Syngman Rhee issued a directive to Koreans that carried a distinctly exilic and transnational tone. He called upon Koreans in the U.S. mainland, Hawai'i, the Philippines, Korea, Japan, and all Japanese-occupied territories to give all that they had in the fight against the common foe: "Every armed Japanese is your enemy, and you visit upon them the fury of an unconquerable people. To fight for America is to fight for Korea."[42] The second generation understood the larger significance of their involvement in the war effort.

The KMLCA leader Mary Chun Lee expressed some of her views through the local press and directly addressed the responsibility of Korean Christians in the United States. Freedom of religion had been taken away in Korea by the Japanese. At the same time, Lee admonished her readers about the indifference that many Americans of all backgrounds often exhibited regarding their faith. Her message targeted the younger generation in particular. One senses in Lee's words not only an urgency and passion, but also an equation of the cause of independence in Korea with Christianity.[43]

Given their shared roots in the KMCLA, Lee would have known Susan Ahn, the daughter of patriot Ahn Chang-ho (An Ch'ang-ho) whose recollection about the KMCLA as a young child opened Chapter 4. By the time of World War II, Ahn had grown up to join the United States Navy and had become a pioneering Asian American woman in the military.[44] Her family, led by her mother, Helen, had deep roots in the church, and Ahn's church family took pride in of one of its own. Susan Ahn had graduated from San Diego State College in 1939 with a degree in education and had worked as a local journalist in the Korean American press in Los Angeles. As a petty officer and naval trainer, Ahn linked her military service to her late father: "In our family we have always tried to live up to the spirit of our father. Though he spent his entire life trying to wrest Korea from Japanese domination, he believed in America—so much so that he came here in 1903 to learn the ways of American democracy to take back to his people—and I honor him in wearing this uniform."[45] In addition to sending young women and men to serve in the military, Korean American congregations sought to make sense of the war, guided by their pastoral leadership and prayer and through community service. In a published sermon excerpt, the Reverend P. K. Yoon of the Korean Presbyterian Church addressed the suffering and pain that those serving in the war faced, but also acknowledged the difficult circumstances for parents, spouses, other family members, and friends. Those on the home front faced the prospect of worry and concern for loved ones involved in the military. Yoon called on his listeners to draw upon the spiritual power available to them through God, reminding them of Jesus as a man of sorrows. Referencing the writing of St. Paul, the pastor situated the sacrifices of the war within the context of faith and liberation. To live or to die, one could be confident that one was with Christ: "Yes, to die for the cause of building God's kingdom in the hearts of men, or to die in defence of human liberty, homes, and country for the present and future generations is to gain these things."[46]

In an unsigned Christmas reflection in 1943, the author wondered where people might find peace in a time of war of such global proportions. The writer commented that wherever people resisted the forces of evil so present in the world, one would find the spirit of Christ and goodwill renewed:

> It is no accidental symbol that the life of Jesus on earth should have been marked by struggle and violence. His very birth was signaled by Herod's order slaying the babes of Bethlehem and his life one of pursuit and persecution, and then his death by crucifixion. But no other man born of woman has come to mean so much in the lives of generations of men and women. His resurrection was the fulfillment of the spirit, and today, that spirit is struggling for resurgence in our own lives.[47]

A sermon given at the KMCLA in 1942 continued the theme of placing the war in a context of faith. The message reminded people that a humble man from Nazareth had conquered more than all of the empires and armies the world had known. German and Japanese visions of world domination proved no match for followers of Jesus living out their faith. "I appeal to you young men and women, born of Korean parentage, learn from Jesus the secrets of how to become doers of golden deeds, how to become healing factors among your society instead of destroyers."[48]

Pastors and laypeople used words to explore the relationship between faith and war in the pages of the Korean American press. Some Korean American Christians in southern California acted out their understanding through community service. Members of the second generation formed the Korean Christian Association, whose first project was to send care packages to Korean Americans who had joined the military. The KMCLA donated funds to support the work of the association, as did the Korean National Revolutionary Party.[49]

## Wartime Liberation

The KMCLA and the Korean National Revolutionary Party (KNRP) might seem like an odd combination of sponsors, but the linkages between these organizations continued and extended some church members' progressive vision of faith and politics.[50] In particular, the war years gave rise to the establishment of a Los Angeles branch of the KNRP and its publication of the leftist newspaper *Korean Independence*. The organization traced its roots to a conference held in Nanking, China, in 1935, when leftist Korean independence groups from China, Manchuria, and the United States joined forces to create the KNRP to form a unified front. This coalition stood in contrast to the diplomatic approach of the organizations allied with the Korean Provisional Government. The KNRP advocated a military strategy and had been engaged in guerilla warfare against Japan and looked to socialist Russia for its cues rather than to the United States. The KNRP, along with the Sino-Korean People's League, represented leftist elements within the Korean American community.[51] Neither of these organizations commanded the loyalties of many Korean Americans, but one study noted that the KNRP drew to its ranks people from the entire spectrum of the Korean American community, including intellectuals, housewives, manual laborers, and Christian ministers. Supporters in the United States raised funds to help Korean military efforts in China. In addition, picketers protested in front of the Japanese consulate in Los Angeles after the start of the Sino-Japanese War in 1937 and also at the docks of San Pedro harbor against the sale of American scrap metal to Japan.[52] For a time, both the KNRP and the Sino-Korean People's League joined the United Korean Committee, the Korean American effort in April 1941 to bring the disparate organizations fighting for Korean independence under one umbrella to more effectively negotiate with the United States government.[53]

The pages of the *Korean Independence* illustrate the coalescence of progressive politics, Christianity, and the KMCLA. The paper began to publish in Los Angeles in 1943, renting a space on West Jefferson Boulevard near other Korean American community organizations such as the Korean National Association and the Korean Presbyterian Church.[54] While the political views of contributors undoubtedly varied, some writers like Diamond Kimm embraced the leftist orientation of the paper and the KNRP. Serving as a general manager for the newspaper, Kimm represented a newer generation of Korean American leaders who emerged during the 1920s and 1930s. Kilsoo Haan of the Sino-Korean People's League, an organization established in Hawai'i in the early 1930s, often contributed articles to the paper. Haan brought to his leftist activities a religious sensibility forged during his years with the Salvation Army.[55]

The Reverend Chang Key-Hyung of the KMCLA and the Reverend P. K. Yoon of the Korean Presbyterian Church often penned articles for the *Korean Independence,* and news coverage about their churches and their other engagements frequently appeared in the paper. Chang stepped into a vacancy created by the departure of the Reverend Whang Sa-Young, who after ten years of dedicated service took up a pastoral assignment in Hawai'i in 1940.[56] Chang was the first fully bilingual pastor of the congregation, and his extensive educational background signaled a maturation of pastoral leadership and the Korean American population at large. Chang had come to the United States in 1928 and attended the Berkeley Baptist Divinity School in northern California from 1932 to 1936, earning the Bachelor of Theology degree in 1936.[57] Chang continued his studies at Duke University, Princeton Seminary, and the Pacific School of Religion. His wife, Lila Chang, recalled that he always seemed to be in school and that his studies remained a lifelong passion.[58]

Reverend Chang brought dynamic leadership to the church in which his fluency in English enabled him to reach a much broader audience as well as bring greater visibility to the KMCLA. Through his writing and speaking, Chang served as a spokesperson for the Korean American community in southern California. A local newspaper noted that Chang had given a speech to the Rotary Club entitled "The Case for Korea" and that he was the only Asian member of the organization.[59] On another occasion, Chang spoke at the Ambassador Hotel on how Korea had not lost its national integrity despite suffering decades of cruel Japanese oppression.[60] Chang also taught Korean language at the University of California, Los Angeles, and the University of Southern California.[61]

The skills that Chang brought to his post as minister meshed well with the progressive character of the congregation, and he did not shy away from examining the relationship between faith and the social issues of the day. In fact, the KMCLA inaugurated a Sunday evening forum focusing on such issues for church members and the general public. In November 1945, Chang led a discussion entitled "Christianity and Socialism."[62] For the Sociology Department of the Los Angeles Public Library, Chang participated in a panel discussion on the topic of Oriental minorities in an Occidental society. The minister pointed to the reality of "prejudice, discrimination, inequality, and restriction against Oriental groups." At the same time, Chang pointed to the false belief in the superiority or inferiority between races. People, according to Chang, "must be ideologically convinced that without racial democracy there cannot be a complete democracy." Education alone, however important, could not eradicate racism, and Chang advocated for the abolition of existing legal discrimination and for the enactment of positive laws to extend the same democratic rights to Asians that other Americans enjoyed.[63]

Called often to comment on his homeland, Chang situated Korea's anti-imperial and anticolonial struggle as part of a larger global context and also linked it to America's past. Chang suggested that the phrase "Give me liberty or give me death!" served as a rallying cry for the Korean people and framed the events taking place in Korea as embodying the essence of the American Revolution.[64] The article represented a sophisticated reading of current and past events. After citing the American Revolution, Chang argued that Korea needed no "protection" from other powers since partial freedom really meant no freedom at all: "The government of Korea shall be 'the government of the people, by the people, and for the people.'" The invocation of U.S. history is not surprising given the context. And yet, in closing, Chang suggested that while the United States served as an important point of reference, the future of Korea, especially in terms of its economy, needed to follow the example of the Russian Revolution. Chang did not elaborate on this last statement, but it is interesting that he ended his opinion piece on this note.[65]

World War II not only infused a renewed hope into the Korean independence movement, but also created new opportunities for Koreans in the United States to contribute. For some members of the KMCLA, those opportunities included utilization of Japanese and Korean language skills to work in government and university-based jobs. Diamond Kimm served the Office of Strategic Studies as a civilian agent, joining a field experimental unit that planned to send Koreans in the United States with Japanese language skills behind enemy lines. According to the personnel data file, Kimm excelled in his training, but the end of the war prevented the implementation of the program.[66] Despite their service to the United States, KMCLA and KNRP members like Diamond Kimm faced persecution and harassment in the Cold War ethos of the postwar period. People went overseas and to other parts of the country, and the KNRP in Los Angeles disbanded in 1955.[67]

Because socialism was stigmatized both within the Korean American community and in the larger U.S. society, the hardships endured by the left-leaning members of the church have not been discussed much. Perhaps it is only now, with the benefit of time passed, that the stories of these individuals can gain a fairer hearing. It is important to recognize that the liberation struggles that took place involved a range of ideological positions that included socialist understandings of Protestant Christianity. As Gi-Wook Shin and Michael Robinson have pointed out, histories of modern Korea have been constricted by a bipolar universe in which the past serves the political ends of two regimes, North and South, that continue to this day.[68]

While KMCLA members with associations with the KNRP have been cast into the shadows, other persons active in the church have been honored by the Republic of Korea for their sacrifices. Park Kyong-sin arrived in the United States in 1924, having already been an active participant in the independence movement. Park left Korea in 1917 to study at a Bible school in Japan and there met Maria Kim, who encouraged her to get involved. Park returned to Korea and took part in the March First Movement, and she recalled the thrill of hearing the church bells ringing and people running out to the streets waving Korean flags. Park's association with the independence movement made her the target of Japanese police, and she spent a difficult winter in hiding in China, suffering physical hardship and working with the Korean Provisional Government. She left China for Hawai'i and worked for a while as a housekeeper. Park then went to the mainland, married, and taught Korean language at the KMCLA in the late 1920s and early 1930s. Park managed to complete her studies begun in Japan many years earlier through a Bible school in Los Angeles. Throughout her activities at the church, Park continued her support of Korea, working with the Women's Patriotic League and also selling war bonds during World War II. One sees in the expanse of Park's life the role of faith and love of country that marked her activity and sensibility. In an interview given at the end of her life, Park commented: "I've broken all thoughts on anything except to concentrate on preparing to meet my Savior."[69]

A friend and coworker of Park's, Kim Hei-won, gained recognition and honor as a patriot for her work through the Korean National Association and the Korean Women's Patriotic Association in California. An active and longtime member of the KMCLA, Kim left Korea with her mother and

siblings, landing in Hawai'i in 1905. Kim and her family moved from a sugarcane plantation on Maui to Honolulu. She left for the mainland to attend
school and to accept a matchmaking arrangement. Although the schooling
did not materialize, she married in 1913. Kim worked with her children in
tow and coordinated independence work not only throughout California
but also in Mexico.[70]

## Milestones Achieved

World War II generated much activity at the intersection of faith and politics, but other markers of the KMCLA in its ministry to the Korean community during this era included the dedication of a church building in 1945.
The congregation's longtime goal had been a permanent church home. At
the 1940 annual conference held in Oakland, California, Marie Lee, who
had been invited to perform a vocal solo at the gathering, read a written
appeal from the church. The committee in charge of the church building
project asked for financial assistance:

> There are about 130 or more adults and about that many more young peo-
> ple including Sunday School children. During the last ten years, we have
> been moving around from one place to another, a few years here and a few
> years there and . . . even we hold our regular mid-week prayer meetings at
> private homes. Therefore, we are badly handicapped in general church ac-
> tivities, especially leading the young people to the Christian environments.
>     We started this campaign about three years ago to raise the funds to
> build our church building and its project has been endorsed by the Board
> of Missions of Tennessee, by Dr. G. C. Emmons, Bishop W. C. Martin,
> and by the Pacific Conference held at Santa Ana last year. We have received
> a good many subscriptions from the members of our church and also from
> many American friends and from various churches during the last year; but
> still we are a long way off to accomplish the object. The lot for the building
> was purchased last year and completely paid. Now, our desire is to build the
> church before the coming Christmas so we can provide the children with a
> new church to the glory of His Name. Friends and brethren of the Confer-
> ence, won't you please give us a lift?[71]

While the denomination pledged to look into the matter, the church
continued its efforts without much help. In 1941, the church raised fifteen

hundred dollars from among the membership.[72] After the move in 1942, the church moved again, since space opened in downtown Los Angeles because of the incarceration of Japanese Americans along the West Coast during World War II. The annual report of the California Oriental Mission in 1943 did not specifically state the circumstances but recorded that the KMCLA had "come into a substantial church building" of the Normandie Street Japanese Methodist Church. Denominational officials saw the development as a positive one, since the congregation had been "pushed about for years and was becoming discouraged for a lack of a place for their own."[73] Whatever relief the KMCLA experienced in their new church campus did not last long, since the congregation needed to move again when Japanese Americans made their way back to the West Coast as the war came to a close.[74]

The KMCLA learned that a church property located on 29th Street a couple of blocks from the University of Southern California had been placed on sale for $15,500. The church sat near the geographic center of the Korean American community in Los Angeles.[75] In a bold move, the church decided to push forward and open escrow on the building in the spring of 1945, despite having insufficient funds. Chang then headed to northern California and throughout Korean communities in the rest of the state in search of support.[76] In addition to the existing funds and the new moneys, the church needed to raise seventy-five hundred dollars. The denomination made up the difference and approved the purchase. The church finally had a permanent home.[77]

The KMCLA began holding its services in the new church building located at 1267 West 29th Street on 3 June 1945, and many tears flowed.[78] The denomination noted in 1945 that the KMCLA had moved seven times in twelve years, and this accounting did not include the numerous relocations that the church had endured since the founding of the mission in 1904.[79] The new building consisted of a sanctuary able to seat 350 people, a small social room, kitchen, four restrooms, and an office. The Reverend Victor Peters who had been a missionary in Korea and had been deported by Japanese in 1939, oversaw the Sunday school.[80] The church held its open house for the public on 7 October 1945.[81]

Another milestone of sorts involved the coming of age of the second generation, largely English-speaking Korean Americans. The church had a promising group, many of whom had graduated from college.[82] In light of the war, Lucille Chung wrote an article to other second-generation Korean Americans, specifically about the role of women. Chung encouraged her female readers to step up to greater positions of leadership and community service, in part because so many of the second-generation men served in the military. In particular, Chung emphasized the vital role of the churches and the contributions that could be made by Korean American women through teaching youth, participating in the choir, and also in serving the needs of the greater community. No doubt taking cues from her elders, Chung stressed the fact that women have always been the backbone of any nation. Korean American women certainly had been at the heart of the ministry of the KMCLA throughout its history.[83]

Lucille Chung's words resonated with the KMCLA choir, which continued to represent an important locus of fellowship as well as outreach. The choir, in a sense, grew up with the second generation, increasingly becoming a public face of the congregation. In 1944, the Easter service reflected the vibrancy of this segment of the church. Emerging leaders such as Alfred Song and Marie Lee took part as soloists and narrators, and a capacity crowd gathered.[84]

In an effort to reach out to younger members of the community, the church sponsored dinners for Korean American students. Reverend Chang addressed what it meant to represent the future leadership of the community.

Ralph Ahn, the youngest son of independence leader Ahn Chang-ho and Helen Ahn, recalled forming a club within the church called the "Monarchs." With buddies like Howard Choy and Luther Hahn, Ahn played in church sports leagues that reached out to other denominations and to the Korean community at large in southern California. These activities included intra-Asian activities. The immigrant press reported that the Korean Monarchs rallied in the last sixty seconds of a football game against the Chinese Pontiacs to end the contest in a 6 to 6 tie.[85] The Monarchs, with their sharp-looking jackets, also hosted social events for young Korean Americans. Ahn, Choy, and Hahn recalled that the young people received much support from their elders, especially the mothers in the congregation.[86]

## Looking Forward, Looking Back

The KMCLA had come a long way from its reorganization in 1930 to the World War II era. The congregation's constant moving underscored the marginal status of Korean Americans within the denomination and the overall segregation patterns in southern California. The growth of the second generation indicated a maturation and grounding of the community in the United States. And yet, the arrival of students from Korea extended the theme of migration & exile and added a progressive flavor to the ongoing fight for independence in the face of colonialism.

The entry of the United States into World War II had major implications for the church, as its young men and women entered military service and those who stayed behind made their own contributions. The transnational nature of the Korean American community took on greater significance as the war spawned renewed hope for the liberation of the homeland. Church members sifted through the connections between faith and war. Those involved in leftist activity operated from a place of faith through intricate and contentious diasporic networks. The war years also brought other changes, most notably the securing of a permanent church home in 1945, not long before the end of the war.

In the postwar Cold War era, the Methodist denomination sought to implement a plan to phase out non-English-language services in Asian immigrant churches. The move reflected an emphasis on Americanization and the goal of seeing so-called ethnic churches become absorbed into a European American society. The plan did not meet with much success. Churches like the KMCLA had over the course of decades laid a foundation of leadership and provided a framework of meaning and community that addressed the needs of its members. That the KMCLA did not "melt" into the landscape underscored the relationship between religion & race.

The relational themes of religion & race, migration & exile, and colonialism & independence have guided the excavation and reclamation work that has focused on the role of Protestant Christianity in Korean American history in Hawai'i and the mainland. The final chapter of the story told here focuses on a remarkable religiously based publication in which the relational themes come through loud and clear. What follows is an effort to listen to individuals and communities as they speak to these concerns in their own voices.

# SIX

# Voices in the Wilderness:
## *The Korean Student Bulletin*

In October 1922, Julian S. Park left New York City on a three-week tour of
a dozen colleges and universities to visit with Korean and Korean American
students. A graduate of Methodist-related Baldwin-Wallace College in Ohio
and having taken classes at the Presbyterian seminary in Princeton, New
Jersey, Park knew the situation of his fellow students well. The tour initi-
ated his duties as the Korean secretary of the Committee on Friendly Relations Among Foreign Students of the Young Men's Christian Association
(YMCA). The report on Park's trip appeared in the inaugural issue of the
*Korean Student Bulletin* (*KSB*) that served as a news, opinion, and information outlet.[1]

The *Korean Student Bulletin* provides access to the perspectives of students and others who appeared in its pages during the years of its publication from 1922 to 1941.[2] The intertwining relational themes of race &
religion, migration & exile, and colonialism & independence help frame
the discussion of the *KSB* as a marker of the role of religion in the history
of Koreans on the mainland and in Hawai'i. The linkages between race and
religion emerged as writers wrestled with how to understand their Christian
faith in light of the racialization of Koreans within the setting of American race relations. Race represented one of many issues deriving from what
might be termed an applied Christianity. The migration & exile theme took
many forms, but the experience of being an international student itself con-

stituted a form a migration and exile. Another dimension of this relational theme encompassed the second generation and how its members blurred the line between Korean and Korean American. The transnational nature of all Koreans in the United States softened any hard-and-fast distinctions between the foreign- and American-born, even as some commented on the differences. The linkages between colonialism and independence emerged in the ongoing concern for the fate of Korea. The *KSB* faithfully reported on people and events in the Korean diaspora while asking questions about how Christianity related to hopes of freedom and independence.

The *KSB* gave young men and women a space in which to articulate what constituted a kind of wilderness experience as they faced uncertain and difficult times. Protestant Christianity served as a means of exploring and navigating that wilderness against the shadows cast by colonial oppression, economic depression, and increasing global conflict.[3]

## Promoting Friendly Relations

The *Korean Student Bulletin* had a twofold aim: "First, it is to serve all the Korean students in this country in a way to bring them into close contact with the Christian influence and to foster the moral and educational interests among them; secondly, to deepen and widen the interest of American Christians in Korea and her people."[4] These goals formed part of a larger effort by the Committee on Friendly Relations to promote international friendship and understanding under the auspices of the YMCA and in co-operation with American Protestant denominations. Although the committee did not offer financial aid, it did serve as an international network of support that included advising students in their home country as well as placement services to colleges in the United States. Local staff met students once they disembarked at American ports and stations and escorted them to their respective campuses. Self-supporting students could find information about and introductions to possible employers. The work of the committee situated students within a comprehensive network that included campus organizations and Protestant congregations.[5]

The ministry of the Committee on Friendly Relations extended the missionary impulse by connecting the work overseas to college campuses in the United States. Formed in 1911, the committee represented a ministry to students that resonated with broader Protestant efforts to work with Asians in the United States with the aim of supporting missions overseas.[6] The Korean Methodist churches in Honolulu and Los Angeles started under such circumstances. The movement between Korea, Hawai'i, and the mainland underscored the relationship between migrants and exiles; that movement very much included students.

Many of the international students already had attended mission institutions in their home countries, and through those connections, young people left for the United States often with the sponsorship of foreign mission as well as indigenous religious organizations. The programs of the committee also reflected the influence of the Student Volunteer Movement (SVM), which emerged in the late nineteenth century.[7] The YMCA and YWCA became the catalysts for college and seminary students to enter foreign missions. The SVM also hosted large international conferences, called quadrennials, that attracted thousands of college students. Books, pamphlets, and study materials produced under the SVM banner gained wide usage by students in the United States and abroad.[8] The movement spread to Europe and Asia, and the *KSB* carried news of related events such as the Ninth Quadrennial held in Indianapolis in 1924.[9]

Korean students took an active role in the wide range of programs associated with the committee, including the formation of the Korean Student Federation of North America in 1923. The Korean Student Federation served as an organizing and coordinating body for key events, such as the regional summer conferences that brought together international and American students at retreat centers and campgrounds. The conferences helped create spaces for interaction to take place and for friendships to form.[10] In 1937, nearly nine thousand international students from almost one hundred different countries ventured to the United States. Estimates vary regarding the numbers of international students from Korea, and the *KSB* reported numbers ranging from 20 to 250 at different points throughout its publication span (1922–41).[11] Nearly nine hundred Korean students had come to the United States during the period from 1899 to 1940.[12] Of course these numbers did not recognize that many laborers floated in and out of student status depending upon their ability to pay for their schooling. Nor do these figures include second-generation American-born Koreans.

Regardless of these distinctions, students of Korean ancestry found sup-

Korean Student Federation, 1924. Photo courtesy of USC Korean American Digital Archive.

port in the work of the international arm of the YMCA. The Committee on Friendly Relations helped sponsor a secretary for Chinese, Japanese, Koreans, and Filipinos in addition to those who hailed from non-Asian countries. The secretaries traveled throughout the United States and overseas. Each of the Asian groups also published its own bulletin.[13] The Committee on Friendly Relations, based in New York City, provided the structure for the work among international students. Some within the YMCA held up a vision in which students, educated and exposed to an American Christian civilization, might return to their home countries to become leading citizens embodying Protestant ideals. The white-collar, capitalist orientation of the organization has been well documented. Captains of industry and American wealth fueled the rapid growth and expansion of the YMCA in the United States and abroad.[14] As such, one could situate the YMCA as part of a larger American imperial project.

At the same time, an internal critique (as well as appreciation) of American culture and society had long formed part of the missionary enterprise.[15] Moreover, the social gospel movement that reached its peak in the late nineteenth century and in the early decades of the twentieth century made an impact upon the YMCA by asking how Christianity engaged societal concerns such as race relations, labor unrest, urban crime and poverty, and international peace. The movement drew from various traditions and represented an effort by Christians to respond to the massive scale of change taking place around them. Social gospel advocates attempted to address the dilemmas of adapting a religion of an earlier rural America to the pressures of an emergent industrial nation.[16] As the organization extended its work to Asia, leaders like Secretary John R. Mott emphasized that the movement's goal was to foster native leadership:

> Our great idea going out to these countries is to leave them as soon as possible; to plant the Association idea in the hearts and minds of native young men in order that they may propagate the Movement themselves, and let us go home as soon as may be. We are putting this burden on the native shoulders. This great work of evangelization is not supremely for British or American or Continental leaders; it is primarily a Chinese, a Japanese, an Indian, a native enterprise.[17]

The directive targeted YMCA endeavors in Asia, but it also applied to students from Asia and of Asian ancestry in the United States. Accordingly, students found a measure of autonomy and freedom within their organizations and networks. For instance, the *KSB* and its counterparts provided a forum "containing news items and frank expressions of opinion by students from the Far East." Koreans did not shy away from anticolonial discourse regarding their homeland and championing a religious nationalism. Chinese students advocated for their nation as a great civilization certainly deserving of the rights and privileges given to European nations.[18] Moreover, Filipino students spoke out against their in-between status as U.S. nationals barred from access to many facets of American life; on homeland politics, they pointed out that the Philippines merited the same level of independence that Americans enjoyed. Japanese students critiqued the immigration policies of the United States and argued for racial equality to counter discrimination and prejudice directed at Japan.[19] As these perspectives suggest, students from Asia made informed cases for their respective nations, all the while exhibiting a keen awareness of the powerful role of the United States in the international order.

## Racial Sensibilities

Students from Korea critiqued and discussed events taking place in Korea, but they also provided commentary on American society and culture. Race and its relationship to religion, both in the United States and within an international context, drew out the observations of students who wrote for the *KSB*. C. C. Hahn of the University of Southern California assessed the positive and negative elements in American civilization. On the plus side of the ledger, Hahn underscored religion, chiefly Christianity, as shaping the character of the nation. Echoing a familiar refrain, Hahn noted that the country's founders came for religious democracy. On the other hand, widespread economic exploitation coupled with racial prejudice marred American civilization. Hahn focused primarily on immigrants and how their idealized views of the United States so often crumbled under the weight of their actual experience. Hahn cited the example by which the United States barred Chinese laborers from entering the country during lean economic times but recruited them when the need for cheap labor increased. The University of Southern California student did not look kindly upon what he termed a "dirty attitude," nor did he excuse the harm that American companies inflicted directly in Asia. In linking race and economics, Hahn juxtaposed the positive elements of Christianity against the corrosive effects of prejudice and greed.[20]

In another essay, written by an attendee of the 1924 Quadrennial International Student Volunteer Convention, the themes of race and religion intersected both with domestic American concerns and more broadly with the issues of international race relations. In both cases, people at the convention sought "to find places where the spirit of Christ has not been the dominant factor in life, and to picture before the students the world of need and its Christian solution." The writer commented that what emerged during the event was a consciousness of how the various races of the world connect. Technology drove some of this consciousness, as modern transportation and travel brought people into more frequent contact. Some clearly did not welcome such proximity. Delegates experienced the tension between the ideal of living in peace and harmony as Christians and the harsh reality of racial discrimination. Charges of prejudice apparently had made their way through the gathering—unleashing anger, discomfort, and embarrassment. In particular, the author sympathized with African Americans in the southern United States.[21]

In extending the international theme, elder statesman and physician Philip Jaisohn (So Chae'pil) contributed an article to the *KSB* in October 1925 describing his experience at the Institute of Pacific Relations in Honolulu. The conference brought together peoples living around the Pacific Ocean with the intent of fostering an exchange of ideas and greater mutual understanding among the participants. Interracial issues posed a central concern as nations jockeyed for economic and military advantage in the region in which stronger countries exploited weaker ones through territorial aggression. Jaisohn could not provide details of the proceedings for reasons of confidentiality, but he mentioned that attendees briefly addressed the plight of Korea. Hugh Cynn represented his country at the meeting and did so admirably. Despite the complexities of the interracial conditions in the Pacific region, Jaisohn suggested that the answer could be found in the eighth commandment: Thou shalt not steal. If nations as well as individuals adhered to this principle, then more peace and justice would be evident in international interracial relations.[22]

## Applied Christianity

"A Rule of Life: Comfort the poor, protect and shelter the weak and with all thy might right that which is wrong. Then shall the Lord love thee, and God himself shall be thy great reward."[23] Along with examining issues of race, the pages of the *KSB* enabled writers to work out meanings of their faith for themselves and for their readers. Protestant Christianity assumed a place of privilege within the bulletin though often subsumed in the reportage of news and other related activities. Articles about religion revealed a kind of applied Christianity. In moving from a realm of belief to one of action, a life of service beyond the self emerged as a major theme based on the example of Jesus.

One essayist reminded readers that despite the importance of an education, the ultimate goal remained to live life as Christians fully engaged in the world. The challenge set before students entailed the development of Christian character modeled on the life of Jesus. Character in turn led one to a life of service: "The world needs not so much men who will dazzle it with their learning as it needs men and women who will lift it with their useful lives of earnestness and sincerity. The races of the world need more God-fearing earnest toiling men and women living truly that they may live to bless all about them." In calling them to a life of service, the writer encouraged readers not to heed the pull of materialism and acquisition. Far greater meaning and fulfillment awaited those who looked to Jesus as the guide and rule of life.[24]

Another journalist distinguished between a general belief in human nature or a supreme being to one centered in a personal God in whose image human beings had been created. The writer suggested that faith consisted of a relationship not only with God, but with other human beings. What is interesting in this schema is how the connection between people necessitated working for social righteousness. The embrace of social change and the betterment of society, while worthy in and of themselves, rightly belonged to religion as their source. The appeal to be a blessing to all nations echoed the promise given to Abraham and Sarah in the Hebrew scriptures. The author painted an integrated notion of faith that led to a life of service beneficial to other people, communities in which the believer lived, and by extension, to the world at large.[25]

A key part of that integration related to the plight of a colonized Korea, and Philip Jaisohn related that situation to the Christian faith. Jaisohn had been invited to speak to the Korean Student Federation in 1924 but could not be present, and so he sent his remarks by mail and the *KSB* printed the letter. The bulk of the message had to do with the damage done to the cause of independence by internal divisions and strife, and the call to unity. Jaisohn noted that the Korean Student Federation embodied the hope of the future of Korea, since students represented a new generation of leadership. As such, the patriot reminded his readers that their fates and Korea's intertwined. The failure or success of one would be shared with the other. The nationalism of the letter is what one might expect from such a figure, but he closed his comments by underscoring the critical place of faith as a foundation for Korea's future. Jaisohn painted Korea's cause as a sacred one because of the just nature of Korea's yearning to be a free and independent nation. In a simple turn of phrase, the physician added: "This simple faith will enable you to face death with courage and receive honor and fortune with humble spirit."[26]

## Between Here and There

Philip Jaisohn may have been an American citizen based in the Philadelphia area, but in his commitments and aspirations he remained part of Korea. Many Koreans in the United States simultaneously and in dynamic fashion occupied migrant and exilic spaces, including those who passed through the pages of the *KSB*. Figures who have appeared earlier in the study made their presence known through their writings and activities. Hugh Cynn continued his transnational ties through frequent travels sponsored by the Korean and international YMCA. Others, like Syngman Rhee, based primarily in Hawai'i and the mainland, also spoke through the bulletin. Of course, the experiences of many others less well known surfaced at different points over the course of the publication of the *KSB*. International students from Korea encountered a range of experiences that marked the migration & exile relationship, and second-generation Korean Americans constituted another distinctive subset.

Park Sang Ryup left Korea in August 1926 to begin his journey as an international student, slated to study at Ohio Wesleyan University. In a poignant letter written to his father, Park recounted the experience of being held for a week at the infamous Angel Island Detention Center in San Francisco Bay. He described how he could not sleep the night prior to the ship's arrival because of his anticipation of finally setting foot on the soil of the country that had inhabited his imagination for so long. The joy Park experienced at entering the bay proved short-lived, and the very fog seemed to say, "Don't come. Our country is too clean to admit a poor Oriental student as you." As he left the ship with immigration officials and went in a small motorboat to the white detention barracks, Park could not help but mark the irony of the beauty of the bay at twilight set against the two armed officials who greeted him at the dock. Approximately one hundred Chinese nationals had been pent up in the prisonlike quarters for months on end, and Park compared the center to an exhibit of undesirables from all over the world. The pain and suffering of those detained found expression in

Chinese character poems etched into the very walls of the barracks.[27] How could a Christian nation so enamored of its democracy and liberty treat peoples from other parts of the world in such a fashion? Park's stay lasted a week, and one sensed that he felt fortunate to have gotten out, but he remained haunted by what he had experienced and seen. He ended the letter to inform his father that he had arrived safely at Ohio Wesleyan.[28]

Park's story may have been somewhat unusual in terms of his experience at Angel Island, but like so many students from Korea, he hoped and dreamed of returning to the homeland with an American education. The *KSB* did not often print much demographic information about students, but rather gave more descriptive listings and news about individuals at various institutions. Of the few numbers available, the *KSB* reported that 21 Korean students enrolled at schools during the 1924–25 academic year. By comparison, there were 36 students from India, 62 from Japan, and 328 from China. As U.S. nationals, Filipinos were counted as foreign students.[29] By 1939, approximately 265 students from Korea had come to the United States. In 1937, the Committee on Friendly Relations recorded that California for that year had the largest number of foreign students (1,906), but the committee also indicated that American-born Asians accounted for 735 of that number. Demographic data often depended upon self-reportage, and many individuals went in and out of student status depending upon finances, health, and other issues. The high mobility and sporadic attendance of some students made it difficult to get accurate assessments of the general student profile. In addition, the fact that students overstayed their visas meant that they avoided bringing attention to themselves.[30]

Many young men and women did not realize their aspirations, as they were beset by the realities of student-laborer lives in which they frequently had to interrupt their studies to earn a living. Emily Porcincula Lawsin's study of the *Filipino Student Bulletin* recounts that many college and university students not only did not graduate, but also did not return home.[31] Sometimes differentiated by class—but not always—laborers and students illustrated the ambiguous and shifting nature of migration. For Koreans and Filipinos, colonialism and exile added another layer of experience. In calculating whether to stay or return, colonization muted the pull of family and other ties to the homeland.[32]

Even for those students who received their degrees and went back to

Korea, the time in the United States rendered them as transnational peoples in which they belonged to more than one place, but perhaps not wholly to any. A biographical article published in 1927 featured L. George Paik, who after a decade in the United States returned to Korea to take up a teaching post at the Chosen Christian College in Seoul. A product of missionary education and sponsorship, Paik had been groomed to play a leading role in Korea's burgeoning Protestant movement. The star student earned an array of degrees from American schools: B.A. (Park College), M.A. and Th.B. (Princeton Seminary) and Ph.D. (Yale University). The article proudly listed Paik's many accomplishments, including his fluency in the Korean, Japanese, Chinese (Mandarin), and English languages, as well as his scholarly work in biblical Greek, Latin, Hebrew, and German. Paik clearly represented the elite segment of international students from Korea. The accumulation of cosmopolitan and cultural capital made Paik not only Korean but also a figure who could and did cross many boundaries. He became a leader in Korean higher education and a prominent church person in his home country and abroad.[33]

If student-laborers from Korea who traversed the Pacific Ocean and negotiated life in the United States provide glimpses into the relationship between migration and exile, then it might seem less likely that this theme would apply second-generation Korean Americans. As U.S. citizens by birth, the children of immigrants in places like Honolulu and Los Angeles had only a rudimentary grasp of Korean language and history, and few had ever been to Korea. Nevertheless, the experiences of the second generation underscore another dimension of migration & exile. Of course, every immigrant group's second generation in the United States has had to grapple with its in-betweenness. The ties to ancestry through families and immigrant institutions coexisted with exposure to the larger society through schooling and popular culture.[34] This in-betweenness, however, has not been uniform. Korean Americans encountered an enduring racism reserved for those groups who have been more or less permanently designated as the racial "other" in the United States, even accounting for the shifting constructions of "race" over time and place.[35]

A report based on the Korean secretary's travel in 1929 included an extended discussion of the second generation, prompted apparently by time spent in the Korean American community in Los Angeles. The American-born and Korean-born students did not have much interaction, and the tensions between the two groups stemmed from differences in age, sensibilities, and life experiences. Chinese and Japanese students also faced similar circumstances. The article recommended that the two groups of students seek to interact and learn from one another and suggested that the YMCA, YWCA, and churches could facilitate interaction and exchange more broadly.[36]

In May 1930, the *KSB* dedicated an issue largely to the second generation. Numerous articles offered commentaries on the topic, including a pointed essay by Martha Choy. She did not take kindly to being referred to as a "problem" and especially bristled at critiques by international students: "But my indignation is aroused every time a braggadocio, sweetly deluded into believing himself the epitome of Korean learning and patriotism feels the urge to hand out hackneyed bits of wisdom. 'Tis no learning in him but pedantry; no patriotism, but chauvinism." Choy's reaction stemmed in part from her own assessment of how she had once idealized Korea and the prospect of someday visiting the land of her ancestors. Inspired by the patriotism she witnessed as a child growing up in Hawai'i, Choy had envisioned becoming a Korean Joan of Arc. Time had tempered her adolescent attitudes toward Korea, as well as the international students she encountered. Given her experience, one might have expected Choy to claim more of an American identity, but her essay seemed more about clarifying and carving out space for the second generation within a more inclusive sense of what it meant to be Korean. She counseled greater tolerance, even as she clearly set forth a defense of the second generation.[37]

Another essay by journalist Y. Kang, also from Hawai'i, sketched out several problem areas for the second generation. Language, according to Kang, had become a major stumbling block. Korean Americans not only struggled with Korean language acquisition but also lacked a solid grasp of the English language. Only a small minority of university and top-tier high school graduates possessed a good command of English. Kang stated that most members of the second generation stood nowhere definitely and that churches needed to play a greater role, since the condition they faced involved moral and existential concerns. As Martha Choy wanted to create space for the second generation, Kang advocated an identity in which no contradiction existed in being 100 percent American citizen and 100 percent Korean patriot.[38]

Helen Lim provided her own version of how the second generation could integrate a sense of self based on what she saw taking place in Los Angeles. Rather than viewing American-born Koreans as a "problem," Lim instead envisioned the possibility of blending the best of two civilizations. Because of Japanese colonialism, the future of the peninsular nation rested with the second generation, since they embodied a Koreanness that would endure beyond their parents. According to Lim, the churches, and in her case the Korean Methodist Church of Los Angeles, held a key place in helping the second generation reach its potential. Lim pointed out that young men and women exercised leadership skills through church life, leading services and taking greater responsibilities within the community. Music provided another venue in which the second generation could use their talents to bring recognition to Korean Americans in the eyes of the larger public.[39]

Several years after the special issue, an honors student at Mt. Holyoke College, Anne Kim, wrote about the dilemma faced by second-generation Korean Americans—namely, that they were by no means full-fledged Americans nor were they fully Korean. Kim eloquently expressed the sentiments held by many of her peers:

> In this land of freedom, he is not free. He will always have the label of yellow man and be treated as such. If he remains in this "free and equal" country he will always be patronized and looked down upon by the white man. He will not have equal footing on which he can compete with the white man. . . . As long as he remains in this country he will always be treated as inferior and not as an equal to his white neighbor.

Kim's candid words underscored the racialization of Korean Americans and the limits of U.S. citizenship for the second generation in particular. Interestingly, even though Kim recognized the ways in which a move to Korea created serious challenges for the American-born, she still advocated the homeland as an outlet for those with ambitions.[40]

The future loomed large for every Korean student, as many struggled simply to stay in school and to complete their varied programs. A colonized Korea and, in Anne Kim's estimation, an America in which Asians could not get a fair chance each presented young people with daunting barriers. During the end of the run of the *KSB* in the late 1930s and early 1940s, Japan's war with China meant that Korea's people and resources would be pressed into even greater service to the Japanese empire seeking to mold East Asia in its own image. In the United States, the lingering effects of the Great Depression placed Koreans, already on the margins, in a more precarious economic position. In this context, perhaps the most serious commentary on the status of Korean students came from a Princeton Seminary student named Y. Hahn. Writing in 1940, Hahn specifically addressed fellow students from Korea who may have been tempted to not return home.[41]

Hahn urged readers to look to the Christian faith as a guide and a source of hope, especially the close of Jesus' earthly ministry. The fickle crowd who had cheered Jesus' entry to Jerusalem turned against him a short while later. Hahn reminded his readers of the sorrow of Mary and the other women who witnessed the death of Jesus on the cross. While acknowledging the reality of that sorrow, he also pointed to the fact that Christians knew that Good Friday did not represent the finale. Resurrection ultimately defined Christianity and set it apart from other religious traditions. Hahn pointed to the need in the homeland for those with resurrection hope to walk the difficult path of sacrificial service because of the example set by Jesus, Mary Magdalene, and the early apostles and martyrs of the church:

> Now "our Jerusalem" is not Los Angeles, Chicago, New York, or Washington, D.C., but it is *Seoul,* the capital of our homeland. Our mission is the re-building of "our Jerusalem." Do our friends warn us not to enter the city, as Agabus warned St. Paul with the prophetic sign of binding feet and hands? Let us look beyond the gloomy predictions to the Divine Will which will guide our way toward "our Jerusalem."[42]

The migration & exile relationship encompassed a range of individuals who surfaced in the pages of the *Korean Student Bulletin,* from elder statesmen who as exiles worked diligently on behalf of Korean independence to students, both foreign- and native-born. Some young men and women enjoyed the privilege of full-time study, but most worked their way through school with interruptions and, in some cases, unrealized dreams. Irrespective of citizenship, generation, or class, all of the writers in the *KSB* could identify with an in-betweenness that marked their condition as Korean and American Christians seeking to find their way in a transnational and troubled world.

## Sacred Cause of Liberty

> In the golden age of Asia
> Korea was one of its lamp-bearers
> And that lamp is waiting
> To be lighted once again
> For the illumination
> In the East
> —Rabindranath Tagore[43]

Migration & exile, in a geographic and spiritual sense, stemmed from the realities of colonialism and the struggle for independence. The hope of a Korea free from Japanese rule rested in the hearts of Koreans spread across continents, spurring concerted action and creating contention and strife. Students occupied an importance place in the workings of the community, as seen in the pages of the *KSB*. The fate of Korea elicited varied responses from writers. Many of them saw their homeland within a biblical framework. Korea, like Israel, sought divine deliverance from its oppressors. In addition, conference proceedings, editorial columns, discussion forums, and news stories all demonstrated a dedication to keeping alive Korea's sacred cause of liberty.[44]

The future Christian educator L. George Paik reported his attendance at an interdenominational student conference held in the Chicago area at the end of 1925. Paik noted the full agenda of panels, topics, and resolutions, but one element of the gathering seemed to make a lasting impression. A contingent of Filipino students passionately presented their case for the independence of the Philippines before their European American colonizers. These students operated within a Christian setting to critique religion as complicit with colonialism, but also offered an example of a faith-based approach to the concerns of their homeland.[45]

Other writers must have picked up on the sentiments expressed by Paik as they pondered how their faith informed their aspirations and actions for Korea. One columnist in 1931 commented on how the momentum and energy from the March First Movement had been waning under the tightening control of the Japanese. The author noted that the change in colonial policy to ease overt controls and restrictions masked more covert and subtle ways that the Japanese operated in Korea. International students, among others, faced an "agonizing" test in working on behalf of Korea's freedom. The writer invoked the language of building the kingdom of God and asked readers whether they possessed the devotion to consecrate their lives to this cause. The very future of the nation depended on it.[46]

Another commentator took a hard look at the role of faith and the international order during the Christmas season of 1931 and found much lacking. A call to action formed the core of the message, prodding readers to stretch beyond the comfortable. The words evince the writer's frustration: "Christ and his followers went out to teach and to alleviate the suffering of the people. The Christian churches must practice these principles and bring these ideals into effect. We cannot stand by and let events take their own course." Despite the real challenges that lay before them, readers needed to prove themselves worthy of the fellowship of Christ: "Peace and goodwill are accomplished by righteous planning and fearless activity. Let us gird up our loins and do something about it."[47]

Perhaps students of every era have been impatient to tackle the issues of their day. In a symposium hosted by the *KSB*, several students offered their perspectives on Korea's needs. Chyung Yil Hyung, a seminarian in New York, suggested that a greater percentage of Korea's population be given access to education. Only about a third of Korean children went to school, according to Chyung, and hearts and minds could not be cultivated without a foundation in education. In addition, those working on the farms of Korea suffered under high taxes, depressed prices, and difficult working conditions. Leadership remained a pressing concern for the nation: "We need not only men and women with brain power, but men and women who are spiritual giants, individuals that can lift the crowds above the fog and mist of depression and show them the dawn of the 'Greater Korea.'"[48]

Others in the discussion forum reinforced the idea of leadership. T. H. Chun of the Pacific School of Religion in Berkeley, California, emphasized that leadership entailed a sacrificial love exemplified by Jesus, who laid down his life for others. From a societal standpoint, Chun advanced the idea of a reconstruction of the nation based upon a social justice that applied to the political and economic realms.[49] A student from the Teachers College at Columbia University stressed leadership experienced in self-help, promoting unity and democratic mass education. Moreover, in addressing the material concerns of the nation, the writer continued, one should not forget the spiritual and how the two must go hand in hand in moving Korea forward.[50]

Maria Kim of Biblical Seminary also raised the issue of leadership, but in the context of a Korea free to manage its own affairs.[51] Instead of looking to others, Koreans had to fend for themselves and fight. An important part of these efforts included genuine leadership independent in thought, but dependent upon God. She also juxtaposed individual initiative and a cooperative spirit. Kim looked to the biblical witness: "As the Israelites in Egypt in their distress cried unto God for deliverance and He raised up Moses as their deliverer, so we Koreans at home and abroad must cry unto God that He would raise up a like leader who will lead us out of bondage unto the promised land of plenty."[52]

While it is debatable whether Maria Kim's prayer for a Korean Moses had been answered, the *KSB* certainly carried news about important leaders within the Korean diaspora. Many of these figures had been influenced by Protestant Christianity and had spent significant time in the United States.[53] The bulletin reported on the assassination of patriot Pak Yong-man in China in October 1928 and its reverberations through the Korean community in Hawai'i.[54] A graduate of the University of Nebraska, Pak advocated a military approach to Korean independence and had established academies on the mainland, in Hawai'i, and in East Asia.[55] The same issue contained an article featuring Helen Kim, a leading figure in higher education in Korea.[56] Kim had graduated from the Methodist-related Ewha, the prestigious college for women, and then had gone on to the United States to continue her studies at Ohio Wesleyan, Boston University, and Columbia University. The *KSB* noted that Kim received her Ph.D. from Teachers College at Columbia in 1931 and that she was the first Korean woman to earn an American doctorate.[57] As dean and eventually president of Ewha and a Christian lay leader, Kim worked on broad social reforms in Korea through her alma mater and through the YWCA.

Physician and statesman Philip Jaisohn served as an adviser and role model for both international and native-born students connected to the Korean Student Federation. Jaisohn wrote in the *KSB* about compatriot Ahn Chang-ho (An Ch'ang-ho), who had been imprisoned by the Japanese and died in Seoul in March 1938.[58] Jaisohn had not known Ahn very well, but a connection existed between the two in that Ahn had been inspired by

Ahn Chango-ho Memorial Service, Los Angeles, 1938. Photo courtesy of USC Korean American Digital Archive.

Jaisohn's lectures given at the Independence Club in Korea. Jaisohn noted the contributions that Ahn had made in California through the Korean National Association and the Young Korean Academy.[59] Ahn worked tirelessly for unity and spiritual and moral regeneration among Koreans to lay a foundation for self-rule.[60]

Kim Kiusic (Kim Kyu-sik), former chief delegate of Korea to the Paris Peace Conference in 1919, represented another person with strong missionary ties.[61] The *KSB* reported in its May-June 1933 issue that Kim had been touring the country to garner American support for China and Korea in light of Japan's invasion of Manchuria.[62] One of the first families of American Protestant missionaries in Korea, the Underwoods, took the orphaned Kim under its wing and sponsored him to attend Roanoke College in Virginia, a Lutheran-affiliated school. Kim graduated as valedictorian in 1903 and returned to Korea as secretary to Horace G. Underwood and remained active with the Korean YMCA and in missionary-affiliated education. To avoid the Japanese, Kim went into exile and embarked on a long and winding journey of nationalist politics that took him to France, the United States, China, and Mongolia. He also worked across a wide political spectrum from right to left and certainly became a major player in diasporic politics.[63]

Despite these and other able leaders, Korea during the era of the publication of the *KSB* suffered under colonialism without much hope of relief. An incident involving derogatory language used by three male Japanese high school students toward three female Korean students in the southwest region near the city of Kwangju in October 1929 set off demonstrations that by early 1930 had spread to nearly sixty thousand students in about two hundred schools. The events in Kwangju formed part of a larger set of student-based nationalist activities in Korea that protested curricular issues such as the prohibition against the teaching of Korean language and history.[64] The *KSB* provided ample print space to cover the events taking place. One response took the form of a heartfelt unsigned prayer. In its tone and content, the prayer can be read as a lament regarding the Kwangju demonstrations, but it can also be understood as speaking to the larger issue of colonial oppression within the context of Christian faith:

> Father, where is thy justice? Must righteousness ever be crushed in the hands of injustice? Must the will to live that Thou hast given be trampled down so mercilessly? Must humanity succumb to brutality? Must brotherhood suffer under the tyranny of bloodshed?
>
> O Lord, where is thy love that led the people of Israel to the land of milk and honey from the yoke of Egypt? Where is thy wrath that destroyed the wickedness of Sodom and Gomorrha [sic]?

The words of the prayer express the writer's anguish and echo the psalms of the Hebrew scriptures. There is a raw honesty to the prayer in which courage crumbles, hope fades, and faith wanes. The writer wondered if there would ever be a day in which love and justice reigned and asked God to speak louder, since the people could not hear through the silence. Like Jesus before the cross, Koreans remained a forsaken people longing for redemption and deliverance.[65]

## Fare Thee Well

As a publication by and for students, the *Korean Student Bulletin* regularly reported news of comings and goings. Perhaps it is fitting that the last issue of the *KSB* in April 1941 marked the untimely passing of Alexander Hurh, who had served as the secretary for Korean students for the previous seven years.[66] Like many others, Hurh had been educated in Protestant mission schools in Korea and had then arrived at the University of Michigan in 1924 to earn both a B.A. and an M.A. in history. Hurh had to work his way through school, and it seems likely that financial pressures forced him to end his postgraduate studies at Columbia University and to take the position as Korean secretary.[67]

At the memorial service, held in New York City at the Korean Methodist Church on 4 January 1941, the *KSB* noted that both Koreans and Americans filled the sanctuary to capacity and spilled outside the doors of the church. The Korean Methodist Church and Institute had been founded in the early 1920s, and it made sense that the service took place there, as it had been the central gathering place for Koreans in New York City. The church had come into being in the aftermath of the March First Movement in 1919, and independence had been woven into its mission from the start. Located near Columbia University on 115th Street, the church had for many years served students, political exiles, and the small Korean American community in the area. The designation of "institute" along with "church" signified its more expansive mission.[68]

The confluence of religion and race could be seen in those in attendance at the church that day—students, YMCA staff, church members, former missionaries, and friends. Most people at the memorial service shared a Protestant faith, but there nevertheless remained a marker that set Koreans apart from non-Koreans. Race framed the language of Christian service and witness by underscoring the difference between Hurh and his people and those of European descent living in the United States. Tributes to Hurh emphasized the ways in which he fostered "mutual understanding and esteem between these two peace loving nations."[69] The working of religion and race did not escape the notice of the writers of the *KSB,* who commented upon the reality of racism in American society—a reality not easily overcome outside and within the Christian fold.

Along with religion & race, one sees in the life journey of Alexander Hurh and in the lives of so many of the students the complexities of migration & exile. Hurh had come to the United States to get an education, intending to return to his homeland afterward, but by the time of his death at age thirty-eight, he had spent almost half of his life outside of Korea.[70] Hurh's position as Korean secretary, however, enabled him to keep abreast of events in the homeland through the steady flow of students from Korea to the United States and back again. Migration and exile, of course, were not strange themes to the Christian faith, and students made the connections throughout their journeys.[71]

For all of the students crossing paths with the *Korean Student Bulletin,* Korea's fate as a colonized nation sparked religious visions of independence. Some looked to the Israelites' captivity and release from Egypt as a source of hope and encouragement. Others spoke about the pressing need for leadership, asking God to raise up a Moses for Korea. News of important leaders filled the pages of the bulletin over the years, and so did prayers seeking justice for those suffering under the yoke of oppression.

Much had taken place since the first Korean secretary, Julian S. Park, left New York City in the autumn of 1922 to tour college and university campuses until the unfortunate death of Korean secretary Alexander Hurh in 1941. The pages of the *Korean Student Bulletin* served as a printed record of the many lives that spanned a Korean diaspora marked in part by the relationships between religion & race, migration & exile, and colonialism & independence. The sorrows surrounding Hurh's passing in January 1941 mixed with uncertainty in the wake of Pearl Harbor by the year's end. The reality of a world at war also brought with it a renewed hope of a free Korea.

The joy felt by Koreans everywhere at the war's end in 1945 proved short-lived, as the United States and the Soviet Union occupied a divided Korea, supplanting the Japanese.[72] Koreans in the United States took part in the scramble at the end of the war and in the postwar period by sending supplies for relief and through exiled leadership that became part of the political jockeying. Two delegations from Hawai'i and the mainland made their way to Korea in December 1945 and January 1946 and lobbied to exert Korean agency into the political process of determining the country's fate. The division of the peninsula at the thirty-eighth parallel by the superpowers foreshadowed things to come and a different kind of heartbreak for Koreans who had fought so long and hard for their nation.[73]

Contention preceded heartbreak, as the factional nature of the Korean communities in the United States did little to regain control over the homeland. The efforts to create a united front broke down toward the end of the war, and claims and counterclaims by the United Korean Committee representatives as well as Syngman Rhee and his followers added to the confusion.[74] The fact that the United States government recognized neither party clearly indicated that the U.S. agenda in Korea had little to do with restoring sovereignty to its people. In that sense, the United States proved remarkably consistent in its behavior over the decades. Rhee's eventual ascendancy in 1948 to become the first president of the Republic of Korea (South Korea) spoke as much to U.S. foreign policy as it did to Korean efforts to direct their own fate.

Margaret Pai recalled the disappointments that followed the war's end that indeed undermined the relief of having many loved ones return home from the military. She noted that Koreans had believed the Soviet and U.S. presence in Korea to be a temporary measure until Japan had been defeated. As the realities of a new occupation of Korea set in, so did the accompanying woes. Syngman Rhee's election to the presidency of South Korea may have been great news to those at the Korean Christian Church, but not so for many others. Pai stated: "My mother and father and other Methodists greeted Rhee's ascension as head of their country with only mild enthusiasm." It is telling that Korean Americans interpreted the news of Korea and its postwar condition by church affiliation. Moreover, Pai's parents, despite many years in the United States, still viewed Korea as *their* country—a fact based on their exclusion from naturalization, but also a condition of their status as migrants and exiles.[75]

That mild enthusiasm reported by Pai turned to outright anger when the politics of pro- and anti-Rhee camps spilled into the churches. Many of the members of the Korean Methodist Church in Honolulu had fought for independence. As aging men and women, they desired to visit their homeland before they passed on. In a move that generated great bitterness, Rhee denied them entry to Korea based upon the local independence and church politics of earlier decades.[76] The contentiousness of community-based factionalism haunted the postwar future of Koreans in the United States even as the legacy of colonialism took new forms in the homeland.[77] Migration to the United States also continued, and as religion had shaped the experiences of so many from 1903 through 1945, it has played a central role in the lives of Koreans in the United States ever since.

# Epilogue

On a March evening in 2004, I attended a celebration of the Los Angeles Korean United Methodist Church (LAKUMC). One hundred years earlier, Florence Sherman and Hugh Cynn launched the Korean mission that the congregation claimed as the founding of the church. The members and friends of the LAKUMC that evening paid tribute to the history that connected the two points in time. Those instrumental in the founding of the mission, no doubt, would have given thanks for a congregation that had faithfully attended to the wide-ranging needs of Korean Americans over the course of a century.

It is difficult to imagine from those humble beginnings that the Los Angeles metropolitan area currently has the largest concentration of Koreans outside Korea and that the overall population of Koreans in the United States today stands at approximately 1.5 million persons. Less surprising, given the narrative presented here, is the fact that Christian churches occupy the heart of these communities. As stated earlier, some estimates suggest that 80 percent of Koreans in the United States today claim an affiliation with Christianity. Like many other groups in our nation's past, Koreans have looked to their churches for social services, racial-ethnic solidarity, and spiritual meaning and comfort in the turbulence that is part and parcel of the migration process.[1] In that sense, Koreans who have arrived since 1965 share affinities with those who made their way to the United States in the early decades of the twentieth century. At the same time, some might suggest that the contemporary religious milieu has taken a conservative turn, reflecting developments within Korean Christianity since the end of World War II and the Korean War that have filtered through to leaders and churches in the United States.[2] Nevertheless, the structures and sensibilities of Christianity have been a central and important presence within Korean America for over one hundred years.[3]

Much contemporary religious activity has been associated with the large-scale migration from Asia and Latin America to the United States since the passage of the 1965 Immigration Act.[4] Moreover, legislative acts in the 1970s and 1980s regarding migrants and refugees from countries such as Vietnam, Cambodia, and Laos have influenced the shaping of the Asian American population during the past several decades.[5] Some scholars have noted the role that religion has played in the latest chapter of immigration to the United States.[6] One study published in 2001 states that more than 30 million people have arrived over the course of the previous thirty years, adding an unprecedented scale and depth to the religious diversity of the nation.[7] Asians in the United States have contributed to this diversity through traditions such as Buddhism and Hinduism, but they have also done so through the diversification of Christianity—something lost on those who do not realize that Christianity represents the largest religious grouping among Asian Americans (46 percent).[8] A major shift has been well under way in which Christianity should no longer be envisioned as a preserve of Western Europe and the United States, but as a global religion increasingly defined by Asia, Africa, and Latin America.[9]

*Contentious Spirits* has shifted the perspective back in time to reclaim a history that is little known. In so doing, this study has argued that religion is the most significant window into Korean American history, because it addressed the fullness of human experience reflected in its structures and sensibilities. Three relational themes framed the discussion as well as deepened the argumentation. The theme of religion & race delved into the racialization of Koreans in the United States. While religion did not create a shield against racism, a Korean American Christianity did help adherents to find a sense of self and community in its midst. The second theme, migration & exile, illustrated how religion drove the transnational migration of Koreans to the United States and how that migration also included the exilic. Colonialism & independence, the third theme, interpreted how a religious nationalism crossed boundaries to engage in anticolonial activities connected to the homeland as well as to the United States. The stories told here not only document forgotten stories, but also ask how those stories serve as a guide in rethinking foundational dimensions of American society and culture within a more expansive and inclusive and less exceptional frame.

These relational themes, then, point to the larger significance of this narrative. Paying careful attention to the confluence of religion and race opens up ways of seeing episodes in our nation's history that have often been overlooked. The Montgomery Bus Boycott in 1955, for instance, and the refusal of Rosa Parks to give up her seat on the bus and the launching of Martin Luther King Jr. onto the national scene make little sense without asking how religion and race imbued the events that unfolded in that particular space and time and formed the core of resistance. Those events in Alabama, moreover, drew upon a long tradition stretching back to independent black churches begun in the late 1700s. Similarly, the stories of farmworkers in California associated with César Chávez, Dolores Huerta, and Philip Vera Cruz must be read against the deeply rooted popular Catholicism that included the devotion to and ritual surrounding Our Lady of Guadalupe. An intentional religion and spirituality grounded the efforts of these union activists in mobilizing people for their cause. These examples suggest how religious contact and exchange as well as conquest and resistance are enmeshed in complex racial formations.

The theme of migration & exile underscores how Koreans and so many other groups occupied an ambiguous and ambivalent transnational space in the United States. Movement from one place to another always involved negotiation of the homeland with what one encountered in a new place, and how individuals and communities made that transition took myriad forms. The linear progression from immigrant to American under the umbrella of assimilation is unsatisfactory because it stresses uniformity in a process characterized by difference. The issue of race, to name only one factor, has had and continues to have a profound effect on that phenomenon described as becoming American. Dynamic and shifting racial distinctions and hierarchies have shaped the continuum between inclusion and exclusion and still are very much at work. In addition, this study has lifted up exile as one of the dimensions of experience that is often left out of the equation, but nevertheless has been very much part of our collective past and present.

The final relational theme of colonialism & independence places a spot-light on the United States as a colonial power. Though few would dispute this fact today, there has been a long arc of denial regarding the United States as a colonizer that continues to prove resilient. The case of Koreans grounds U.S. colonialism in the sugarcane plantations of Hawai'i and in an internal colonialism on the mainland. Koreans inherited an expansive and adaptive system with enduring consequences, especially for African Americans, Latinos, Native Americans, and other Asians. Protestant Christianity proved to be a double-edged sword, implicated in the machinations of empire abroad and at home, but also a key building block in visions of liberation and resistance that fueled aspirations, actions, and imaginations.

The history and ongoing presence of Koreans in the United States highlights the importance of religion for American society and culture, and in a broader sense, how religion is an ever-salient dimension of world affairs. Despite predictions of secularization, the death of God, and the collapse of the so-called mainline Protestant denominations, religion has continued to thrive in the United States. The fact that migration has fueled a good part of this dynamism and growth domestically also points to the vibrancy of religion in other parts of the world and how religion has been very much a part of the transnational traffic that has intensified with technology.

Sociologist Peter Berger, who has wrestled with secularization theory for several decades, has written about resurgent religion that has proved wrong theorists who claimed that modernization would necessarily lead to the decline of religion in society and in the minds of individuals. Even in Western Europe, where the theory has found most traction, Berger suggests that religion has survived even though institutions have declined. While modernization has had secularizing effects, it has also produced strong countermovements, and one does not need to look far for such examples in our contemporary context. Berger reminds us that the relationship between religion and modernity is a complex one, and he calls for case studies that might help untangle some of that complexity.[10]

In that vein, *Contentious Spirits* has examined the structures and sensibilities of Protestant Christianity that have deeply shaped the history of Koreans in the United States. If modernity erodes established certainties, then Christianity offered Koreans a new way of seeing the world during a time of tremendous upheaval marked by migration, exile, racialization, colonialism, and the struggle for independence. Religion represented an engagement with modernity that is still ongoing, and the story is far from complete. This study has argued that no other lens has been more salient than religion, and in that regard, the case of Korean Americans points to the need for thoughtful and sustained analysis of the role of religion in the United States. Of course, religion often has been dismissed as a relic of the old world or because it is an inherently elusive and messy social phenomenon. And yet, to neglect religion in the analysis of national and global affairs is to do so at great peril.[11]

# Notes

## Introduction

1. The late Elder Whamok Lee (1898–1997) is featured in K. W. Lee, with Luke and Grace Kim, "Home Is Where the Soul Is," *KoreAm Journal* 16, no. 2 (February 2005): 50–59. The account focuses on her son, Warren Lee, author of *A Dream for South Central: The Autobiography of an Afro-Americanized Korean Christian Minister* (Seoul, Korea: Christian Literature Society, 1994). In the article, Elder Lee's name is spelled Hwa Mok Lee, but she used the spelling Whamok Lee.

2. That migration to this country has never been a uniform experience is made all too evident in the passage of the Naturalization Act of 1790, which limited citizenship to free whites—a restriction that was not fully removed for Asians until 1952. The Chinese Exclusion Act of 1882 also began a string of exclusionary measures aimed at multiple Asian groups that culminated in the 1924 Immigration Act. For overviews on Asian American history, see Sucheng Chan, *Asian Americans: An Interpretive History* (Boston: Twayne, 1991); and Ronald Takaki, *Strangers from a Different Shore: A History of Asian Americans* (Boston: Little, Brown, 1989). See also, Bill Ong Hing, *Making and Remaking Asian America Through Immigration Policy, 1850–1990* (Stanford, CA: Stanford University Press, 1993).

3. As historian Sucheng Chan (*Asian Americans,* 145) points out, the 1965 Immigration Act, the 1975 Indochina Migration and Refugee Assistance Act, the 1980 Refugee Act, and the 1987 Amerasian Homecoming Act together created the legal structure surrounding the migration of Asians to the United States during the past forty years.

4. The figure of 1.5 million Korean Americans is based upon the 2006 estimate

of the U.S. Census Bureau, published in the newsletter *Facts for Features*, Asian/Pacific American Heritage Month, March 3, 2008, p. 1 (http://www.census.gov/Press-Release/www/releases/archives/facts_for_features_special_editions/011602.html). For a general overview of Korean Americans, see Won Moo Hurh, *The Korean Americans* (Westport, CT: Greenwood Press, 1998).

5. Pei-te Lien and Tony Carnes, "The Religious Demography of Asian American Boundary Crossing," in Tony Carnes and Fenggang Yang, eds., *Asian American Religions: The Making and Remaking of Borders and Boundaries* (New York: New York University Press, 2004), 48–49. Of the total figure (79 percent), Protestants accounted for 69 percent and Catholics 11 percent. The following are the percentages for the remaining categories: None (6 percent), Not Sure (1 percent), Other (3 percent), Refused to Answer (6 percent). The survey data for church attendance were for the New York City area. The directory listing of churches consisted of 3,402 Protestant churches, and a separate directory identified 154 Catholic parishes in the United States. Lien and Carnes cite *Modern Buddhism*, a Korean journal, for the figure of one hundred Buddhist temples in the United States.

6. The scholarship on Korean American religion continues to grow at a steady clip: David K. Yoo and Ruth H. Chung, eds., *Religion and Spirituality in Korean America* (Urbana: University of Illinois Press, 2008); Rebecca Y. Kim, *God's Whiz Kids: Korean American Evangelicals on Campus* (New York: New York University Press, 2006); Elaine Howard Ecklund, *Korean American Evangelicals: New Models of Civic Life* (New York: Oxford University Press, 2006); Su Yon Pak et al., *Singing the Lord's Song in a New Land: Korean American Practices of Faith* (Louisville, KY: Westminster John Knox Press, 2005); Sharon A. Suh, *Being Buddhist in a Christian World: Gender and Community in a Korean American Temple* (Seattle: University of Washington Press, 2004); Okyun Kwon, *Buddhist and Protestant Korean Immigrants: Religious Beliefs and Socioeconomic Aspects of Life*, The New Americans (New York: LFB Scholarly Publishing, 2003); Young Lee Hertig, *Cultural Tug of War: The Korean Immigrant Family and Church in Transition* (Nashville: Abingdon Press, 2001); Ho-Youn Kwon, Kwang Chung Kim, and R. Stephen Warner, eds., *Korean Americans and Their Religions: Pilgrims and Missionaries from a Different Shore* (University Park: Pennsylvania State University Press, 2001); Jung Ha Kim, *Bridge-makers and Cross-bearers: Korean-American Women and the Church* (Atlanta: Scholars Press, 1997); Victoria H. Kwon, *Entrepreneurship and Religion: Korean Immigrants in Houston, Texas* (New York: Garland, 1997); Ai Ra Kim, *Women Struggling for a New Life: The Role of Religion in the Cultural Passage from Korea to America* (Albany: State University of New York Press, 1996). Too numerous to mention are books that have significant content on Korean American religion as well as book chapters, journal articles, dissertations, and theses.

7. The literature on early Korean American history includes Warren Y. Kim, *Koreans in America* (Seoul: Po Chin Chai, 1971); Bong-Youn Choy, *Koreans in America* (Chicago: Nelson-Hall, 1979); Wayne Patterson, *The Korean Frontier in America: Immigration to Hawai'i, 1896–1910* (Honolulu: University of Hawai'i Press, 1988); Wayne Patterson, *The Ilse: First-Generation Korean Immigrants in Hawai'i, 1903–1973* (Honolulu: University of Hawai'i Press, 2000).

8. I have followed the convention of the spelling *Hawai'i* with the glottal mark because this is how the word is spelled and pronounced in the Hawaiian language. The word *Hawaiian* apparently is not a Hawaiian word but an English word and hence spelled without the glottal mark.

9. Sucheng Chan, introduction to *Quiet Odyssey: A Pioneer Korean Woman in America,* by Mary Paik Lee (Seattle: University of Washington Press, 1990), L.

10. The key structure in the study is the local congregation, and churches provide a framework for studying the major themes examined. In that sense, the literature on American congregations is helpful in documenting how dominant this form of human community has been for the United States throughout much of its history. At the same time, what is presented here is less strictly a case study of congregations and more a use of the congregation as a means of exploring the broader contours of religion in Korean American history. See Nancy Tatum Ammerman, *Congregation and Community* (New Brunswick, NJ: Rutgers University Press, 1996); James P. Wind and James W. Lewis, eds., *American Congregations,* Vol. 2, *New Perspectives in the Study of Congregations* (Chicago: University of Chicago Press, 1998).

11. Henry Goldschmidt, "Introduction: Race, Nation, and Religion," in Henry Goldschmidt and Elizabeth McAlister, eds., *Race, Nation, and Religion in the Americas* (New York: Oxford University Press, 2004), 18–21.

12. Robert A. Orsi, *Between Heaven and Earth: The Religious Worlds People Make and the Scholars Who Study Them* (Princeton, NJ: Princeton University Press, 2005), 1–4.

13. Howard Winant, *The World Is a Ghetto: Race and Democracy Since World War II* (New York: Basic Books, 2001), 3.

14. The notion of benefit draws from George Lipsitz, *The Possessive Investment in Whiteness: How White People Profit from Identity Politics* (Philadelphia: Temple University Press, 1998).

15. In offering this critique, I am of course borrowing from those who have long recognized the intertwining of religion and race. Perhaps the most influential body of work has come from the study of African American religious traditions. See Timothy E. Fulop and Albert J. Raboteau, eds., *African American Religions: Interpretive Essays in History and Culture* (New York: Routledge, 1996). See also two

recent works on religion and race: Craig R. Prentiss, ed., *Religion and the Creation of Race and Ethnicity: An Introduction* (New York: New York University Press, 2003); and Henry Goldschmidt and Elizabeth McAlister, eds., *Race, Nation, and Religion in the Americas* (New York: Oxford University Press, 2004).

16. David K. Yoo, ed., *New Spiritual Homes: Religion and Asian Americans* (Honolulu: University of Hawai'i Press, 1999), 1–18. The good news is that the scholarship on Asian Americans and religion has grown in recent years. Several anthologies are a good starting point for this literature: Pyong Gap Min and Jung Ha Kim, eds., *Religions in Asian America: Building Faith Communities* (Walnut Creek, CA: Altamira Press, 2002); Jane N. Iwamura and Paul Spickard, eds., *Revealing the Sacred in Asian Pacific America* (New York: Routledge, 2003); Tony Carnes and Fenggang Yang, eds., *Asian American Religions: The Making and Remaking of Borders and Boundaries* (New York: New York University Press, 2004).

17. In his article "More 'Trans—,' Less 'National'" (*Journal of American Ethnic History* 25, no. 4 [Summer 2006]: 74–84), Matthew Frye Jacobsen provides a helpful overview; Rachel Ida Buff's "Transnational Visions: Reinventing Immigration Studies" (*American* Quarterly 57 [December 2005]: 1263–72) is a review essay of recent works. For a helpful review and critique of U.S. immigration history, see Hasia R. Diner, "History and the Study of Immigration: Narratives of the Particular," in Caroline B. Brettell and James F. Hollified, eds., *Migration Theory: Talking Across Disciplines* (New York: Routledge, 2008), 31–49. Diner discusses the lack of theory in U.S. immigration history and the persistence of American exceptionalism. A helpful introduction to the field is Jon Gjerde, ed., *Major Problems in American Immigration and Ethnic History* (Boston: Houghton Mifflin, 1998).

18. Historian Thomas Bender has been a leading voice among U.S. historians on this issue: Thomas Bender, ed., *Rethinking American History in a Global Age* (Berkeley: University of California Press, 2002); and Thomas Bender, *A Nation Among Nations: America's Place in World History* (New York: Hill & Wang, 2006).

19. As a guide to this literature, see Charles Hirschman, Philip Kasinitz, and Josh DeWind, eds., *The Handbook of International Migration: The American Experience* (New York: Russell Sage Foundation, 1999); Nancy Foner, Ruben G. Rumbaut, and Steven J. Gold, eds., *Immigration Research for a New Century: Multidisciplinary Perspectives* (New York: Russell Sage Foundation, 2000); Douglas S. Massey et al., *Worlds in Motion: Understanding International Migration at the End of the Millennium* (Oxford: Oxford University Press, 1998).

20. Nancy Foner, "What's New About Transnationalism? New York Immigrants Today and at the Turn of the Century," *Diaspora* 6, no. 3 (1997): 355–75.

21. See the special issue edited by Erika Lee and Naoko Shibusawa, "What Is Transnational Asian American History? Recent Trends and Challenges," *Journal*

*of Asian American Studies* 8, no. 3 (October 2005): vii–xvii; and Mae M. Ngai, "Asian American History—Reflections on the De-centering of the Field," *Journal of American Ethnic History* 25, no. 4 (Summer 2006): 97–108.

22. Hurh, *Korean Americans,* 106.

23. Fred Harvey Harrington, *God, Mammon, and the Japanese: Dr. Horace Allen and Korean-American Relations, 1884–1905* (Madison: University of Wisconsin Press, 1944).

24. There are of course other groups who have experienced exile in the United States, and an interesting case study that also has religion as a centerpiece is Thomas A. Tweed, *Our Lady of the Exile: Diasporic Religion at a Cuban Catholic Shrine* (New York: Oxford University Press, 1999).

25. Diaspora is sometimes distinguished from the transnational in terms of a sense of belonging to a common ancestry that extends beyond any particular state. Independence movement leaders and to some extent most Koreans abroad sensed a connection to the homeland and to other Koreans scattered in different places. For more on Asian diasporas and their relationship with Asian and Asian American studies, see Rhacel S. Parreñas and Lok C. D. Siu, eds., *Asian Diasporas: New Formations, New Conceptions* (Stanford, CA: Stanford University Press, 2007). The editors offer a helpful definition and discussion in their introduction.

26. These comments about homemaking draw upon Yen Le Espiritu, *Home Bound: Filipino American Lives Across Cultures, Communities, and Countries* (Berkeley: University of California Press, 2003), especially chap. 1, "Home Making."

27. See Bruce Cumings, *Korea's Place in the Sun: A Modern History* (New York: W. W. Norton, 1997); and Peter Duus, *The Abacus and the Sword: The Japanese Penetration of Korea, 1895–1910* (Berkeley: University of California Press, 1995), 413–23. I borrow the phrase "community of memory" from Takaki, *Strangers from a Different Shore,* page 10, and Takaki references the phrase from Robert Bellah et al., *Habits of the Heart.*

28. Gi-Wook Shin, *Ethnic Nationalism in Korea: Genealogy, Politics, and Legacy* (Stanford, CA: Stanford University Press, 2007), 8–14.

29. Andre Schmid, *Korea Between Empires, 1895–1919* (New York: Columbia University Press, 2002), 19–22 and chap. 7.

30. Oscar Campomanes, "New Formations of Asian American Studies and the Question of U.S. Imperialism," *Positions* 5, no. 2 (Fall 1997): 533–37.

31. See Ann Laura Stoler, ed., *Haunted by Empire: Geographies of Intimacy in North American History* (Durham, NC: Duke University Press, 2006), especially chap. 2, which focuses on the comparison of North American history and postcolonial studies; and Amy Kaplan and Donald E. Pease, eds., *Cultures of United States Imperialism* (Durham, NC: Duke University Press, 1993).

32.  Edna Bonacich and Lucie Cheng, "Introduction: A Theoretical Orientation to International Labor Migration," in Lucie Cheng and Edna Bonacich, eds., *Labor Immigration Under Capitalism: Asian Workers in the United States Before World War II* (Berkeley: University of California Press, 1984), 1–56. Although there is much to critique in their formulation, the essay still stands as an important call for theorizing early Asian migration.

33.  For some helpful works on the imperial history of Hawai'i, see Jonathan Kay Kamakawiwo'ole Osorio, *Dismembering Lahui: A History of the Hawaiian Nation to 1887* (Honolulu: University of Hawai'i Press, 2002); Noenoe K. Silva, *Aloha Betrayed: Native Hawaiian Resistance to American Colonialism* (Durham, NC: Duke University Press, 2004); Haunani-Kay Trask, *From a Native Daughter: Colonialism and Sovereignty in Hawai'i*, rev. ed. (Honolulu: University of Hawai'i Press, 1999); Elizabeth Buck, *Paradise Remade: The Politics of Culture and History in Hawai'i* (Philadelphia: Temple University Press, 1993).

34.  Patterson, *Korean Frontier in America*, 48–50.

35.  William R. Hutchison, *Errand to the World: American Protestant Thought and Foreign Missions* (Chicago: University of Chicago Press, 1987). On colonialism in East Asia, see Tani E. Barlow, ed., *Formations of Colonial Modernity in East Asia* (Durham, NC: Duke University Press, 1997); and Gi-Wook Shin and Michael Robinson, *Colonial Modernity in Korea* (Cambridge, MA: Harvard University Asia Center, 1999).

36.  Robert Blauner, *Racial Oppression in America* (New York: Harper & Row, 1972).

37.  Nicholas De Genova, "Introduction: Latino and Asian Racial Formations at the Frontiers of U.S. Nationalism," in Nicholas De Genova, ed., *Racial Transformations: Latinos and Asians Remaking the United States* (Durham, NC: Duke University Press, 2006), 10–11. De Genova discusses the importance of Latino and Asian formations within the context of the black-white binary. Native Americans provide the key, since they are the prototype of the outsider who can never be assimilated into "white" America, and that status is extended to Asians and Latinos (and Latin America and Asia) to provide coherence and wholeness to the white supremacy of the U.S. nation-state.

38.  Nadia Kim's recently published study on Korean Americans makes a persuasive case that immigrants have been transnationally racialized within a U.S. imperial framework that well precedes their arrival to the United States, back to the era of World War II. My point is that the process actually goes back to the late nineteenth century. Nadia Y. Kim, *Imperial Citizens: Koreans and Race from Seoul to LA* (Stanford, CA: Stanford University Press, 2008).

39.  Shin and Robinson, *Colonial Modernity in Korea*; Barlow, *Formations of Colonial Modernity*.

40. In addressing the shortcomings of a black/white binary, my point is not to underestimate the importance of this frame, but to suggest how it must be held in check with other racial formations in the United States. For a good statement on the ongoing and foundational place of race as black/white, see Joe R. Feagin, *Racist America: Roots, Current Realities, and Future Reparations* (New York: Routledge, 2001).

## Chapter 1

Chapter title: The title, "God's Chosŏn People," is a play on words in which the notion of the Jews as God's chosen people (later adopted by Christians) is intermingled with the term for the Chosŏn era (1392–1910), the last dynastic kingdom to reign in Korea. From my experience, there is also a sense in which many Korean American Christians (and Korean Christians) believe that God has especially chosen Korean peoples to be a vanguard of the kingdom of God. One scholar notes that some Korean Christians view themselves as the New Israel. See Don Baker, "Christianity Koreanized," in Hyung Il Pai and Timothy R. Tangherlini, eds., *Nationalism and the Construction of Korean Identity* (Berkeley: Institute of East Asian Studies, University of California, 1998), 124. Such beliefs, of course, are by no means unique to Koreans or Korean Americans.

The word *Chosŏn,* which approximates "dynastic freshness," or a land where the "morning is fresh," appeared in fifth-century Chinese documents as the first legendary Korean state. The linguistic information about *Chosŏn* is taken from Keith Pratt and Richard Rutt, *Korea: A Historical and Cultural Dictionary* (Surrey, England: Curzon Press, 1999), 232–33.

1. Peter Hyun, *Man Sei! The Making of a Korean American* (Honolulu: University of Hawai'i Press, 1986), 5. This account differs from the account given by the Reverend Soon Hyun in his autobiography, in which only a friend saw him off. Soon Hyun, "My Autobiography," unpublished manuscript, Center for Korean Studies, University of Hawai'i, Manoa, 78. No date is listed on the document.

2. The term *Manse* will appear in various forms in this chapter, reflecting the English spelling of Korean words in source materials. As noted in the introduction, the McCune-Reischauer system has guided the romanization of Korean words, but matters have been complicated by a number of factors, such as retaining romanization in source materials.

3. Hyun, *Man Sei!* 1. The capitalized words at the beginning of the quote are taken directly from the book.

4. Hyun, *Man Sei!* 6–11. Historian Ki-baik Lee notes that more than 2 million persons directly participated in fifteen hundred separate gatherings in all but seven of Korea's 218 county administrations. According to Japanese records, there were

nearly 50,000 arrests, approximately 7,500 killed, and nearly 16,000 injured. Some 715 houses were destroyed, including 47 churches and 2 schools. Lee makes a case that actual numbers far exceeded these official statistics. See Ki-baik Lee, *A New History of Korea,* trans. Edward W. Wagner with Edward J. Shultz (Cambridge, MA: Harvard University Press, 1984), 344–45. Bruce Cumings cites numbers close to those listed above but attributes these to Korean nationalist figures with Japanese numbers much lower: 553 killed and more than 12,000 arrested. Bruce Cumings, *Korea's Place in the Sun: A Modern History* (New York: W. W. Norton, 1997), 155.

5. Choy Hai-Arm, "Mansae," *Korean Student Bulletin,* October–November 1937, 1, 6. The bulletin was part of the Committee of Friendly Relations Among Foreign Students, affiliated with the International Young Men's Christian Association (YMCA), and is featured in Chapter 6.

6. Choy Hai-Arm, "Mansae," *Korean Student Bulletin,* February–March 1938, 1, 7–8.

7. I have not been able to locate further information about Choy, though this is not untypical of those who were occasional contributors to publications.

8. Chung-Shin Park, *Protestantism and Politics in Korea* (Seattle: University of Washington Press, 2003), 49.

9. Don Baker, introduction to Robert E. Buswell Jr., ed., *Religions of Korea in Practice* (Princeton, NJ: Princeton University Press, 2007). Baker's essay provides a helpful overview of the religious pluralism of Korea.

10. Kenneth M. Wells, *New God, New Nation: Protestants and Self-Reconstruction Nationalism in Korea, 1896–1937* (Honolulu: University of Hawai'i Press, 1990), 21–25.

11. James Huntley Grayson, *Korea: A Religious History* (London: Routledge Curzon, 2002), 140–46; see also Duk-Whang Kim, *A History of Religions in Korea* (Seoul: Daeji Moonhwa-sa, 1988), chaps. 3–6.

12. Wells, *New God, New Nation,* 21–22.

13. Grayson, *Korea,* 137–39, 184.

14. Cumings, *Korea's Place in the Sun,* 115–20; Grayson, *Korea,* 198–202. For a more detailed analysis, see Albert L. Park, "Visions of the Nation: Religion and Ideology in 1920s and 1930s Rural Korea" (Ph.D. diss., University of Chicago, 2007).

15. Wells, *New God, New Nation,* 25–26; Spencer J. Palmer, *Korea and Christianity: The Problem of Identification with Tradition* (Seoul: Royal Asiatic Society, Korea Branch, 1967), 3–18.

16. David Chung, *Syncretism: The Religious Context of Christian Beginnings in Korea* (Albany: State University of New York Press, 2001), 107–8.

17. Ibid., 179.

18. Cumings, *Korea's Place in the Sun,* 43.

19.  See for example, L. George Paik, *The History of Protestant Missions in Korea, 1832–1910* (Pyeng Yang, Korea: Union Christian College Press, 1929). I have used the spelling of Pyeng Yang given in the publication information in Paik's book instead of the standardized spelling, P'yŏngyang. Don Baker, "Christianity Koreanized," in Hyung Il Pai and Timothy R. Tangherlini, eds., *Nationalism and the Construction of Korean Identity* (Berkeley. Institute of East Asian Studies, University of California, 1998), 108–25.; Chung, *Syncretism*; Martha Huntley, *Caring, Growing, Changing: A History of the Protestant Mission in Korea* (New York: Friendship Press, 1984).

20.  Mark R. Mullins and Richard Fox Young, eds., *Perspectives on Christianity in Korea and Japan: The Gospel and Culture in East Asia* (Lewiston, NY: Edwin Mellen Press, 1995), xiv–xxii.

21.  Robert E. Buswell Jr. and Timothy S. Lee, eds., *Christianity in Korea* (Honolulu: University of Hawai'i Press, 2006), 1.

22.  Donald N. Clark, "History and Religion in Modern Korea: The Case of Protestant Christianity," in Lewis R. Lancaster and Richard K. Payne, eds., *Religion and Society in Contemporary Korea* (Berkeley: Institute for Asian Studies, University of California, 1997), 169.

23.  Paik, *History of Protestant Missions*, 151.

24.  Huntley, *Caring, Growing, Changing*, 128.

25.  Palmer, *Korea and Christianity*, 69–77.

26.  Grayson, *Korea*, 158–59.

27.  Paik, *History of Protestant Missions*, 109–14. For an extended treatment of Allen, see Fred Harvey Harrington, *God, Mammon, and the Japanese: Dr. Horace Allen and Korean-American Relations, 1884–1905* (Madison: University of Wisconsin Press, 1944).

28.  Park, *Protestantism and Politics*, 23.

29.  Wells, *New God, New Nation*, 32.

30.  Paik, *History of Protestant Missions*, 354–60.

31.  Ibid., 360–65.

32.  Ibid., 364.

33.  Park, *Protestantism and Politics*, 29.

34.  Wells, *New God, New Nation*, 33.

35.  Paik, *History of Protestant Missions*, 173–90. In addition to American Protestant missionaries, others from England, Australia, and Canada were in Korea, as were some independent missionaries. Paik details who these various groups were.

36.  There are a number of general histories of U.S. religion, including Sydney E. Alhstrom, *A Religious History of the American Peoples* (New Haven, CT: Yale University Press, 1972); and Catherine Albanese, *America, Religions, and Religion* (Belmont, CA: Wadsworth, 1999).

37. Paik, *History of Protestant Missions,* 191.

38. Ibid., 193; Huntley, *Caring, Growing, Changing,* 76.

39. Huntley, *Caring, Growing, Changing,* 80–81, 159–68. Other leaders included Helen Kim and Sister Agneta Chang, as profiled in Donald N. Clark, "Mothers, Daughters, Biblewomen, and Sisters: An Account of 'Women's Work' in the Korea Mission Field," in *Christianity in Korea* (see note 21), 167–92. Also see Choi Hee An, *Korean Women and God: Experiencing God in a Multi-religious Colonial Context* (Maryknoll, NY: Orbis Press, 2005).

40. Park, *Protestantism and Politics,* 4.

41. Ibid. 4–5.

42. Ibid., 35.

43. Ibid., 34–35.

44. Huntley, *Caring, Growing, Changing,* 169–73.

45. Kyong-bae Min, "National Identity in the History of the Korean Church," translated by Yi Sun-ja, in Chai-shin Yu, ed., *Korea and Christianity* (Fremont, CA: Asian Humanities Press, 2004), 122; Wi Jo Kang, *Christ and Caesar in Modern Korea: A History of Christianity and Politics* (Albany: State University of New York Press, 1997).

46. Wells, *New God, New Nation,* 44–46.

47. This sequence of events is taken from Michael E. Robinson, *Cultural Nationalism in Colonial Korea, 1920–1925* (Seattle: University of Washington Press, 1988), 17–24.

48. Park, *Protestantism and Politics,* 23–29.

49. Wells, *New God, New Nation,* 26–27.

50. Paik, *History of Protestant Missions,* 77–78; Wells, *New God, New Nation,* 27–29; see also Harrington, *God, Mammon, and the Japanese.*

51. Park, *Protestantism and Politics,* 16–17.

*Chapter 2*

1. Chemulp'o was the former name of the western port city now known as Inch'on, located near Seoul.

2. Soon Hyun, "My Autobiography," unpublished manuscript, Center for Korean Studies, University of Hawai'i , Manoa, 61–62.

3. Ibid., 63–64.

4. Two different birth dates for Hyun appear in various documents: 21 March 1878 and 21 March 1879. I have chosen the 1879 date because it is listed in Hyun's autobiography (p. 9) as well as in a War Department personnel form. The assumption is that Hyun would have listed the date of his birth in both of these contexts.

In contrast, Hyun's death certificate lists his birth date as 21 March 1878, as does a brief biographical sketch that is part of his collected works digitized by the University of Southern California as part of its Korean American Digital Archives collection. Hyun died on 11 August 1968 in Los Angeles. Both the War Department form and the death certificate can be accessed at http://digarc.usc.edu:8089/cispubsearch/objectdetails.jsp?objectname=kada-m605 (Death certificate) and http://digarc.usc.edu:8089/cispubsearch/objectdetails.jsp?objectname=kada-m365 (War Department document).

5. Two general histories of Korea are Ki-baik Lee, *A New History of Korea,* trans. Edward W. Wagner with Edward J. Shultz (Cambridge, MA: Harvard University Press, 1984); and Bruce Cumings, *Korea's Place in the Sun: A Modern History* (New York: W. W. Norton, 1997). Two works that focus on the role of Protestant Christianity in Korea are Chung-Shin Park, *Protestantism and Politics in Korea* (Seattle: University of Washington Press, 2003); and Kenneth M. Wells, *New God, New Nation: Protestants and Self-Reconstruction Nationalism in Korea, 1896–1937* (Honolulu: University of Hawai'i Press, 1990).

6. Hyun, "My Autobiography," 9, 50–57.

7. Ronald Takaki, *Pau Hana: Plantation Life and Labor in Hawai'i, 1835–1920* (Honolulu: University of Hawai'i Press, 1983), 24–29; Edward D. Beechert, *Working in Hawai'i: A Labor History* (Honolulu: University of Hawai'i Press, 1985), 235. Milton Murayama captures a sense of racial hierarchy and divide and rule in his classic novel *All I Asking for Is My Body* (Honolulu: University of Hawai'i Press, 1959), 28–29, 33.

8. Wayne Patterson, *The Korean Frontier in America: Immigration to Hawai'i, 1896–1910* (Honolulu: University of Hawai'i Press, 1988), 47–50. Patterson provides a detailed overview of the migration process on pages 92–102.

9. Yŏng-ho Ch'oe, "The Early Korean Immigration: An Overview," in Yŏng-ho Ch'oe, ed., *From the Land of Hibiscus: Koreans in Hawai'i* (Honolulu: University of Hawai'i Press, 2007), 15–18.

10. Hyun, "My Autobiography," 59–61; Patterson, *Korean Frontier in America,* 49–50, 94.

11. Patterson, *Korean Frontier in America,* 92–94.

12. The history of American Protestant missions in Hawai'i includes early laudatory and triumphal accounts that have been countered with stinging critique. For contrasting perspectives on the general history of Hawai'i that include discussion of missionaries, see Gavan Daws, *Shoal of Time* (New York: Macmillan, 1968); and Jonathan Kay Kamakawiwo'ole Osorio, *Dismembering Lahui: A History of the Hawaiian Nation to 1887* (Honolulu: University of Hawai'i Press, 2002).

13. Takaki, *Pau Hana,* 16–18.

14. Ibid., 18–21.

15. Osorio, *Dismembering Lahui,* 9–13.

16. Noenoe K. Silva, *Aloha Betrayed: Native Hawaiian Resistance to American Colonialism* (Durham, NC: Duke University Press, 2004), 1–13.

17. Osorio, *Dismembering Lahui,* 11–13.

18. Elizabeth Buck, *Paradise Remade: The Politics of Culture and History in Hawai'i* (Philadelphia: Temple University Press, 1993), 63–76, 164–71.

19. Wayne Patterson, *The Ilse: First-Generation Korean Immigrants in Hawai'i, 1903–1973* (Honolulu: University of Hawai'i Press, 2000), 11–17.

20. Bong-Youn Choy, *Koreans in America* (Chicago: Nelson-Hall, 1979), 320–24. The quote is taken from an oral history interview conducted by the author.

21. Takaki, *Pau Hana,* 8–9, 59–60.

22. Choy, *Koreans in America,* 96–97.

23. Patterson, *The Ilse,* 11.

24. Ronald Takaki, *Strangers from a Different Shore: A History of Asian Americans* (Boston: Little, Brown, 1989), 142–55.

25. Gary Pak, *A Ricepaper Airplane* (Honolulu: University of Hawai'i Press, 1998), 22–24; Brenda L. Kwon, *Beyond Ke'eamoku Street: Koreans, Nationalism, and Local Culture in Hawai'i* (New York: Garland, 1999), 118–19.

26. Bernice B. H. Kim, "The Koreans in Hawai'i" (Master's thesis, University of Hawai'i, 1937), 138–39.

27. Hyun, "My Autobiography," 63–68; Alex R. Vergara, ed., *Waves: The United Methodist Church of Hawai'i Centennial Jubilee* (Koloa, HI: Taylor, 1988), 22.

28. Vergara, *Waves,* 22.

29. Kingsley K. Lyu, "Korean Nationalist Activities in Hawai'i and the Continental United States, 1900–1945, Part I: 1900–1919," *Amerasia Journal* 4, no. 1 (1977): 31.

30. Warren Y. Kim, *Koreans in America* (Seoul: Po Chin Chai, 1971), 29.

31. Patterson, *The Ilse,* 55–67.

32. Ibid., 55–56; chap. 5 goes into more detail on the exodus from plantation to city.

33. Ibid., 56–58; Kim, *Koreans in America,* 137–38.

34. *Fifty Years of St. Luke's Church, Honolulu, Hawai'i,* October 1957, 15–16. This history of the church was part of the church files, and I thank Michael Kim, long-time member and treasurer of the church, for letting me photocopy various materials from the church files during my visit in May 2004. A brief history of St. Luke's, including material discussed here, is also found in Patterson, *The Ilse,* 58–60.

35. *Fifty Years of St. Luke's,* 16–17; C. Fletcher Howe, *The First Fifty Years of St. Elizabeth's Church, Honolulu, Hawai'i* (Honolulu: Advertiser Publishing, 1952), 18–19. Pahk was also known by his Korean name, Sang Ha Park.

36. *Fifty Years of St. Luke's,* 16–19; Howe, *First Fifty Years,* 20–21.

37. *Fifty Years of St. Luke's,* 17–19.

38. Interview with Michael Kim, 31 May 2004, Honolulu, Hawai'i. Kim showed me around the grounds of the church, and he noted that church members lovingly took care of the physical plant every Saturday. The church at the time of the interview had an aging membership of fewer than fifty persons, and Kim stated that the lack of younger members was an issue of concern for the future of the church; *Fifty Years of St. Luke's,* 21.

39. *Journal of Hawaiian Mission,* 1907, 18. Comity agreements were such that many groups could work among the Japanese because their numbers were so large.

40. Romanization using the McCune-Reischauer guide is given in parentheses when available.

41. *Journal of Hawaiian Mission,* 1907, 25.

42. *Journal of the Hawaiian Mission,* 1912, 14; 1908, 26.

43. *Journal of Hawaiian Mission,* 1905, 25; 1907, 24; 1908, 11.

44. Interview with Stella Haan, 4 October 1999, Santa Cruz, CA.

45. Ibid.

46. *Journal of Hawaiian Mission,* 1908, 36; 1912, 15.

47. Vergara, *Waves,* 21; Yŏng-ho Ch'oe, "History of Korean Church: A Case Study of Christ United Methodist Church, 1903–2003," in Ilpyong J. Kim, ed., *Korean Americans: Past, Present, and Future* (Elizabeth, NJ: Hollym, 2004), 38; Yŏng-ho Ch'oe, "A Brief History of the Christ United Methodist Church, 1903–2003," in *Christ United Methodist Church, 1903–2003: A Pictorial History* (Seoul: Qumran, 2003), 37. There is a discrepancy in the name of the predecessor group to the church as well as the church name itself. Vergara states that the Korean Evangelical Society then became the First Korean Church, while Ch'oe cites the names Korean Methodist Mission and Honolulu Korean Methodist Church. These sources, however, agree on the dates and the persons involved. It is the case that the church has had several names over the years.

48. Ch'oe, "History of Korean Church," 40–41. Because there are resources like the essays by Yŏng -ho Ch'oe that provide an overview of the history of the church, the treatment of the church's history will be selective to highlight various aspects of the congregation's religious life.

49. Ch'oe, "Brief History," 37–38.

50. Ibid., 38. This incident is recorded by many others already cited in this chapter, and it will be taken up in more detail in Chapter 3.

51. Ch'oe, "Brief History," 39–40. Also see Kim, *Koreans in America,* 57–59; Patterson, *The Ilse,* 100–101; and Richard S. Kim, "Korean Immigrant (Trans)Nationalism: Diaspora, Ethnicity, and State-Making, 1903–1945" (Ph.D. diss., University of Michigan, 2002). This brief treatment is not meant to downplay

the significance of the independence politics among Korean Americans in Hawai'i, but rather to focus on the implications for the religious communities. A fuller discussion of the practice of religious nationalism follows in the next chapter.

52. The break between the Korean Methodist Church and the Korean Christian Church will be discussed more fully in Chapter 3.

53. Emma Shin, "Korean Methodist Episcopal Church," 1928, box A5, Romanzo Adams Social Research Laboratory Student Papers (A1979:042c), University Archives, University of Hawai'i at Manoa, page 2, 9–10. This paper is part of the Romanzo Adams Social Research Laboratory (RASRL) Confidential Files located in Special Collections, University of Hawai'i at Manoa.

54. Shin, "Korean Methodist Episcopal Church," 1, 3–4, 7–8; Alice Chai, "Korean Women in Hawaii, 1903–1945," in Hilah F. Thomas and Rosemary Skinner Keller, eds., *Women in New Worlds: Historical Perspectives on the Wesleyan Tradition* (Nashville, TN: Abingdon Press, 1981), 328–44, 425–27.

55. Margaret K. Pai, *The Dreams of Two Yi-Min* (Honolulu: University of Hawai'i Press, 1989).

56. Ibid., 2–3. The spelling and ordering of the names of the author's parents are taken from the book.

57. Pai, *Dreams of Two Yi-Min*, 4.

58. Chai, "Korean Women in Hawaii," 328.

59. Chung Sook is the Korean name of the author, Margaret Pai. Pai, *Dreams of Two Yi-Min*, 7.

60. Pai, *Dreams of Two Yi-Min*, 8–33.

61. Ibid., 34–42. There were other issues regarding the tensions between Rhee and the Methodist missions that are addressed in the next chapter.

62. Barbara Bennett Peterson, "Dora Kim Moon," in Barbara Bennett Peterson, ed., *Notable Women of Hawai'i* (Honolulu: University of Hawai'i Press, 1984), 271–72.

63. Ibid., 273.

64. Ch'oe, "History of Korean Church," 48; Bennett Peterson, "Dora Kim Moon," 274.

65. Bennett Peterson, "Dora Kim Moon," 271–74.

66. Ch'oe, "History of Korean Church," 47.

67. "What the Korean Young People in Hawai'i Expect of the Christian Church," *American-Korean* 5, no. 1 (2 June 1929): 3–4.

68. Patterson, *The Ilse*, 151–68.

69. Lili M. Kim, "How Koreans Repealed Their 'Enemy Alien' Status: Korean Americans' Identity, Culture, and National Pride in Wartime Hawai'i," in Yŏng-ho Ch'oe, ed., *From the Land of Hibiscus: Koreans in Hawai'i* (Honolulu: University of Hawai'i Press, 2007), 195–219.

70. Ch'oe, "History of Korean Church," 49.

71. Ibid., 49–50.

72. Letter from Lim Doo Hwa to Brother Pak, 22 June 1944. The correspondence is part of the archives of the Christ United Methodist Church. Materials have been collected in binders marked with various dates. The letters from World War II are in the 1944–45 binder. I thank Donna Lee and other members of the church for helping me access these papers.

73. Letter from Soon S. Chun to Lim Doo Hwa, 23 November 1944, Christ United Methodist Church Archives, binder 1944–45.

74. Letter of John Pai to Lim Doo Hwa, 4 May 1944, Christ United Methodist Church Archives, binder 1944–45.

75. Letter from Thomas Park to Lim Doo Hwa, 24 June 1944, Christ United Methodist Church Archives, binder 1944–45.

76. Ch'oe, "History of Korean Church," 50–51.

77. Patterson, *The Ilse*, 67. Religious statistics are difficult to come by since they are largely self-reported, but these figures give some sense of the dominant place of Protestant Christianity among Korean Americans.

78. Hyun, "My Autobiography," 63–69; 104; Peter Hyun, *In the New World: The Making of a Korean American* (Honolulu: University of Hawai'i Press, 1991), ix.

79. Hyun, "My Autobiography," 73–86.

80. Peter Hyun, *Man Sei! The Making of A Korean American* (Honolulu: University of Hawai'i Press, 1986), xii.

81. Ibid., 27, 91–92.

82. Hyun, "My Autobiography," 98–103. The falling out with Rhee, as was the case for many Korean immigrants and exiles, remained a sore point for Hyun and for his children, Peter and David Hyun, who have been fiercely protective of their father's legacy.

83. Hyun, *In the New World*, 8–9, 34–35.

84. Ibid., 36–37.

85. Ibid., 37.

86. Ibid., 37–39.

87. Hyun, "My Autobiography," 103–4.


## Chapter 3

1. A version of this chapter was published as "Nurturing Religious Nationalism: Korean Americans in Hawai'i," in Laurie Maffly-Kipp, Leigh E. Schmidt, and Mark Valeri, eds., *Practicing Protestants: Histories of Christian Life in America, 1630–1965* (Baltimore: Johns Hopkins University Press, 2006), 100–117. Reprinted with permission of the Johns Hopkins University Press.

2. The South Korean government has donated more than six hundred thousand dollars toward the total cost of the project, estimated to cost $2.8 million. Burl Burlingame, "Soul Survivor," *Honolulu Star-Bulletin*, 14 August 2000.

3. On lived religion, see David D. Hall, ed., *Lived Religion in America* (Princeton, NJ: Princeton University Press, 1997); and Robert A. Orsi, ed., *Gods of the City: Religion and the American Urban Landscape* (Bloomington: Indiana University Press, 1999).

4. As Conrad Cherry reminds us, "Two chief revelatory events for the civil religion are the American Revolution (joined with the entire constitutional period) and the American Civil War. The first was a moment when God delivered the colonies from Pharaoh Britain and the 'evils' of the Old World. . . . The Civil War was the nation's first real 'time of testing' when God tried the permanence of the Union or, in some interpretations, brought judgment upon his wayward people." Conrad Cherry, ed., *God's New Israel: Religious Interpretations of American Destiny*, rev. ed. (Chapel Hill: University of North Carolina Press, 1998), 11.

5. Albert J. Raboteau, *Fire in the Bones: Reflections on African American Religious History* (Boston: Beacon Press, 1995), 4.

6. Ho-Youn Kwon, Kwang Chung Kim, and R. Stephen Warner, eds., *Korean Americans and Their Religions: Pilgrims and Missionaries from a Different Shore* (University Park: Pennsylvania State University Press, 2001); Warren Y. Kim, *Koreans in America* (Seoul: Po Chin Chai, 1971); Bong-Youn Choy, *Koreans in America* (Chicago: Nelson-Hall, 1979); Won Moo Hurh, *The Korean Americans* (Westport, CT: Greenwood Press, 1998).

7. For background on this issue, see Bruce Cumings, *Korea's Place in the Sun: A Modern History* (New York: W. W. Norton, 1997); and Gi-Wook Shin and Michael Robinson, eds., *Colonial Modernity in Korea* (Cambridge, MA: Harvard University Asia Center, 1999).

8. For a general overview of Asian American history, see Ronald Takaki, *Strangers from a Different Shore: A History of Asian Americans* (Boston: Little Brown, 1989); and Sucheng Chan, *Asian Americans: An Interpretive History* (Boston: Twayne, 1991). The literature on race in the United States is vast, but some key studies include Alexander Saxton, *The Rise and Fall of the White Republic: Class Politics and Mass Culture in Nineteenth-Century America* (New York: Verso, 1990); Michael Omi and Howard Winant, *Racial Formations in the United States: From the 1960s to the 1990s*, 2nd ed. (New York: Routledge, 1994); Gary Gerstle, *American Crucible: Race and Nation in the Twentieth Century* (Princeton, NJ: Princeton University Press, 2001); and George Lipsitz, *The Possessive Investment in Whiteness: How White People Profit from Identity Politics* (Philadelphia: Temple University Press, 1998).

9. President Woodrow Wilson's Fourteen Points speech was delivered before a joint session of the U.S. Congress on 8 January 1918 in an effort to sketch out a just

and lasting peace in the context of World War I. For Koreans and Korean Americans, the emphasis on the self-determination of nations gave voice to efforts that they had been engaged in well before Korea was annexed by Japan in 1910. For more background on Wilson and the speech, see Arthur S. Link, *Wilson the Diplomatist: A Look at His Major Foreign Policies* (Baltimore: Johns Hopkins University Press, 1957); Arthur S. Link et al., eds., *The Papers of Woodrow Wilson*, Vol. 45, *November 11, 1917–January 15, 1918* (Princeton, NJ: Princeton University Press, 1984).

10. James Huntley Grayson, *Korea: A Religious History* (London: Routledge Curzon, 2002), 155. For general background on Christianity in Korea, see Allen D. Clark, *A History of the Church in Korea* (Seoul: Christian Literature Society of Korea, 1971); Donald N. Clark, *Christianity in Modern Korea* (Lanham, MD: University Press of America, 1986); and Chung-Shin Park, *Protestantism and Politics in Korea* (Seattle: University of Washington Press, 2003).

11. The standard work on Protestant missions is L. George Paik, *The History of Protestant Missions in Korea, 1832–1910* (Pyeng Yang, Korea: Union Christian College Press, 1929).

12. Kenneth M. Wells, *New God, New Nation: Protestants and Self-Reconstruction Nationalism in Korea, 1896–1937* (Honolulu: University of Hawai'i Press, 1990), 16–17, 40.

13. Don Baker, "Christianity Koreanized," in Hyung Il Pai and Timothy R. Tangherlini, eds., *Nationalism and the Construction of Korean Identity* (Berkeley: Institute of East Asian Studies, University of California, 1998), 118–20.

14. Cumings, *Korea's Place in the Sun*, 157–60.

15. Wi Jo Kang, *Christ and Caesar in Modern Korea: A History of Christianity and Politics* (Albany: State University of New York Press, 1997), 39–42.

16. Wells, *New God, New Nation*, 1–20.

17. It is beyond the scope of this chapter to fully examine the sources of this division. Despite their many commonalities, Rhee and Pak differed in their vision for how best to achieve independence for Korea. Rhee favored diplomacy and a close alliance with the United States, while Pak advocated a militaristic approach in which Koreans abroad would spearhead an armed invasion of the peninsula coordinated with independence efforts in Korea. Wayne Patterson provides some background on the divided nature of the Korean American community in Hawai'i: *The Ilse: First-Generation Korean Immigrants in Hawai'i, 1903–1973* (Honolulu: University of Hawai'i Press, 2000), 100–101.

18. For more background, see Ronald Takaki, *Pau Hana: Plantation Life and Labor in Hawai'i, 1835–1920* (Honolulu: University of Hawai'i Press, 1983).

19. The College of Hawai'i, founded in 1907, became the University of Hawai'i in 1920, and the University of Hawai'i, Manoa, in 1972.

20. Bernice B. H. Kim, "The Koreans in Hawai'i" (Master's thesis, University of

Hawai'i, 1937), 140–42; Kingsley K. Lyu, "Korean Nationalist Activities in Hawai'i and the Continental United States, 1900–1945, Part I, 1900–1919," *Amerasia Journal* 4, no. 1 (1977): 47, 77.

21.  Choy, *Koreans in America,* 260–61. Also, Yŏng-ho Ch'oe, "Syngman Rhee in Hawai'i: His Activities in the Early Years, 1913–1915," in Yŏng-ho Ch'oe, ed., *From the Land of Hibiscus: Koreans in Hawai'i* (Honolulu: University of Hawai'i Press, 2007), 53–88. Ch'oe also mentions the pro-Japanese comments made by Methodist Bishop Merriman Harris when he visited Hawai'i in 1908.

22.  Syngman Rhee, *The Spirit of Independence: A Primer of Korean Modernization and Reform,* trans. Han-Kyo Kim (Honolulu and Seoul: University of Hawai'i Press and the Institute for Modern Korean Studies, Yonsei University, 2001), 1–18. Kim provides a brief but helpful biographical sketch: Translator's Introduction, 1–21.

23.  Kim, Translator's Introduction, 1–5.

24.  Rhee, *Spirit of Independence,* 280–83, 1–14; Robert T. Oliver, *Syngman Rhee: The Man Behind the Myth* (New York: Dodd, Mead, 1954), 113–26. Oliver's biography is unquestioningly favorable toward Rhee, but he had access to Rhee's personal papers, and the work contains useful information. Richard C. Allen (*Korea's Syngman Rhee: An Unauthorized Portrait* [Rutland, VT: C. E. Tuttle, 1960]) is far more critical, but Allen often depends upon Oliver for details and facts about Rhee's activities.

25.  Choy, *Koreans in America,* 79, 83–85; Rhee, *Spirit of Independence,* 1–18. This section of the text is a brief biography of Rhee written by the translator, Han-Kyo Kim.

26.  Oliver, *Syngman Rhee,* 109–14.

27.  Kim, "Koreans in Hawai'i," 142–43.

28.  Choy, *Koreans in America,* 261–62; Oliver, *Syngman Rhee,* 123.

29.  Ki-Baik Lee, *A New History of Korea,* trans. Edward W. Wagner with Edward J. Shultz(Cambridge, MA: Harvard University Press, 1984), 340–44; Michael E. Robinson, *Cultural Nationalism in Colonial Korea, 1920–1925* (Seattle: University of Washington Press, 1988), 3–13.

30.  Kim, "Koreans in Hawai'i," 143–45.

31.  Lyu, "Korean Nationalist Activities," 48–51. Many of the Korean language schools that operated under religious auspices also provided Korean Americans shelter from efforts by the territorial government of Hawai'i to curb foreign language instruction to foster greater standard English language acquisition (versus pidgin English).

32.  Quoted from Lyu, "Korean Nationalist Activities," 79. Ironically, in 1934 Rhee married Francesca Donner, an Austrian, who would become the first First Lady of the Republic of Korea (South Korea).

33. Choy, *Koreans in America,* 118–19. I have made only passing mention of the Comrade Society/Tongjihoe because others have written more about the group. Especially helpful is Richard S. Kim, "Korean Immigrant (Trans)Nationalism: Diaspora, Ethnicity, and State-Making, 1903–1945" (Ph.D. diss., University of Michigan, 2002).

34. "Objectives and Aims of the K.C.C." Is a memo with excerpts from Syngman Rhee's writings on the Korean Christian Church reported to be in the possession of the Reverend Richard C. Kimm in 1945. I thank Bessie Park, a longtime member of the church, for lending me documents from her personal papers, including this item.

35. Lyu, "Korean Nationalist Activities," 79–85.

36. "History of Korean Missions Inc.," unpublished paper, no date, in the Korean Christian Church files, Honolulu. This organization continues to oversee the churches, which now number three: Honolulu, Wahiawa, and Hilo.

37. Kim, *Koreans in America,* 67.

38. Interview with Helen Chung, 4 April 2000, Honolulu.

39. Kim, *Koreans in America,* 67.

40. Winifred Lee Namba, "Nodie Kimhaikim Sohn," in Barbara Bennett Peterson, ed., *Notable Women of Hawai'i* (Honolulu: University of Hawai'i Press, 1984), 356–57.

41. The suggestion to include material on the Makiki Christian Church and the First Chinese Church of Christ came from an anonymous reviewer of the manuscript for Stanford University Press.

42. The information about the church architecture is taken from the Web site of the Makiki Christian Church: http://www.makikichristianchurch.org/history.htm.

43. The Web site for the First Chinese Church of Christ: http://kanalu68.brinkster.net/fccc/newfccc.asp?que=short.

44. *Honolulu Star-Bulletin,* 23 April 1938.

45. Lyu, "Korean Nationalist Activities," 80–81; *Honolulu Star-Bulletin,* 23 April 1938.

46. The date of the dedication is taken from the program produced for the event. I thank Bessie Park for giving me a copy of the program.

47. The large mixed-race population in Hawai'i (including Koreans) also complicates discussions about racial categories.

48. Ference Szasz, *Religion in the Modern American West* (Tucson: University of Arizona Press, 2002).

49. Because assimilation has been (and, to an extent, still is) such a dominant framework for understanding immigration and settlement in the United States, it

is often the case that historians have understudied how many groups have found other ways to engage (or not engage) the nation. American exceptionalism has also contributed to the tendency to view the United States as somehow categorically different from other nations in the processes of nation-building, especially in relation to colonial and imperial endeavors. Works on Korean nationalism have also been helpful in thinking about the nationalisms of Korean American Christians, including Chong-sik Lee, *The Politics of Korean Nationalism* (Berkeley: University of California Press, 1963); and Elaine H. Kim and Chungmoo Choi, eds., *Dangerous Women: Gender and Korean Nationalism* (New York: Routledge, 1998). An interesting point of comparison for the study of religious nationalism might include Asian Indian Sikhs, Irish Catholics, and Korean Protestant immigrants in the United States, since all three groups were active during the first part of the twentieth century.

50. "The Changing Role of the Korean Christian Church," spring 1965, Student Papers, Romanzo Adams Social Research Laboratory records, A1979:042c, box 9, Hamilton Library, University of Hawai'i at Manoa. No author is listed. The quote is taken from page 5 of the paper.

51. "Changing Role of the Korean Christian Church," 6, 10.

*Chapter 4*

1. The mission/church, as this chapter documents, underwent different configurations and names over the years and is today the Los Angeles Korean United Methodist Church.

2. John Cha, *Willow Tree Shade: The Susan Ahn Cuddy Story* (Los Angeles[?]: Korean American Heritage Foundation, 2002), 55.

3. This chapter draws upon material from David K. Yoo and Hyung-ju Ahn, *Faithful Witness: A Centennial History of the Los Angeles Korean United Methodist Church, 1904–2004* (Los Angeles: Los Angeles Korean United Methodist Church, 2004). Permission to reprint granted by the Los Angeles Korean United Methodist Church.

4. Works on Christianity in Korea include Chung-Shin Park, *Protestantism and Politics in Korea* (Seattle: University of Washington Press, 2003); Wi Jo Kang, *Christ and Caesar in Modern Korea: A History of Christianity and Politics* (Albany: State University of New York Press, 1997); Allen D. Clark, *A History of the Church in Korea* (Seoul: Christian Literature Society of Korea, 1971); and Donald N. Clark, *Christianity in Modern Korea* (Lanham, MD: University Press of America, 1986); Don Baker, "Christianity Koreanized," in Hyung Il Pai and Timothy R. Tangherlini, eds., *Nationalism and the Construction of Korean Identity* (Berkeley: Institute of East Asian Studies, University of California, 1998), 118–20.

5. The concept of internal colonialism has a long history, but my usage is largely indebted to the work of sociologist Robert Blauner and his application of the term to the United States. Robert Blauner, *Racial Oppression in America* (New York: Harper & Row, 1972).

6. Eldon G. Ernst, "The Emergence of California in American Religious Historiography," *Religion and American Culture* 11, no. 1 (Winter 2001): 31–52. Even with the influx of Protestants from the Midwest to Los Angeles, Ernst notes that the presence of Pentecostals and other groups meant that Protestantism was internally diverse. Michael E. Engh, *Frontier Faiths: Church, Temple, and Synagogue in Los Angeles, 1846–1888* (Albuquerque: University of New Mexico Press, 1992), 212; Howard DeWitt, *The Fragmented Dream: Multicultural California* (Dubuque, IA: Kendall/Hunt, 1996), xiii. See also Tomas Almaguer, *Racial Fault Lines: The Historical Origins of White Supremacy in California* (Berkeley: University of California Press, 1994).

7. Sandra Sizer Frankiel, *California's Spiritual Frontiers: Religious Alternatives in Anglo-Protestantism, 1850–1910* (Berkeley: University of California Press, 1988), 61–62. It should be noted that Frankiel did not mention Koreans, but East Asians.

8. A number of fine studies on race and southern California have examined the interactions among various communities that are usually studied separately, and such comparative work is very welcome. My point is that people within such communities had fairly limited contact with those outside because of language and social barriers, even in cases when there may have been close physical proximity. Among the recent studies, see Mark Wild, *Street Meeting: Multiethnic Neighborhoods in Early Twentieth-Century Los Angeles* (Berkeley: University of California Press, 2005); and Allison Varzally, *Making a Non-White America* (Berkeley: University of California Press, 2008). The study by Josh Sides, *L.A. City Limits: African American Los Angeles from the Great Depression to the Present* (Berkeley: University of California Press, 2003), problematizes, among other things, the notion that Los Angeles was a racial haven for African Americans.

9. One could argue that racial barriers continue to exert influence among Protestant Christians in the United States today. Michael O. Emerson and Christian Smith, *Divided by Faith: Evangelical Religion and the Problem of Race in America* (New York: Oxford University Press, 2000); Curtiss Paul DeYoung et al., *United by Faith: The Multiracial Congregation as an Answer to the Problem of Race* (New York: Oxford University Press, 2003); Kathleen Garces-Foley, *Crossing the Ethnic Divide: The Multiethnic Church on a Mission* (New York: Oxford University Press, 2005).

10. Hyung June Moon, "The Korean Immigrants in America: The Quest for Identity in the Formative Years, 1903–1918," (Ph.D. diss., University of Nevada, Reno, 1976), 92–98. Although Moon limited his study to the years 1903–18, he pro-

vides a very detailed and fairly comprehensive portrait of Koreans in Hawai'i and on the mainland in terms of occupation, social organization, and the like.

11.  Helen Lewis Givens, "The Korean Community in Los Angeles County" (Master's thesis, University of Southern California, 1939).

12.  U.S. Bureau of the Census, *Fifteenth Census of the United States: 1930,* vol. 3, *Population, Reports by States,* Part 1, Alabama–Missouri (Washington, DC: Government Printing Office, 1932), 233. Tracking the census figures for Koreans in California and Hawai'i during the early decades of the twentieth century underscored the arbitrary and racialized nature of the data collection. For instance, Koreans appear as a separate category in some years but are lumped together under "Other" at other points. In most cases, the category of "Other" is not further specified. Moreover, while Koreans certainly represented a small part of the overall population, the issue of numbers did not prevent census takers from providing detailed tabulations of foreign-born whites. In addition, given that Koreans represented a migratory, transient, and largely foreign-born population, census workers would have had a difficult time getting an accurate account. For these reasons, and more importantly, because of the importance of Koreans in the United States for a transnational community, numbers hardly tell the whole story.

13.  George Heber Jones, "Memoir of Dr. Harry C. Sherman," *Official Minutes of the 17th Annual Meeting of the Korea Mission, Methodist Episcopal Church,* May 1901, 69–71.

14.  "Mrs. Florence M. Sherman," *Harvester,* 16, no. 3 (January 1916), 646–51. *The Harvester* was the monthly magazine published by the First Methodist Episcopal Church in Los Angeles.

15.  *Korea Repository,* August 1898, 308.

16.  *Korea Repository,* September 1898, 315.

17.  Jones, "Memoir," 69–71.

18.  Ibid., 70. Jones makes a reference to a "Heung-u," and Hugh Cynn's Korean name was spelled "Heung-wu."

19.  Chong-sik Lee, *Syngman Rhee: The Prison Years of a Young Radical* (Seoul: Yonsei University Press, 2001), 39–47. I thank Young-Ik Lew of Yonsei University for providing me with a copy of Lee's book.

20.  Jones, "Memoir," 71; "Mrs. Florence M. Sherman" *Harvester,* 16, no. 3 (January 1916), 649.

21.  "A New Mission," *Harvester,* 5, no. 2 (October–November 1904), 3.

22.  Ibid.

23.  Robert T. Handy, *We Witness Together: A History of Cooperative Home Missions* (New York: Friendship Press, 1956).

24.  Mia Tuan, *Forever Foreigners or Honorary Whites? The Asian Ethnic Experience Today* (New Brunswick, NJ: Rutgers University Press, 1998).

25. Ki-Baik Lee, *A New History of Korea*, trans. Edward W. Wagner with Edward J. Shultz (Cambridge, MA: Harvard University Press, 1984), 305.

26. "Korean Work" and "Korean Work in Los Angeles," *Official Journal of the Ninth Annual Session of the Pacific Japanese Mission of the Methodist Episcopal Church*, 4–6 September 1908, 25–26.

27. "Report of the Los Angeles Korean Methodist Episcopal Mission for 1909," *Journal of the Fifth Session of the Hawai'i Mission of the Methodist Episcopal Church*, 16–20 March 1910, 33–34.

28. Harold Garnet Black, "The Church of the Lighted Cross: History of the First Methodist Church of Los Angeles, California," *Horizon*, 1932, 32; K. W. Lee with Luke and Grace Kim, "Seeding Hope and Social Justice," *KoreAm Journal* (May 2005): 44–51.

29. Hugh Heung-wo Cynn, *The Rebirth of Korea: The Reawakening of the People, Its Causes, and the Outlook* (New York: Abingdon Press, 1920), 129–35. Quote taken from p. 129.

30. Lee, *Syngman Rhee*, 185–87. This information is based upon notes from an interview of Cynn by Robert T. Oliver in Korea in April 1949. Oliver was a close associate of Rhee's and wrote an authorized and highly favorable biography, *Syngman Rhee: The Man Behind the Myth* (New York: Dodd, Mead, 1954).

31. "Report of the Los Angeles Korean Methodist Episcopal Mission for 1909," *Journal of the Fifth Session of the Hawai'i Mission of the Methodist Episcopal Church*, 16–20 March 1910, 34.

32. Cynn, *Rebirth of Korea*, 15–16.

33. "Assaulted by His Own People: Korean Diplomat Is Attacked in San Francisco," *Los Angeles Times*, 23 March 1908, p. 11; Bong-Youn Choy, *Koreans in America* (Chicago: Nelson-Hall, 1979), 146–49. I used Choy's spellings of the names of the individuals involved.

34. "Assaulted by His Own People." The quote is taken from the *Los Angeles Times* article. The newspaper article identified the speaker as Lee, but Yi is one of several ways to anglicize the Korean name. As I mentioned in the previous note, I have followed Choy's lead in listing the speaker as Yi Hak-hyun. It is telling that the newspaper headline of the story read "Assaulted by His Own People: Korean Diplomat Is Attacked in San Francisco." While Stevens was technically a representative of the Korean government, it is ironic that the headline ignores the context of what is reported in the article.

35. Choy, *Koreans in America*, 147–49; Warren Y. Kim, *Koreans in America* (Seoul: Po Chin Chai, 1971), 78–84.

36. "Coreans Tell How They Planned to Kill Him," *San Francisco Chronicle*, 24 March 1908; "Durham Stevens Succumbs to Wounds," *San Francisco Chronicle*, 26 March 1908.

37. "Murder Verdict in Chang Case," *San Francisco Chronicle*, 24 December 1908; "Light Penalty for I. W. Chang," *San Francisco Chronicle*, 3 January 1909; Choy, *Koreans in America*, 147–49; Kim, *Koreans in America*, 78–84. Kim states that the jury reached its verdict on 22 December 1908, while the *Chronicle* story dated 24 December relates that the jury reached its verdict the day before. In his dissertation, Richard S. Kim notes that after his release, Chang lived in San Francisco until 1930, when he committed suicide after many years of battling depression. Kim also notes that Chun Myung Woon was released without bail before the trial and fled to Manchuria. Richard S. Kim, "Korean Immigrant (Trans)Nationalism: Diaspora, Ethnicity, and State-Making, 1903–1945" (Ph.D. diss., University of Michigan, 2002), 52–66, 78–80.

38. Kang, *Christ and Caesar*, 38–42.

39. "How Stevens Won Enmity," *Los Angeles Times,* 25 March 1908, p. II 1.

40. Ibid.

41. Ibid.

42. Mary Paik Lee, *Quiet Odyssey: A Pioneer Woman in America* (Seattle: University of Washington Press, 1990).

43. Sonia Shinn Sunoo, *Korean Kaleidoscope: Oral Histories,* vol. 1, *Early Korean Pioneers, 1903–1905* (Davis, CA: Korean Oral History Project, Sierra Mission Area, United Presbyterian Church, 1982), 35. For some reason, Henry Chung changed his name to Henry Chung de Young in 1923 and worked for twenty years as a salesman for La Choy Food Products (and related businesses), an "oriental" food company started by his colleague Ilhan New. See Henry Chung, *Korea and the United States Through War and Peace, 1943–1960* (Seoul: Yonsei University Press, 2000). The information about his name and employment is taken from the foreword by Young-Ick Lew, p. xvi.

44. *Pacific Methodist Advocate*, 19 June 1924.

45. Ibid.

46. Harold Garnet Black, "The Church of the Lighted Cross: History of the First Methodist Church of Los Angeles, California" *Horizon*, 1932, 32; K. W. Lee with Luke and Grace Kim, "Seeding Hope and Social Justice," *KoreAm Journal* (May 2005): 44–51.

47. Woong-min Kim, "History and Ministerial Roles of Korean Churches in the Los Angeles Area" (D.Min. diss., Claremont School of Theology, Claremont, CA, 1981), 23–24.

48. Ibid.

49. *New Korea*, 25 August 1909; 1 September 1909.

50. *New Korea*, 1 September 1909; *Korean Student Bulletin*, February 1923.

51. "Mother W. B. Stewart," *Korean Student Bulletin*, December 1929; Woong-

min Kim, "History and Ministerial Roles," 19–20; Choy, *Koreans in America,* 109, 277; Joe Blackstock, "Shunned Koreans Had a Remarkable Friend," *Inland Valley Daily Bulletin,* 23 March 2007, www.dailybulletin.com/ourpast/ci_5510842; "History of First Presbyterian Church," http://myfpc-upland.com/History.htm. The use of threat and intimidation in this incident apparently did not result in an attack, perhaps because Koreans had weapons. Stewart's husband, William Boyd Stewart, was a younger brother of Los Angeles–based Union Oil founder Lyman Stewart.

52. Do-Hyung Kim and Yŏng-ho Ch'oe, "The March First Movement of 1919 and Koreans in Hawai'i," in Yŏng-ho Ch'oe, ed., *From the Land of Hibiscus: Koreans in Hawai'i* (Honolulu: University of Hawai'i Press, 2007), 124.

53. "Korean Representatives to the Peace Conference," *Freedom and Peace Under Japan?* 1, no. 1 (March 1919): 7. This publication would eventually become the *Korea Review,* published in Philadelphia. I thank Richard S. Kim for lending me his copies of the *Korea Review;* Choy, *Koreans in America,* 152–53.

54. Erez Manela, *The Wilsonian Moment: Self-Determination and the International Origins of Anticolonial Nationalism* (New York: Oxford University Press, 2007).

55. Michael E. Robinson, *Cultural Nationalism in Colonial Korea, 1920–1925* (Seattle: University of Washington Press, 1988), 3; Peter Hyun, *Man Sei! The Making of a Korean American* (Honolulu: University of Hawai'i Press, 1986), xi–4; Timothy S. Lee, "A Political Factor in the Rise of Protestantism in Korea: Protestantism and the 1919 March First Movement," *Church History* 69, no. 1 (March 2000): 116–42.

56. "A Letter to the Christian Churches of America," *Korea Review* 1, no. 3 (May 1919): 66. This publication became the *Korea Review* later in 1919, but in this first issue did not appear to have a title except: "Freedom and Peace with Korea Under Japan?"

57. "Philadelphia Congress," *Korea Review* 1, no. 3 (May 1919): 90; Richard S. Kim, "Inaugurating the American Century: The 1919 Philadelphia Korean Congress, Korean Diasporic Nationalism, and American Protestant Missionaries," *Journal of American Ethnic History* 26, no. 1 (Fall 2006): 50–76.

58. *Korea Review* 1, no. 5 (July 1919): 13–14.

59. *Korea Review* 2, no. 10 (December 1920): 1.

60. *New Korea,* 3 April 1919, as quoted in Woong-min Kim, "History and Ministerial Roles," 21–22.

61. Jessie M. Martin, "Molly Hong Min," in Barbara Bennett Peterson, ed., *Notable Women of Hawaii* (Honolulu: University of Hawai'i Press, 1984), 265–67.

62. *New Korea,* 14 February 1924; 27 March 1924.

63. *New Korea,* 6 March 1924.

64. Choy, *Koreans in America,* 263.

65. Woong-min Kim, "History and Ministerial Roles," 40–43; Choy, *Koreans in America,* 263.

66. *New Korea,* 28 August 1926.

67. *Pacific Methodist Advocate,* 2 September 1926, 4.

68. *New Korea,* 23 September 1926.

69. *New Korea,* 12 May 1927; Choy, *Koreans in America,* 263.

70. *New Korea,* 15 December 1927.

71. *New Korea,* 23 October 1930.

72. *New Korea,* 21 July 1909; Kim, *Koreans in America,* 18–20.

73. *New Korea,* 6 September 1917.

74. *The Yearbook of the Methodist Episcopal Church, South,* 1927, 310–11.

75. Moon, "Korean Immigrants in America"; Warren Kim (*Koreans in America*), and Bong-Youn Choy (*Koreans in America*) all provide an occupational profile for Korean Americans.

76. The Gentleman's Agreement of 1907–8 was aimed at Japanese laborers, but because of Japan's role in Korea, it also affected Koreans. Family reunification allowed under the agreement opened a window for Japanese and Korean women to migrate—a loophole closed by the Immigration Act of 1924. Protectorate status (1905) and annexation (1910) meant that fewer Koreans left the country, since Japan channeled labor for its own ends. Kim, *Koreans in America,* 22–23.

77. *The Yearbook of the Methodist Episcopal Church, South,* 1940, 371.

78. *New Korea,* 5 July 1928.

79. *Pacific Methodist Advocate,* 5 July 1928, 6.

80. *Los Angeles Times,* 13 July 1928, 1; 16 July 1928, 5; 17 July 1928, 1. A Korean delegate, Kim Kwan-Six, a graduate from Syracuse University, was elected as one of the vice presidents.

81. *The Yearbook of the Methodist Episcopal Church, South,* 1927, 310–11.

## Chapter 5

1. This chapter draws upon material from David K. Yoo and Hyung-ju Ahn, *Faithful Witness: A Centennial History of the Los Angeles Korean United Methodist Church* (Los Angeles: Los Angeles Korean United Methodist Church, 2004). Permission granted to reprint from the Los Angeles Korean United Methodist Church.

2. *New Korea (Shinhan Minbo),* 15 January 1931.

3. *Pacific Methodist Advocate,* 10 July 1930, 10.

4. Yŏng-ho Ch'oe makes reference to missionaries' pro-Japanese sentiments in

"A Brief History of the Christ United Methodist Church, 1903–2003," in *Christ United Methodist Church, 1903–2003: A Pictorial History* (Honolulu: Christ United Methodist Church, 2003), 38.

5. Helen Lewis Givens, "The Korean American Community in Los Angeles County" (Master's thesis, University of Southern California, 1939), 22–28.

6. Ibid., 22.

7. *New Korea*, 19 March 1936; 13 August 1936.

8. *New Korea*, 11 October 1934.

9. *The Yearbook of the Methodist Episcopal Church, South*, 1938, 326–27.

10. Ibid.

11. *The Yearbook of the Methodist Episcopal Church, South*, 1934, 26.

12. *New Korea*, 28 November 1935.

13. *New Korea*, 26 January 1933; 27 July 1933.

14. *Seventieth Anniversary of the Korean United Presbyterian Church* (Los Angeles: Korean United Presbyterian Church, 1976), 58–59.

15. *Seventieth Anniversary*, 59.

16. *New Korea*, 12 March 1936.

17. *Los Angeles Times,* 30 April 1938, A2.

18. Woong-min Kim, "History and Ministerial Roles of Korean Churches in the Los Angeles Area" (D.Min. diss., Claremont School of Theology, Claremont, CA, 1981), 41–43.

19. *Pacific Korean Weekly,* 3 December 1939.

20. *New Korea*, 18 August 1938.

21. *New Korea*, 8 June 1939.

22. *New Korea*, 12 December 1935.

23. Givens, "Korean Community," 26.

24. *New Korea,* 19 January 1939.

25. Givens, "Korean Community," 27.

26. *New Korea*, 21 August 1941.

27. *New Korea*, 29 May 1941.

28. Warren Y. Kim, *Koreans in America* (Seoul: Po Chin Chai, 1971), 22–23.

29. *New Korea*, 1 September 1938.

30. There is an excellent and varied literature related to Chinese exclusion, and among the many fine studies are Erika Lee, *At America's Gates: Chinese Immigration During the Exclusion Era, 1882–1943* (Chapel Hill: University of North Carolina Press, 2003); Bill Ong Hing, *Making and Remaking Asian America Through Immigration Policy, 1850–1990* (Stanford, CA: Stanford University Press, 1993); and Alexander Saxton, *The Indispensable Enemy: Labor and the Anti-Chinese Movement in* California (Berkeley: University of California Press, 1971). For a general history,

see Sucheng Chan, *Asian Americans: An Interpretive History* (Boston: Twayne, 1991); Ronald Takaki, *Strangers from a Different Shore: A History of Asian Americans* (Boston: Little, Brown, 1989).

31. Kenneth M. Wells, *New God, New Nation: Protestants and Self-Reconstruction Nationalism in Korea, 1896–1937* (Honolulu: University of Hawai'i Press, 1990), 16–20.

32. *NAPKO Project of OSS* (Seoul: Ministry of Patriots and Veterans Affairs, 1992), 755; "Diamond Kimm, Central Intelligence Agency File," University of Southern California, Korean American Digital Archive, Record ID: kada-m18295, http://digarc.usc.edu/search/controller/view/kada-m18295.html. The limited biographical information on Kimm notes that he attended both the University of Southern California and the Colorado School of Mines during the period from 1928 to 1938, and he focused his studies in geology and mining, apparently with the hope that he might help Korea develop in this area.

33. *New Korea*, 10 March 1938.

34. *The Yearbook of the Methodist Episcopal Church, South*, 1938, 322–27.

35. *New Korea*, 15 May 1941.

36. Givens, "Korean Community," 26.

37. *Pacific Methodist Advocate*, 15 September 1932, 12.

38. James W. May, "Methodism in the United States," in Nolan B. Harmon, ed., *The Encyclopedia of World Methodism* (Nashville, TN: Methodist Publishing House, 1974), 1563.

39. "Pearl Harbor and Korea," *Voice of Korea*, 7 December 1943, 3. This journal was published by the Korean Affairs Institute in Washington, DC. The journal letterhead indicated that the Korean Affairs Institute was "A Non-Profit Organization 'Devoted to Freedom.'"

40. For much more detail on Korean Americans during the war, see Lili M. Kim, "The Pursuit of Imperfect Justice: The Predicament of Koreans and Korean Americans on the Homefront During World War II" (Ph.D. diss., University of Rochester, 2001).

41. *New Korea*, 22 January 1942.

42. *New Korea*, 1 January 1942.

43. *New Korea*, 26 June 1941.

44. I have made reference here to Susan Ahn, rather than Susan Ahn Cuddy, since she was single when she enlisted. John Cha, *Willow Tree Shade: The Susan Ahn Cuddy Story* (Los Angeles[?]: Korean American Heritage Foundation, 2002).

45. *New Korea*, 15 April 1943; 11 November 1943.

46. *New Korea*, 29 October 1942.

47. *New Korea*, 23 December 1943.

48. *New Korea*, 24 December 1942.

49. *New Korea*, 23 September 1943.

50. Both the KMCLA and the KNRP took part in a coalition of organizations in southern California under the banner of the Korean Christian Association.

51. For a more detailed overview of the leftist activity of the Korean independence movement, see Richard S. Kim, "Korean Immigrant (Trans)Nationalism: Diaspora, Ethnicity, and State-Making, 1903–1945" (Ph.D. diss., University of Michigan, 2002), especially chap. 5.

52. Bong-Youn Choy, *Koreans in America* (Chicago: Nelson-Hall, 1979), 120–21.

53. The dissertations of Richard S. Kim, "Korean Immigrant (Trans)Nationalism," and Lili M. Kim, "Pursuit of Imperfect Justice," discuss the United Korean Committee, as does Anne Soon Choi, "Unity for What? Unity for Whom? The United Korean Committee of North America, 1941–1945," in Yŏng-ho Ch'oe, ed., *From the Land of Hibiscus: Koreans in Hawaii* (Honolulu: University of Hawai'i Press, 2007), 220–55.

54. Kim, *Koreans in America,* 69–70.

55. Kim, "Korean Immigrant (Trans)Nationalism," chap. 5. Anne Choi's article on the United Korean Committee also contains information on Kilsoo Haan.

56. *Journal and Proceedings of Third Session of the California Oriental Mission of the Methodist Church,* 1941, 23.

57. *New Korea*, 14 June 1928; 14 May 1936. The school is now called the American Baptist Seminary of the West. I thank Annie Russell, Registrar, American Baptist Seminary of the West, for tracking down Key H. Chang's record from the school's archives. The Bachelor of Theology (B.Th.) degree was the precursor to the Bachelor of Divinity (B.D.) that has since become the Master of Divinity (M.Div.).

58. Interview by phone with Lila Chang, 4 July 2003.

59. *Korean Independence*, 5 January 1944.

60. *Korean Independence*, 17 January 1945.

61. *New Korea*, 7 May 1942.

62. *Korean Independence,* 28 November 1945.

63. *Korean Independence*, 29 March 1944.

64. *Korean Independence*, 24 November 1943.

65. Ibid.

66. "Diamond Kimm, Central Intelligence Agency File," University of Southern California, Korean American Digital Archive, Record ID: kada-m18295, http://digarc.usc.edu/search/controller/view/kada-m18295.html; *NAPKO Project of OSS* (Seoul: Ministry of Patriots and Veterans Affairs, 1992), 755.

67. "Diamond Kimm, Central Intelligence Agency File"; Choy, *Koreans in America,* 121.

68. Gi-Wook Shin and Michael Robinson, eds., *Colonial Modernity in Korea* (Cambridge, MA: Harvard University Asia Center, 1999), 1–18.

69. Sonia Shinn Sunoo, ed. and trans., "Park Kyung-Shin," in *Korean Picture Brides: 1903–1920, A Collection of Oral Histories* (Philadelphia: Xlibris, 2002), 132–53.

70. Sonia Shinn Sunoo, ed. and trans., "Kim Hei-Won," in *Korean Picture Brides: 1903–1920, A Collection of Oral Histories* (Philadelphia: Xlibris, 2002), 154–66.

71. *Journal and Proceedings of the Second Session of the California Oriental Mission of the Methodist Church*, 1940, 16.

72. *Journal and Proceedings of the Third Session of the California Oriental Mission of the Methodist Church*, 1941, 12.

73. *Journal and Proceedings of the Fortieth Annual Session of the California Oriental Mission of the Methodist Church*, 1943, 16.

74. *Journal and Proceedings of the Forty-second Annual Session of the California Oriental Mission and the First Annual Session of the California Oriental Provisional Conference of the Methodist Church*, 1945, 20.

75. Ibid, 34.

76. *Korean Independence*, 6 June 1945.

77. *Journal and Proceedings*, 1945, 34.

78. *Korean Independence*, 30 May 1945.

79. *Journal and Proceedings*, 1945, 20.

80. *Korean Independence*, 5 January 1944; 10 October 1945.

81. *Korean Independence*, 3 October 1945; 10 October 1945.

82. *Pacific Methodist Advocate*, 30 October 1941, 1420.

83. *Korean Independence*, 24 November 1943.

84. *Korean Independence*, 13 April 1944.

85. *New Korea*, 1 January 1942.

86. Interview with Ralph Ahn, Howard Choy, Nellie Choy, and Luther Hahn, Los Angeles, 10 June 2003.

## Chapter 6

1. "Mr. Yelton Introduces the Korean Secretary" and "Report on College Visitation," *Korean Student Bulletin*, December 1922. The *Korean Student Bulletin will* hereafter be cited as *KSB*.

2. The last regular issue of the *KSB* appears to have been the March–April 1940 issue, though nothing in the issue itself indicated that it would be the end. The date 1941 is listed as the end point because of a special issue in April 1941 in honor of Alexander Hurh, who died of an illness in January 1941. Hurh had served as the Korean secretary.

3. The bulletin had a broad geographical focus, since students went to school throughout the United States, but California and Hawai'i still proved to be centers of activity, as reflected in many of the writings discussed in this chapter.

4. "The Bulletin Is," *KSB*, December 1922.

5. "Committee on Friendly Relations Among Foreign Students," *KSB*, December 1922.

6. C. Howard Hopkins, *History of the Y.M.C.A. in North America* (New York: Association Press, 1951), 629–30.

7. Michael Parker, *The Kingdom of Character: The Student Volunteer Movement for Foreign Missions, 1886–1926* (Lanham, MD: University Press of America, 1998).

8. H. M. Goodpasture, "Student Volunteer Movement for Foreign Missions," in Daniel G. Reid et al., eds., *Dictionary of Christianity in America* (Downers Grove, IL: InterVarsity Press, 1990), 1143.

9. "My Impressions of the Ninth Quadrennial International Student Volunteer Convention in Indianapolis," *KSB*, February 1924.

10. Regional groups formed, affiliated with the national work of the committee, like the Korean Christian Students Association of Los Angeles.

11. *KSB*, October 1925; March–April 1939.

12. Warren Y. Kim, *Koreans in America* (Seoul: Po Chin Chai, 1971), 22–23.

13. For information on the other Asian groups, see Timothy Tseng, "Religious Liberalism, International Politics, and Diasporic Realities: The Chinese Students Christian Association of North America, 1909–1951," *Journal of America–East Asian Relations* 5, nos. 3–4 (Fall–Winter 1996), 305–30; David K. Yoo, *Growing Up Nisei: Race, Generation, and Culture Among Japanese Americans of California, 1924–1949* (Urbana: University of Illinois Press, 2000), 59–63; and Emily Porcincula Lawsin, "Pensionados, Paisanos, and Pinoys: An Analysis of the Filipino Student Bulletin, 1929–1933," *Filipino American National Historical Society Journal* 4 (1996): 33–33P.

14. Hopkins, *History of the Y.M.C.A.*, 6, 594–604. The stories of the intensive and massive fund-raising campaigns in various cities in the United States (and in other locales) suggest the capitalist storehouse that funded the YMCA and other American Protestant ventures at home and abroad.

15. For a helpful study of American Protestant missions, see William R. Hutchison, *Errand to the World: American Protestant Thought and Foreign Missions* (Chicago: University of Chicago Press, 1987).

16. Mark A. Noll, *A History of Christianity in the United States and Canada* (Grand Rapids, MI: W. B. Eerdmans, 1992), 304–7.

17. Mott as quoted in Hopkins, *History of the Y.M.C.A.*, 657. The social gospel in the United States is far more complex than the couple of sentences devoted to the movement here. There is a considerable body of work that has been identified

with the movement, as well as studies about the movement. Among the secondary literature, see C. Howard Hopkins, *The Rise of the Social Gospel in American Protestantism, 1865–1915* (New Haven, CT: Yale University Press, 1940); Ronald C. White and C. Howard Hopkins, *The Social Gospel: Religion and Reform in Changing America* (Philadelphia: Temple University Press, 1976); and Christopher H. Evans, ed., *The Social Gospel Today* (Louisville, KY: Westminster John Knox Press, 2001).

18. Jun Xing, *Baptized in the Fire of Revolution: The American Social Gospel and the YMCA in China, 1919–1937* (Bethlehem, PA: Lehigh University Press, 1996). This work provides a good case study of how the YMCA's student movement's embrace of the social gospel played out in China during a volatile era.

19. "Foreign Students in U.S.A.," *KSB*, May–June 1937.

20. C. C. Hahn, "The Good and Bad Elements of American Civilization," *KSB*, January 1926.

21. "My Impressions of the Ninth Quadrennial International Student Volunteer Convention in Indianapolis," *KSB*, February 1924.

22. Philip Jaisohn, "Institute of Pacific Relations," *KSB,* October 1925.

23. Attributed to Alfred the Great (c. 849–99), quoted in *KSB,* January 1926.

24. "The Christian Challenge," *KSB*, February 1923.

25. "Faith in a Personal God," *KSB*, April 1923.

26. "Dr. Jaisohn's Letter to the Convention," *KSB*, September 1924.

27. Angel Island serves as a prominent marker in the Asian American history of exclusion and racism and the role of the nation-state. Many studies examine the history of Asian Americans (especially Chinese Americans) and Angel Island, including Sucheng Chan, *Asian Americans: An Interpretive History* (Boston: Twayne, 1991); Ronald Takaki, *Strangers from a Different Shore: A History of Asian Americans* (Boston: Little, Brown, 1989); Him Mark Lai, Genny Lim, and Judy Yung, *Island: Poetry and History of Chinese Immigrants on Angel Island, 1910–1940* (Seattle: University of Washington Press, 1999); Erika Lee, *At America's Gates: Chinese Immigration During the Exclusion Era* (Chapel Hill: University of North Carolina Press, 2003); and Laurence Yep and Kathy S. Yep, *The Dragon's Child: A Story of Angel Island* (New York: HarperCollins, 2008).

28. "On Entering the U.S.: A Letter from a Korean Student to His Father," *KSB*, November–December 1938. Sang Ryup Park later worked in Los Angeles on the leftist newspaper linked to the Korean National Revolutionary Party, *Korean Independence*. See Chapter 5 for more on this subject.

29. "Number of Foreign Students Admitted to U.S.," *KSB*, October 1925.

30. "Korean Students in America," *KSB*, March–April 1939; "Foreign Students in USA," *KSB*, May–June 1937.

31. Lawsin, "Pensionados, Paisanos, and Pinoys," 33D–E.

32. On religion and migration in the Filipino American experience, see Steffi San Buenaventura, "Filipino Folk Spirituality and Immigration: From Mutual Aid to Religion," in David K. Yoo, ed., *New Spiritual Homes: Religion and Asian Americans* (Honolulu: University of Hawai'i Press, 1999), 52–86.

33. "Dr. Paik Returns to Korea to Teach," *KSB,* November 1927.

34. There are many fine studies of second generation Americans, including Deborah Dash Moore, *At Home in America: Second Generation New York Jews* (New York: Columbia University Press, 1981); Jere Takahashi, *Nisei/Sansei: Shifting Japanese American Identities and Politics* (Philadelphia: Temple University Press, 1997); and Marjorie Lee, "*Hu-Jee*: The Forgotten Second Generation of Chinese America, 1930–1950," (Master's thesis, University of California, Los Angeles, 1984). For a general overview of U.S. immigration history, see Thomas Archdeacon, *Becoming American: An Ethnic History* (New York: Free Press, 1983); and Roger Daniels, *Coming to America: A History of Immigration and Ethnicity in American Life* (New York: Harper Perennial, 2002).

35. Joe R. Feagin, *Systemic Racism: A Theory of Oppression* (New York: Routledge, 2006).

36. "The Secretary's Trip to the Pacific Coast," *KSB,* October 1929.

37. "Confessions of an American-Born Korean," *KSB*, May 1930.

38. "Our Second Generation Is a Problem," *KSB,* May 1930.

39. "Problems of the Second Generation in Los Angeles," *KSB*, May 1930.

40. "Whither American-Born Korean," *KSB*, March–April 1935.

41. "The Sanction of the Christian Worker," *KSB*, March–April 1940.

42. Ibid.

43. The Nobel Laureate's poem appeared in the October 1929 issue of the *KSB* in what appeared to be a copy of a handwritten message from Tagore, dated 28 March 1929.

44. The identification of God and nation is a tradition firmly grounded in the American experience extending from colonial times to the period under discussion, including the Protestant missionary enterprise. Helpful texts on this theme include Ernest L. Tuveson, *Redeemer Nation: The Idea of America's Millennial Role* (Chicago: University of Chicago Press, 1968); and Robert T. Handy, *A Christian America: Protestant Hopes and Historical Realities* (New York: Oxford University Press, 1971).

45. "Evanston Conference," *KSB,* March 1926.

46. "Meeting the Supreme Test," *KSB*, March 1931.

47. "Christianity and World Peace," *KSB*, December 1931.

48. "Mass Education, Improvement of Agriculture, Spiritual Leadership," *KSB*, March 1931.

49. "Love, Faithful Leadership and Economic Justice," *KSB*, March 1931. See

Kenneth M. Wells, *New God, New Nation: Protestants and Self-Reconstruction Nationalism in Korea, 1896–1937* (Honolulu: University of Hawai'i Press, 1990).

50. "Spirit and Matter Must Go Together," *KSB*, March 1931.

51. Biblical Seminary is today New York Theological Seminary. The school was founded in 1900 as a nondenominational Protestant institution. For more information, see www.nyts.edu.

52. "Initiative but Cooperative Leadership," *KSB*, March 1931.

53. This intentionally brief discussion of important leaders is meant only to offer a quick composite sketch of those who appeared in the pages of the *KSB* and to provide a few additional details by way of context. Many of these individuals are discussed in previous chapters. Other key leaders, especially those who did not have a connection with the United States and Protestant Christianity, did not get much press. Information about the leaders who appear in the *KSB* (and these others) is available in the literature of Korean and Korean American studies. Some helpful texts include Chong-Sik Lee, *The Politics of Korean Nationalism* (Berkeley: University of California, Berkeley, 1963); Bruce Cumings, *Korea's Place in the Sun: A Modern History* (New York: W. W. Norton, 1997); Ki-baik Lee, *A New History of Korea,* trans. Edward W. Wagner with Edward J. Shultz (Cambridge, MA: Harvard University Press, 1984); Bong-Youn Choy, *Koreans in America* (Chicago: Nelson-Hall, 1977); and Kim, *Koreans in America.*

54. "News Items from Hawai'i," *KSB*, December 1928.

55. Choy, *Koreans in America,* 85–87.

56. "An Appreciation of Miss Helen Kim," *KSB*, December 1928.

57. "New Ewha Head," *KSB*, May–June 1939.

58. "Chang Ho Ahn Dies at 61; Champion of Korea's Freedom," *KSB*, February–March 1938; "My Impression of Ahn Chang-Ho," *KSB*, April–May 1938.

59. "My Impression of Ahn Chang-Ho," *KSB*, April–May 1938.

60. Choy, *Koreans in America,* 80–83.

61. Kiusic Kim as well as Kiusic Kimm were anglicized spellings of Kim Kyu-sik, and the spelling here is what appeared in the bulletin.

62. "Dr. Kiusic Kim in America," *KSB*, May–June 1935.

63. Key S. Ryang, "Kim Kyu-Sik as a Common Man and a Political Leader," *Korea Observer* 13, no. 1 (Spring 1982): 36–54.

64. Lee, *A New History of Korea,* 363–64.

65. "In Defense of Justice: A Prayer," *KSB*, February 1930.

66. While most records indicate that the last regular issue of the *KSB* appeared in March–April 1940, the tribute to Hurh was published as a special issue in April 1941.

67. *KSB*, April 1941. In the November–December 1934 issue of the *KSB* an-

nouncing his appointment, Hurh was identified as a Ph.D. candidate in history at Columbia University.

68. Ellen Lee, *The Planted Seed: History of the English Language Ministry of the Korean Methodist Church and Institute* (New York: Korean Methodist Church and Institute, 1995), 13–17; Kim, *Koreans in America,* 36–37; Choy, *Koreans in America,* 256.

69. *KSB,* April 1941.

70. Based upon the information in the special issue of the *KSB,* Hurh, by my calculation, was born in 1903, came to the United States at the age of twenty-one in 1924, and died in 1941 at the age of thirty-eight.

71. *New Korea,* 9 January 1941. The article listed Hurh as thirty-six years old.

72. Earlier chapters provide more details regarding the wartime years in Hawai'i and California in regard to religion and Korean American history. For a fuller treatment of Korean Americans and World War II, see Lili M. Kim, "The Pursuit of Imperfect Justice: The Predicament of Koreans and Korean Americans on the Homefront During World War II" (Ph.D. diss., University of Rochester, 2001).

73. Kim, *Koreans in America,* 146–48. Much has been written about these events, and these comments touch briefly upon the end of the war and its influence on Koreans in the United States and to the extent possible, the role of religion.

74. Choy, *Koreans in America,* 180–81.

75. Margaret K. Pai, *The Dreams of Two Yi-Min* (Honolulu: University of Hawai'i Press, 1989), 144–45.

76. Yŏng-ho Ch'oe, "A Brief History of the Christ United Methodist Church," in *Christ United Methodist Church, 1903–2003: A Pictorial History* (Seoul: Qumran, 2003), 44–45.

77. In my conversations and interviews with children of these first immigrants as part of the research for this book, I was struck by how Rhee's actions deeply hurt these men and women who had given so much for the cause of independence. Moreover, the children continued to carry those sentiments long after their parents had died.

## *Epilogue*

1. For an overview, see David K. Yoo and Ruth H. Chung, eds., *Religion and Spirituality in Korean America* (Urbana: University of Illinois Press, 2008).

2. Characterizations of Korean and Korean American Christianity run the risk of oversimplifying complex developments, and thus the statement of a conservative turn within contemporary Korean American churches must take such concerns into account. Chung-Shin Park, *Protestantism and Politics in Korea* (Seattle: University

of Washington Press, 2003) provides a framework for understanding the relationship between religion and politics in Korea over the course of the twentieth century. Park notes that much of Korean Christianity since World War II has been conformist in nature, as Christians increasingly became part of the ruling establishment. These developments have had an influence upon how Korean American Christianity has taken shape in the United States. Progressive elements within Korean and Korean American Protestant Christianity have been a distinct minority.

3. Scholars studying Korean Americans more generally have commented on the place of churches within the more recent experience of this community: Won Moo Hurh, *The Korean Americans* (Westport, CT: Greenwood Press, 1998); Pyong Gap Min, *Caught in the Middle: Korean Merchants in America's Multiethnic Cities* (Berkeley: University of California Press, 1996); Kyeyoung Park, *The Korean American Dream: Immigrants and Small Business in New York City* (Ithaca, NY: Cornell University Press, 1997); and In-Jin Yoon, *On My Own: Korean Businesses and Race Relations in America* (Chicago: University of Chicago Press, 1997).

4. In focusing on the post-1965 period and more contemporary issues in the epilogue, I have not dealt with the era from 1945 to 1965, in which the power and presence of United States in its relationship with South Korea had direct ties to the military wives, adoptees, and international students who came to the United States. See Ji-Yeon Yuh, *Beyond the Shadow of Camptown: Korean Military Brides in America* (New York: New York University Press, 2002); Jae Ran Kim, "Waiting for God: Religion and Korean American Adoption," in David K. Yoo and Ruth H. Chung, eds., *Religion and Spirituality in Korean America* (Urbana: University of Illinois Press, 2008), 83–99; and Jane Jeong Trenka et al., eds., *Outsiders Within: Writing on Transnational Adoption* (Cambridge, MA: South End Press, 2006); Hurh, *Korean Americans*.

5. Sucheng Chan, *Asian Americans: An Interpretive History* (Boston: Twayne, 1991), 145–65.

6. Among the works more generally on post-1965 immigration and religion, see R. Stephen Warner and Judith G. Wittner, eds., *Gatherings in Diaspora: Religious Communities and the New Immigration* (Philadelphia: Temple University Press, 1998); and Helen Rose Ebaugh and Janet Saltzman Chafetz, *Religion and the New Immigrants*, abridged student edition (Walnut Creek, CA: Altamira Press, 2000). A number of anthologies examine religion within Asian American communities, including David K. Yoo, ed., *New Spiritual Homes: Religion and Asian Americans* (Honolulu: University of Hawai'i Press, 1999); Pyong Gap Min and Jung Ha Kim, eds., *Religions in Asian America: Building Faith Communities* (Walnut Creek, CA: Altamira Press, 2002); Jane N. Iwamura and Paul Spickard, eds., *Revealing the Sacred in Asian and Pacific America* (New York: Routledge, 2003); and Tony Carnes

and Fenggang Yang, eds., *Asian American Religions: The Making and Remaking of Borders and Boundaries* (New York: New York University Press, 2004). This listing does not do justice to the many fine studies that focus on a particular group or theme.

7.  Diana L. Eck, *A New Religious America: How a "Christian Country" Has Become the World's Most Religiously Diverse Nation* (New York: Harper San Francisco, 2001).

8.  Pei-te Lien and Tony Carnes, "The Religious Demography of Asian American Boundary Crossing," in Tony Carnes and Fenggang Yang, eds., *Asian American Religions: The Making and Remaking of Borders and Boundaries* (New York: New York University Press, 2004), 40. A small sampling of works on Asian American Christianity: Fumitaka Matsuoka, *Out of Silence: Emerging Themes in Asian American Churches* (Cleveland: United Church Press, 1995); Peter C. Phan, *Christianity with an Asian Face: Asian American Theology in the Making* (Maryknoll, NY: Orbis Press, 2003); Fumitaka Matsuoka and Eleazar S. Fernandez, eds., *Realizing the America of Our Hearts: Theological Voices of Asian Americans* (St. Louis: Chalice Press, 2003); Mary F. Foskett and Jeffrey Kah-Jin Kuan, eds., *Ways of Being, Ways of Reading: Asian American Biblical Interpretation* (St. Louis: Chalice Press, 2006); Tat-Siong Benny Liew, *What Is Asian American Biblical Hermeneutics? Reading the New Testament* (Honolulu: University of Hawai'i Press, 2008).

9.  Mark R. Mullins and Richard Fox Young, eds., *Perspectives on Christianity in Korea and Japan: The Gospel and Culture in East Asia* (Lewiston, NY: Edwin Mellen, 1995), xxii; Mark A. Noll, *The New Shape of World Christianity: How American Experience Reflects Global Faith* (Downers Grove, IL: IVP Academic, 2009); Lamin Sanneh, *Disciples of All Nations: Pillars of World Christianity* (New York: Oxford University Press, 2007).

10.  Peter L. Berger, ed., *The Desecularization of the World: Resurgent Religion and World Politics* (Grand Rapids, MI: William B. Eerdmans, 1992), 3–18; William R. Hutchison, *Between the Times: The Travail of the Protestant Establishment in America, 1900–1960* (Cambridge: Cambridge University Press, 1989); Robert Wuthnow, *The Restructuring of American Religion: Society and Faith Since World War II* (Princeton, NJ: Princeton University Press, 1988); Wade Clark Roof and William McKinney, *American Mainline Religion: Its Changing Shape and Future* (New Brunswick, NJ: Rutgers University Press, 1987). For a general history, see Mark A. Noll, *A History of Christianity in the United States and Canada* (Grand Rapids, MI: William B. Eerdmans, 1992).

11.  Berger, *Desecularization of the World,* 18.

# Bibliography

*Archives, Collections, and Private Papers*

Bessie Park Papers, Honolulu
Center for Korean Studies, University of Hawai'i, Manoa
Christ United Methodist Church Archives, Honolulu
Claremont School of Theology Library Archives, Claremont, CA
Graduate Theological Union Library Archives, Berkeley, CA
Korean American Digital Archive, University of Southern California, Los Angeles
Korean Christian Church Files, Honolulu
Hamilton Library, Special Collections, University of Hawai'i, Manoa
Hawai'i-Pacific Collection, University of Hawai'i, Manoa
Hawai'i State Library, Honolulu
Hoover Institution Archives, Stanford University, Stanford, CA
Korean Christian Church Files, Honolulu
Los Angeles Korean United Methodist Church Files, Los Angeles
Presbyterian Historical Society, Philadelphia, PA
Romanzo Adams Social Research Laboratory (RASRL) Collection, University of Hawai'i, Manoa
Saint Luke's Episcopal Church Files, Honolulu
Special Collections, University of California, Santa Cruz

*Denominational and Church Records*

*Fifty Years of St. Luke's Church, Honolulu, Hawai'i,* October 1957.
*Journal and Proceedings of the California Oriental Mission of the Methodist Church*

*Journal of the Hawaiian Mission of the Methodist Episcopal Church*
*Official Journal of the Pacific Japanese Mission of the Methodist Episcopal Church*
*Official Minutes of the Korea Mission, Methodist Episcopal Church*
*Seventieth Anniversary of the Korean United Presbyterian Church of Los Angeles*
*The Yearbook of the Methodist Episcopal Church South*


## Interviews

Ralph Ahn, Howard Choy, Nellie Choy, and Luther Hahn, 10 June 2003, Los Angeles
Lila Chang (phone), 14 July 2003, Los Angeles
Helen Chung, 4 April 2000, Honolulu
Stella Haan, 4 October 1999, Santa Cruz, CA
Steven Jhu, 4 April 2000, Honolulu
Michael Kim, 31 May 2004, Honolulu
T. Samuel Lee, 12 August 1999; 31 May 2004, Honolulu
Warren Lee, 7 October 2004, San Anselmo, CA.
Bessie Park, 7 April 2000, Honolulu
Elaine Woo, 3 June 2004, Honolulu


## Newspapers and Periodicals

*The American-Korean* (Honolulu, HI)
*Facts for Features* (Washington, DC)
*Harvester* (Los Angeles, CA)
*Honolulu Star-Bulletin*
*Horizon* (Los Angeles, CA)
*Inland Valley Daily Bulletin* (Ontario, CA)
*KoreAm Journal* (Los Angeles, CA)
*Korean Independence* (Los Angeles, CA)
*Korean Student Bulletin* (Chicago, IL and New York)
*Korea Observer* (Seoul, Korea)
*Korea Repository* (Seoul, Korea)
*Korea Review* (Philadelphia, PA)
*Los Angeles Times*
*New Korea (Shinhan Minbo)* (San Francisco, CA and Los Angeles, CA)
*Pacific Korean Weekly* (Honolulu, HI)
*Pacific Methodist Advocate* (San Francisco, CA)
*San Francisco Chronicle*
*Voice of Korea* (Washington, DC)

*Other Sources*

Albanese, Catherine. *America, Religions, and Religion.* Belmont, CA: Wadsworth, 1999.

Alhstrom, Sydney E. *A Religious History of the American Peoples.* New Haven, CT: Yale University Press, 1972.

Allen, Richard C. *Korea's Syngman Rhee: An Unauthorized Portrait.* Rutland, VT: C. E. Tuttle, 1960.

Almaguer, Tomas. *Racial Fault Lines: The Historical Origins of White Supremacy in California.* Berkeley: University of California Press, 1994.

Ammerman, Nancy Tatum. *Congregation and Community.* New Brunswick, NJ: Rutgers University Press, 1996.

An, Choi Hee. *Korean Women and God: Experiencing God in a Multi-religious Colonial Context.* Maryknoll, NY: Orbis Press, 2005.

Archdeacon, Thomas. *Becoming American: An Ethnic History.* New York: Free Press, 1983.

Baker, Don. "Christianity Koreanized." In *Nationalism and the Construction of Korean Identity*, edited by Hyung Il Pai and Timothy R. Tangherlini, 108–25. Berkeley: Institute of East Asian Studies, University of California, 1998.

———. Introduction to *Religions of Korea in Practice,* edited by Robert E. Buswell Jr., 1–31. Princeton, NJ: Princeton University Press, 2007.

Barlow, Tani E., ed. *Formations of Colonial Modernity in East Asia.* Durham, NC: Duke University Press, 1997.

Beechert, Edward D. *Working in Hawai'i: A Labor History.* Honolulu: University of Hawai'i Press, 1985.

Bellah, Robert N., Richard Madsen, William Sullivan, Ann Swidler, and Steven Tipton. *Habits of the Heart: Individualism and Commitment in American Life.* New York: Harper & Row, 1985.

Bender, Thomas. *A Nation Among Nations: America's Place in World History.* New York: Hill & Wang, 2006.

———, ed. *Rethinking American History in a Global Age.* Berkeley: University of California Press, 2002.

Bennett Peterson, Barbara, "Dora Kim Moon." In Barbara Bennett Peterson, ed., *Notable Women of Hawai'i,* 271–72. Honolulu: University of Hawai'i Press, 1984.

Berger, Peter L., ed. *The Desecularization of the World: Resurgent Religion and World Politics.* Grand Rapids, MI: William B. Eerdmans, 1992.

Blauner, Robert. *Racial Oppression in America.* New York: Harper & Row, 1972.

Bonacich, Edna, and Lucie Cheng. "Introduction: A Theoretical Orientation to International Labor Migration." In *Labor Immigration Under Capitalism: Asian Workers in the United States Before World War II,* edited by Lucie Cheng and Edna Bonacich, 1–56. Berkeley: University of California Press, 1984.

Buck, Elizabeth. *Paradise Remade: The Politics of Culture and History in Hawai'i.* Philadelphia: Temple University Press, 1993.

Buenaventura, Steffi San. "Filipino Folk Spirituality and Immigration: From Mutual Aid to Religion." In *New Spiritual Homes: Religion and Asian Americans,* edited by David K. Yoo, 52–86. Honolulu: University of Hawai'i Press, 1999.

Buff, Rachel Ida. "Transnational Visions: Reinventing Immigration Studies." *American Quarterly* 57 (2005): 1263–72.

Busk, Elizabeth. *Paradise Remade: The Politics of Culture and History in Hawai'i.* Philadelphia: Temple University Press, 1993.

Buswell, Robert E., Jr., and Timothy S. Lee, eds. *Christianity in Korea.* Honolulu: University of Hawai'i Press, 2006.

Campomanes, Oscar. "New Formations of Asian American Studies and the Question of U.S. Imperialism." *Positions* 5, no. 2 (1997): 523–50.

Carnes, Tony, and Fenggang Yang, eds. *Asian American Religions: The Making and Remaking of Borders and Boundaries.* New York: New York University Press, 2004.

Cha, John. *Willow Tree Shade: The Susan Ahn Cuddy Story.* Los Angeles[?]: Korean American Heritage Foundation, 2002.

Chai, Alice. "Korean Women in Hawaii, 1903–1945." In *Women in New Worlds: Historical Perspectives on the Wesleyan Tradition,* edited by Hilah F. Thomas and Rosemary Skinner Keller, 328–44, 425–27. Nashville, TN: Abingdon Press, 1981.

Chan, Sucheng. *Asian Americans: An Interpretive History.* Boston: Twayne, 1991.

Cherry, Conrad, ed. *God's New Israel: Religious Interpretations of American Destiny,* rev. ed. Chapel Hill: University of North Carolina Press, 1998.

Ch'oe, Yŏng-ho. "A Brief History of the Christ United Methodist Church, 1903–2003." In *Christ United Methodist Church, 1903–2003: A Pictorial History.* Honolulu: Christ United Methodist Church, 2003.

———. "The Early Korean Immigration: An Overview." In *From the Land of Hibiscus: Koreans in Hawai'i,* edited by Yŏng-ho Ch'oe, 11–40. Honolulu: University of Hawai'i Press, 2007.

———. "History of Korean Church: A Case Study of Christ United Methodist Church, 1903–2003." In *Korean Americans: Past, Present, and Future,* edited by Ilpyong J. Kim, 38–62. Elizabeth, NJ: Hollym, 2004.

———. "Syngman Rhee in Hawai'i: His Activities in the Early Years, 1913–1915."

In *From the Land of Hibiscus: Koreans in Hawai'i,* edited by Yŏng-ho Ch'oe, 53–88. Honolulu: University of Hawai'i Press, 2007.

Choi, Anne Soon. "Unity for What? Unity for Whom? The United Korean Committee of North America, 1941–1945." In *From the Land of Hibiscus: Koreans in Hawai'i,* edited by Yŏng-ho Ch'oe, 220–55. Honolulu: University of Hawai'i Press, 2007.

Choy, Bong-Youn. *Koreans in America.* Chicago: Nelson-Hall, 1979.

Chung, David. *Syncretism: The Religious Context of Christian Beginnings in Korea.* Albany: State University of New York Press, 2001.

Chung, Henry. *Korea and the United States Through War and Peace, 1943–1960.* Seoul: Yonsei University Press, 2000.

Clark, Allen D. *A History of the Church in Korea.* Seoul: Christian Literature Society of Korea, 1971.

Clark, Donald N. *Christianity in Modern Korea.* Lanham, MD: University Press of America, 1986.

———. "History and Religion in Modern Korea: The Case of Protestant Christianity." In *Religion and Society in Contemporary Korea*, edited by Lewis R. Lancaster and Richard K. Payne, 169–213. Berkeley: Institute for Asian Studies, University of California, 1997.

———. "Mothers, Daughters, Biblewomen, and Sisters: An Account of 'Women's Work' in the Korea Mission Field." In *Christianity in Korea*, edited by Robert E. Buswell Jr. and Timothy S. Lee, 167–92. Honolulu: University of Hawai'i Press, 2006.

Cumings, Bruce. *Korea's Place in the Sun: A Modern History.* New York: W. W. Norton, 1997.

Cynn, Hugh Heung-wo. *The Rebirth of Korea: The Reawakening of the People, Its Causes, and the Outlook.* New York: Abingdon Press, 1920.

Daniels, Roger. *Coming to America: A History of Immigration and Ethnicity in American Life.* New York: Harper Perennial, 2002.

Daws, Gavan. *Shoal of Time: A History of the Hawaiian Islands.* New York: Macmillan, 1968.

De Genova, Nicholas. "Introduction: Latino and Asian Racial Formations at the Frontiers of U.S. Nationalism." In *Racial Transformations: Latinos and Asians Remaking the United States,* edited by Nicholas De Genova, 1–20. Durham, NC: Duke University Press, 2006.

DeWitt, Howard. *The Fragmented Dream: Multicultural California.* Dubuque, IA: Kendall/Hunt, 1996.

DeYoung, Curtiss Paul, Michael O. Emerson, George Yancey, and Karen Chai

Kim. *United by Faith: The Multiracial Congregation as an Answer to the Problem of Race*. New York: Oxford University Press, 2003.

Diner, Hasia R. "History and the Study of Immigration: Narratives of the Particular." In *Migration Theory: Talking Across Disciplines*, edited by Caroline B. Brettell and James F. Hollified, 31–49. New York: Routledge, 2008.

Duus, Peter. *The Abacus and the Sword. The Japanese Penetration of Korea, 1895–1910*. Berkeley: University of California Press, 1995.

Ebaugh, Helen Rose, and Janet Saltzman Chafetz. *Religion and the New Immigrants*, abridged student edition. Walnut Creek, CA: Altamira Press, 2000.

Eck, Diana L. *A New Religious America: How a "Christian Country" Has Become the World's Most Religiously Diverse Nation*. New York: Harper San Francisco, 2001.

Ecklund, Elaine Howard. *Korean American Evangelicals: New Models of Civic Life*. New York: Oxford University Press, 2006.

Emerson, Michael O., and Christian Smith. *Divided by Faith: Evangelical Religion and the Problem of Race in America*. New York: Oxford University Press, 2000.

Engh, Michael E. *Frontier Faiths: Church, Temple, and Synagogue in Los Angeles, 1846–1888*. Albuquerque: University of New Mexico Press, 1992.

Ernst, Eldon G. "The Emergence of California in American Religious Historiography." *Religion and American Culture* 11, no. 1 (2001): 31–52.

Espiritu, Yen Le. *Home Bound: Filipino American Lives Across Cultures, Communities, and Countries*. Berkeley: University of California Press, 2003.

Evans, Christopher H., ed. *The Social Gospel Today*. Louisville, KY: Westminster John Knox Press, 2001.

Feagin, Joe R. *Racist America: Roots, Current Realities, and Future Reparations*. New York: Routledge, 2001.

———. *Systemic Racism: A Theory of Oppression*. New York: Routledge, 2006.

Foner, Nancy. "What's New About Transnationalism? New York Immigrants Today and at the Turn of the Century." *Diaspora* 6 (1997): 355–75.

Foner, Nancy, Ruben G. Rumbaut, and Steven J. Gold, eds. *Immigration Research for a New Century: Multidisciplinary Perspectives*. New York: Russell Sage Foundation, 2000.

Foskett, Mary F., and Jeffrey Kah-Jin Kuan, eds. *Ways of Being, Ways of Reading: Asian American Biblical Interpretation*. St. Louis: Chalice Press, 2006.

Frankiel, Sandra Sizer. *California's Spiritual Frontiers: Religious Alternatives in Anglo-Protestantism, 1850–1910*. Berkeley: University of California Press, 1988.

Fulop, Timothy E., and Albert J. Raboteau, eds. *African American Religions: Interpretive Essays in History and Culture*. New York: Routledge, 1996.

Garces-Foley, Kathleen. *Crossing the Ethnic Divide: The Multiethnic Church on a Mission*. New York: Oxford University Press, 2005.

Gerstle, Gary. *American Crucible: Race and Nation in the Twentieth Century.* Princeton, NJ: Princeton University Press, 2001.

Givens, Helen Lewis. "The Korean Community in Los Angeles County." Master's thesis, University of Southern California, 1939.

Gjerde, Jon, ed. *Major Problems in American Immigration and Ethnic History*. Boston: Houghton Mifflin, 1998.

Goldschmidt, Henry. "Introduction: Race, Nation, and Religion." In *Race, Nation, and Religion in the Americas*, edited by Henry Goldschmidt and Elizabeth McAlister, 3–31. New York: Oxford University Press, 2004.

Goldschmidt, Henry and Elizabeth McAlister, eds. *Race, Nation, and Religion in the Americas*. New York: Oxford University Press, 2004.

Goodpasture, H. M. "Student Volunteer Movement for Foreign Missions." In *Dictionary of Christianity in America*, edited by Daniel G. Reid, Robert D. Linder, Bruce L Shelley, and Harry S. Stout, 1143. Downers Grove, IL: InterVarsity Press, 1990.

Grayson, James Huntley. *Korea: A Religious History*. London: Routledge Curzon, 2002.

Hall, David D., ed. *Lived Religion in America*. Princeton, NJ: Princeton University Press, 1997.

Handy, Robert T. *A Christian America: Protestant Hopes and Historical Realities*. New York: Oxford University Press, 1971.

———. *We Witness Together: A History of Cooperative Home Missions*. New York: Friendship Press, 1956.

Harrington, Fred Harvey. *God, Mammon, and the Japanese: Dr. Horace Allen and Korean-American Relations, 1884–1905*. Madison: University of Wisconsin Press, 1944.

Hertig, Young Lee. *Cultural Tug of War: The Korean Immigrant Family and Church in Transition*. Nashville: Abingdon Press, 2001.

Hing, Bill Ong. *Making and Remaking Asian America Through Immigration Policy, 1850–1990*. Stanford, CA: Stanford University Press, 1993.

Hirschman, Charles, Philip Kasinitz, and Josh DeWind, eds. *The Handbook of International Migration: The American Experience*. New York: Russell Sage Foundation, 1999.

Hopkins, C. Howard. *History of the Y.M.C.A. in North America*. New York: Association Press, 1951.

———. *The Rise of the Social Gospel in American Protestantism, 1865–1915*. New Haven, CT: Yale University Press, 1940.

Howe, C. Fletcher. *The First Fifty Years of St. Elizabeth's Church, Honolulu, Hawai'i.* Honolulu: Advertiser Publishing, 1952.

Huntley, Martha. *Caring, Growing, Changing: A History of the Protestant Mission in Korea.* New York: Friendship Press, 1984.

Hurh, Won Moo. *The Korean Americans.* Westport, CT: Greenwood Press, 1998.

Hutchison, William R. *Between the Times: The Travail of the Protestant Establishment in America, 1900–1960.* Cambridge: Cambridge University Press, 1989.

———. *Errand to the World: American Protestant Thought and Foreign Missions.* Chicago: University of Chicago Press, 1987.

Hyun, Peter. *In the New World: The Making of a Korean American.* Honolulu: University of Hawai'i Press, 1991.

———. *Man Sei! The Making of a Korean American.* Honolulu: University of Hawai'i Press, 1986.

Hyun, Soon. "My Autobiography." Unpublished manuscript. Center for Korean Studies, University of Hawai'i Manoa, n.d.

Iwamura, Jane N., and Paul Spickard, eds. *Revealing the Sacred in Asian Pacific America.* New York: Routledge, 2003.

Jacobsen, Matthew Frye. "More 'Trans—,' Less 'National.'" *Journal of American Ethnic History* 2, no. 4 (2006): 74–84.

Kang, Wi Jo. *Christ and Caesar in Modern Korea: A History of Christianity and Politics.* Albany: State University of New York Press, 1997.

Kaplan, Amy, and Donald E. Pease, eds. *Cultures of United States Imperialism.* Durham, NC: Duke University Press, 1993.

Kim, Ai Ra. *Women Struggling for a New Life: The Role of Religion in the Cultural Passage from Korea to America.* Albany: State University of New York Press, 1996.

Kim, Bernice B. H. "The Koreans in Hawai'i." Master's thesis, University of Hawai'i, 1937.

Kim, Do-Hyung, and Yŏng-ho Ch'oe. "The March First Movement of 1919 and Koreans in Hawai'i." In *From the Land of Hibiscus: Koreans in Hawai'i,* edited by Yŏng- ho Ch'oe, 123–52. Honolulu: University of Hawai'i Press, 2007.

Kim, Duk-Whang. *A History of Religions in Korea.* Seoul: Daeji Moonhwa-sa, 1988.

Kim, Elaine H., and Chungmoo Choi, eds. *Dangerous Women: Gender and Korean Nationalism.* New York: Routledge, 1998.

Kim, Eleana. "Wedding Citizenship and Culture: Korean Adoptees and the Global Family of Korea." In *Cultures of Transnational Adoption,* edited by Toby Alice Volkman, 49–80. Durham, NC: Duke University Press, 2005.

Kim, Jae Ran. "Waiting for God: Religion and Korean American Adoption." In *Religion and Spirituality in Korean America,* edited by David K. Yoo and Ruth H. Chung, 83–99. Urbana: University of Illinois Press, 2008.

Kim, Jung Ha. *Bridge-makers and Cross-bearers: Korean-American Women and the Church*. Atlanta: Scholars Press, 1997.

Kim, Lili M. "How Koreans Repealed Their 'Enemy Alien' Status: Korean Americans' Identity, Culture, and National Pride in Wartime Hawai'i." In *From the Land of Hibiscus: Koreans in Hawai'i*, edited by Yŏng-ho Ch'oe, 195–219. Honolulu: University of Hawai'i Press, 2007.

———. "The Pursuit of Imperfect Justice: The Predicament of Koreans and Korean Americans on the Homefront During World War II." Ph.D. diss., University of Rochester, 2001.

Kim, Nadia Y. *Imperial Citizens: Koreans and Race from Seoul to LA*. Stanford, CA: Stanford University Press, 2008.

Kim, Rebecca Y. *God's Whiz Kids: Korean American Evangelicals on Campus*. New York: New York University Press, 2006.

Kim, Richard S. "Inaugurating the American Century: The 1919 Philadelphia Korean Congress, Korean Diasporic Nationalism, and American Protestant Missionaries." *Journal of American Ethnic History* 26, no. 1 (Fall 2006): 50–76.

———. "Korean Immigrant (Trans)Nationalism: Diaspora, Ethnicity, and State-Making, 1903–1945." Ph.D. diss., University of Michigan, 2002.

Kim, Warren Y. *Koreans in America*. Seoul: Po Chin Chai, 1971.

Kim, Woong-min. "History and Ministerial Roles of Korean Churches in the Los Angeles Area." D.Min. diss., Claremont School of Theology, Claremont, CA, 1981.

Kwon, Brenda L. *Beyond Ke'eamoku Street: Koreans, Nationalism, and Local Culture in Hawai'i*. New York: Garland, 1999.

Kwon, Ho-Youn, Kwang Chung Kim, and R. Stephen Warner, eds. *Korean Americans and Their Religions: Pilgrims and Missionaries from a Different Shore*. University Park: Pennsylvania State University Press, 2001.

Kwon, Okyun. *Buddhist and Protestant Korean Immigrants: Religious Beliefs and Socioeconomic Aspects of Life*. The New Americans. New York: LFB Scholarly Publishing, 2003.

Kwon, Victoria H. *Entrepreneurship and Religion: Korean Immigrants in Houston, Texas*. New York: Garland, 1997.

Lai, Him Mark, Genny Lim, and Judy Yung. *Island: Poetry and History of Chinese Immigrants on Angel Island, 1910–1940*. Seattle: University of Washington Press, 1999.

Lawsin, Emily Porcincula. "Pensionados, Paisanos, and Pinoys: An Analysis of the Filipino Student Bulletin, 1929–1933." *Filipino American National Historical Society Journal* 4 (1996): 33–33P.

Lee, Chong-sik. *The Politics of Korean Nationalism*. Berkeley: University of California Press, 1963.

————. *Syngman Rhee: The Prison Years of a Young Radical*. Seoul: Yonsei University Press, 2001.

Lee, Ellen. *The Planted Seed: History of the English Language Ministry of the Korean Methodist Church and Institute*. New York: Korean Methodist Church and Institute, 1995.

Lee, Erika. *At America's Gates. Chinese Immigration During the Exclusion Era, 1882–1943*. Chapel Hill: University of North Carolina Press, 2003.

Lee, Erika, and Naoko Shibusawa. "What Is Transnational Asian American History? Recent Trends and Challenges." *Journal of Asian American Studies* 8, no. 3 (2005): vii–xvii.

Lee, Ki-baik. *A New History of Korea*. Translated by Edward W. Wagner with Edward J. Shultz. Cambridge, MA: Harvard University Press, 1984.

Lee, Marjorie. "*Hu-Jee*: The Forgotten Second Generation of Chinese America, 1930–1950." Master's thesis, University of California, Los Angeles, 1984.

Lee, Mary Paik. *Quiet Odyssey: A Pioneer Woman in America*. Seattle: University of Washington Press, 1990.

Lee, Timothy S. "A Political Factor in the Rise of Protestantism in Korea: Protestantism and the 1919 March First Movement." *Church History* 69, no. 1 (2000): 116–42.

Leonard, Karen I. *The South Asian Americans*. Westport, CT: Greenwood Press, 1997.

Lien, Pei-te, and Tony Carnes. "The Religious Demography of Asian American Boundary Crossing." In *Asian American Religions: The Making and Remaking of Borders and Boundaries*, edited by Tony Carnes and Fenggang Yang, 38–51. New York: New York University Press, 2004.

Liew, Tat-Siong Benny. *What Is Asian American Biblical Hermeneutics? Reading the New Testament*. Honolulu: University of Hawai'i Press, 2008.

Link, Arthur S. *Wilson the Diplomatist: A Look at His Major Foreign Policies*. Baltimore: Johns Hopkins University Press, 1957.

Link, Arthur, David W. Hirst, John E. Little, and Fredrick Aandahl, eds. *The Papers of Woodrow Wilson*. Vol. 45, *November 11, 1917–January 15, 1918*. Princeton, NJ: Princeton University Press, 1984.

Lipsitz, George. *The Possessive Investment in Whiteness: How White People Profit from Identity Politics*. Philadelphia: Temple University Press, 1998.

Lyu, Kingsley K. "Korean Nationalist Activities in Hawai'i and the Continental United States, 1900–1945, Part I: 1900–1919." *Amerasia Journal* 4, no. 1 (1977): 23–90.

Maffly-Kipp, Laurie, Leigh E. Schmidt, and Mark Valeri, eds. *Practicing Protestants: Histories of Christian Life in America, 1630–1965*. Baltimore: Johns Hopkins University Press, 2006.

Martin, Jessie M. "Molly Hong Min." In *Notable Women of Hawaii,* edited by Barbara Bennett Peterson, 265–67. Honolulu: University of Hawaii Press, 1984.

Manela, Erez. *The Wilsonian Moment: Self-Determination and the International Origins of Anticolonial Nationalism.* New York: Oxford University Press, 2007.

Massey, Douglas S., Joaquin Arango, Graeme Hugo, Ali Kouaouci, Adela Pellegrino, and J. Edward Taylor. *Worlds in Motion: Understanding International Migration at the End of the Millennium.* Oxford: Oxford University Press, 1998.

Matsuoka, Fumitaka. *Out of Silence: Emerging Themes in Asian American Churches.* Cleveland: United Church Press, 1995.

Matsuoka, Fumitaka, and Eleazar S. Fernandez, eds. *Realizing the America of Our Hearts: Theological Voices of Asian Americans.* St. Louis: Chalice Press, 2003.

May, James W. "Methodism in the United States." In *The Encyclopedia of World Methodism,* edited by Nolan b. Harmon, 1563. Nashville: Methodist Publishing House, 1974.

Miller, Kerby. *Emigrants and Exiles: Ireland and the Irish Exodus to North America.* New York: Oxford University Press, 1985.

Min, Kyong-bae. "National Identity in the History of the Korean Church," translated by Yi Sun-ja. In *Korea and Christianity,* edited by Chai-shin Yu, 121–43. Fremont, CA: Asian Humanities Press, 2004.

Min, Pyong Gap. *Caught in the Middle: Korean Merchants in America's Multiethnic Cities.* Berkeley: University of California Press, 1996.

Min, Pyong Gap, and Jung Ha Kim, eds. *Religions in Asian America: Building Faith Communities.* Walnut Creek, CA: Altamira Press, 2002.

Moon, Hyung June. "The Korean Immigrants in America: The Quest for Identity in the Formative Years, 1903–1918." Ph.D. diss., University of Nevada, Reno, 1976.

Moore, Deborah Dash. *At Home in America: Second Generation New York Jews.* New York: Columbia University Press, 1981.

Mullins, Mark R., and Richard Fox Young, eds. *Perspectives on Christianity in Korea and Japan: The Gospel and Culture in East Asia.* Lewiston, NY: Edwin Mellen Press, 1995.

Murayama, Milton. *All I Asking for Is My Body.* Honolulu: University of Hawai'i Press, 1959.

Namba, Winifred Lee. "Nodie Kimhaikim Sohn." In *Notable Women of Hawai'i,* edited by Barbara Bennett Peterson, 356–57. Honolulu: University of Hawai'i Press, 1984.

*NAPKO Project of OSS.* Seoul: Ministry of Patriots and Veterans Affairs, 1992.

Ngai, Mae M. "Asian American History—Reflections on the De-centering of the Field." *Journal of American Ethnic History* 25, no. 4 (2006): 97–108.

Noll, Mark A. *A History of Christianity in the United States and Canada*. Grand Rapids, MI: William B. Eerdmans, 1992.

———.*The New Shape of World Christianity: How American Experience Reflects Global Faith*. Downers Grove, IL: IVP Academic, 2009.

Oliver, Robert T. *Syngman Rhee: The Man Behind the Myth*. New York: Dodd, Mead, 1954.

Omi, Michael, and Howard Winant. *Racial Formations in the United States: From the 1960s to the 1990s*, 2nd ed. New York: Routledge, 1994.

Orsi, Robert A. *Between Heaven and Earth: The Religious Worlds People Make and the Scholars Who Study Them*. Princeton, NJ: Princeton University Press, 2005.

———, ed. *Gods of the City: Religion and the American Urban Landscape*. Bloomington: Indiana University Press, 1999.

Osorio, Jonathan Kay Kamakawiwo'ole. *Dismembering Lahui: A History of the Hawaiian Nation to 1887*. Honolulu: University of Hawai'i Press, 2002.

Pai, Margaret K. *The Dreams of Two Yi-Min*. Honolulu: University of Hawai'i Press, 1989.

Paik, L. George. *The History of Protestant Missions in Korea, 1832–1910*. Pyeng Yang, Korea: Union Christian College Press, 1929.

Pak, Gary. *A Ricepaper Airplane*. Honolulu: University of Hawai'i Press, 1998.

Pak, Su Yon, Unzu Lee, Jung Ha Kim, and Myung Ji Cho. *Singing the Lord's Song in a New Land: Korean American Practices of Faith*. Louisville, KY: Westminster John Knox Press, 2005.

Palmer, Spencer J. *Korea and Christianity: The Problem of Identification with Tradition*. Seoul: Royal Asiatic Society, Korea Branch, 1967.

Park, Albert L. "Visions of the National: Religion and Ideology in 1920s and 1930s Rural Korea." Ph.D. diss., University of Chicago, 2007.

Park, Chung-Shin. *Protestantism and Politics in Korea*. Seattle: University of Washington Press, 2003.

Park, Kyeyoung. *The Korean American Dream: Immigrants and Small Business in New York City*. Ithaca, NY: Cornell University Press, 1997.

Parker, Michael. *The Kingdom of Character: The Student Volunteer Movement for Foreign Missions, 1886–1926*. Lanham, MD: University Press of America, 1998.

Parreñas, Rhacel S., and Lok C. D. Siu, eds. *Asian Diasporas: New Formations, New Conceptions*. Stanford, CA: Stanford University Press, 2007.

Patterson, Wayne. *The Ilse: First-Generation Korean Immigrants in Hawai'i, 1903–1973*. Honolulu: University of Hawai'i Press, 2000.

———. *The Korean Frontier in America: Immigration to Hawai'i, 1896–1910*. Honolulu: University of Hawai'i Press, 1988.

Phan, Peter C. *Christianity with an Asian Face: Asian American Theology in the Making.* Maryknoll, NY: Orbis Press, 2003.

Pratt, Keith, and Richard Rutt. *Korea: A Historical and Cultural Dictionary.* Surrey, England: Curzon Press, 1999.

Prentiss, Craig R., ed. *Religion and the Creation of Race and Ethnicity: An Introduction.* New York: New York University Press, 2003.

Raboteau, Albert. *Fire in the Bones: Reflections on African American Religious History.* Boston: Beacon Press, 1995.

Rhee, Syngman. *The Spirit of Independence: A Primer of Korean Modernization and Reform,* translated by Han-Kyo Kim. Honolulu and Seoul: University of Hawai'i Press and the Institute for Modern Korean Studies, Yonsei University, 2001.

Robinson, Michael E. *Cultural Nationalism in Colonial Korea, 1920–1925.* Seattle: University of Washington Press, 1988.

Roof, Wade Clark, and William McKinney. *American Mainline Religion: Its Changing Shape and Future.* New Brunswick, NJ: Rutgers University Press, 1987.

Ryang, Key S. "Kim Kyu-Sik as a Common Man and a Political Leader." *Korea Observer* 13, no. 1 (Spring 1982): 36–54.

Saxton, Alexander. *The Indispensable Enemy: Labor and the Anti-Chinese Movement in California.* Berkeley: University of California Press, 1971.

———. *The Rise and Fall of the White Republic: Class Politics and Mass Culture in Nineteenth-Century America.* New York: Verso, 1990.

Schmid, Andre. *Korea Between Empires, 1895–1919.* New York: Columbia University Press, 2002.

Shin, Gi-Wook. *Ethnic Nationalism in Korea: Genealogy, Politics, and Legacy.* Stanford, CA: Stanford University Press, 2007.

Shin, Gi-Wook, and Michael Robinson, eds. *Colonial Modernity in Korea.* Cambridge, MA: Harvard University Asia Center, 1999.

Sides, Josh. *L.A. City Limits: African American Los Angeles from the Great Depression to the Present.* Berkeley: University of California Press, 2003.

Silva, Noenoe K. *Aloha Betrayed: Native Hawaiian Resistance to American Colonialism.* Durham, NC: Duke University Press, 2004.

Spickard, Paul. *Almost All Aliens: Immigration, Race, and Colonialism in American History and Identity.* New York: Routledge, 2007.

Stoler, Ann Laura., ed. *Haunted by Empire: Geographies of Intimacy in North American History.* Durham, NC: Duke University Press, 2006.

Suh, Sharon A. *Being Buddhist in a Christian World: Gender and Community in a Korean American Temple.* Seattle: University of Washington Press, 2004.

Sunoo, Sonia Shinn. *Korean Kaleidoscope: Oral Histories.* Vol. 1, *Early Korean Pio-*

*neers, 1903–1905.* Davis, CA: Korean Oral History Project, Sierra Mission Area, United Presbyterian Church, 1982.

———, ed. and trans. "Kim Hei-Won." In *Korean Picture Brides: 1903–1920, A Collection of Oral Histories,* 154–66. Philadelphia: Xlibris, 2002.

———, ed. and trans. "Park Kyung-Shin." In *Korean Picture Brides: 1903–1920, A Collection of Oral Histories,* 132–53. Philadelphia: Xlibris, 2002.

Szasz, Ference. *Religion in the Modern American West.* Tucson: University of Arizona Press, 2002.

Takahashi, Jere. *Nisei/Sansei: Shifting Japanese American Identities and Politics.* Philadelphia: Temple University Press, 1997.

Takaki, Ronald. *Pau Hana: Plantation Life and Labor in Hawai'i, 1835–1920.* Honolulu: University of Hawai'i Press, 1983.

———. *Strangers from a Different Shore: A History of Asian Americans.* Boston: Little, Brown, 1989.

Trask, Haunani-Kay. *From a Native Daughter: Colonialism and Sovereignty in Hawai'i,* rev. ed. Honolulu: University of Hawai'i Press, 1999.

Trenka, Jane Jeong, Julie Chinyere Oparah, and Sun Yung Shin, eds. *Outsiders Within: Writing on Transnational Adoption.* Cambridge, MA: South End Press, 2006.

Tseng, Timothy. "Religious Liberalism, International Politics, and Diasporic Realities: The Chinese Students Christian Association of North America, 1909–1951." *Journal of America–East Asian Relations* 5, nos. 3–4 (1996): 305–30.

Tuan, Mia. *Forever Foreigners or Honorary Whites? The Asian Ethnic Experience Today.* New Brunswick, NJ: Rutgers University Press, 1998.

Tuveson, Ernest L. *Redeemer Nation: The Idea of America's Millennial Role.* Chicago: University of Chicago Press, 1968.

Tweed, Thomas A. *Our Lady of the Exile: Diasporic Religion at a Cuban Catholic Shrine.* New York: Oxford University Press, 1999.

U.S. Bureau of the Census, *Fifteenth Census of the United States: 1930.* Vol. 3, *Population, Reports by States.* Part 1, Alabama–Missouri (Washington, DC: Government Printing Office, 1932).

Varzally, Allison. *Making a Non-White America.* Berkeley: University of California Press, 2008.

Vergara, Alex R., ed. *Waves: The United Methodist Church of Hawai'i Centennial Jubilee.* Koloa, HI: Taylor, 1988.

Warner, R. Stephen, and Judith G. Wittner, eds. *Gatherings in Diaspora: Religious Communities and the New Immigration.* Philadelphia: Temple University Press, 1998.

Wells, Kenneth M. *New God, New Nation: Protestants and Self-Reconstruction Nationalism in Korea, 1896–1937*. Honolulu: University of Hawai'i Press, 1990.

White, Ronald C., and C. Howard Hopkins. *The Social Gospel: Religion and Reform in Changing America*. Philadelphia: Temple University Press, 1976.

Wild, Mark. *Street Meeting: Multiethnic Neighborhoods in Early Twentieth-Century Los Angeles*. Berkeley: University of California Press, 2005.

Winant, Howard. *The World Is a Ghetto: Race and Democracy Since World War II*. New York: Basic Books, 2001.

Wind, James P., and James W. Lewis, eds. *American Congregations*. Vol. 2, *New Perspectives in the Study of Congregations*. Chicago: University of Chicago Press, 1998.

Wuthnow, Robert. *The Restructuring of American Religion: Society and Faith Since World War II*. Princeton, NJ: Princeton University Press, 1988.

Xing, Jun Xing. *Baptized in the Fire of Revolution: The American Social Gospel and the YMCA in China, 1919–1937*. Bethlehem, PA: Lehigh University Press, 1996.

Yang, Eun Sik. "Korean Women of America: From Subordination to Partnership, 1903–1930." *Amerasia Journal* 11, no. 2 (1984): 1–28.

Yep, Laurence, and Kathy S. Yep. *The Dragon's Child: A Story of Angel Island*. New York: HarperCollins, 2008.

Yoo, David K. *Growing Up Nisei: Race, Generation, and Culture Among Japanese Americans of California, 1924–1949*. Urbana: University of Illinois Press, 2000.

———, ed. *New Spiritual Homes: Religion and Asian Americans*. Honolulu: University of Hawai'i Press, 1999.

Yoo, David K., and Hyung-ju Ahn. *Faithful Witness: A Centennial History of the Los Angeles Korean United Methodist Church, 1904–2004*. Los Angeles: Los Angeles Korean United Methodist Church, 2004.

Yoo, David K., and Ruth H. Chung, eds. *Religion and Spirituality in Korean America*. Urbana: University of Illinois Press, 2008.

Yoon, In-Jin. *On My Own: Korean Businesses and Race Relations in America*. Chicago: University of Chicago Press, 1997.

Yuh, Ji-Yeon. *Beyond the Shadow of Camptown: Korean Military Brides in America*. New York: New York University Press, 2002.

Yung, Judy. *Island: Poetry and History of Chinese Immigrants on Angel Island, 1910–1940*. Seattle: University of Washington Press, 1999.

# Index